WITHDRAWN
UTSA LIBRARIES

International Political Economy Series

Series Editor: **Timothy M. Shaw**, Visiting Professor, University of Massachusetts Boston, USA and Emeritus Professor, University of London, UK

The global political economy is in flux as a series of cumulative crises impacts its organization and governance. The IPE series has tracked its development in both analysis and structure over the last three decades. It has always had a concentration on the global South. Now the South increasingly challenges the North as the centre of development, also reflected in a growing number of submissions and publications on indebted Eurozone economies in Southern Europe.

An indispensable resource for scholars and researchers, the series examines a variety of capitalisms and connections by focusing on emerging economies, companies and sectors, debates and policies. It informs diverse policy communities as the established trans-Atlantic North declines and 'the rest', especially the BRICS, rise.

Titles include:

Leslie Elliott Armijo and Saori N. Katada (*editors*)
THE FINANCIAL STATECRAFT OF EMERGING POWERS
Shield and Sword in Asia and Latin America

Md Mizanur Rahman, Tan Tai Yong, Ahsan Ullah (*editors*)
MIGRANT REMITTANCES IN SOUTH ASIA
Social, Economic and Political Implications

Bartholomew Paudyn
CREDIT RATINGS AND SOVEREIGN DEBT
The Political Economy of Creditworthiness through Risk and Uncertainty

Lourdes Casanova and Julian Kassum
THE POLITICAL ECONOMY OF AN EMERGING GLOBAL POWER
In Search of the Brazil Dream

Toni Haastrup, and Yong-Soo Eun (*editors*)
REGIONALISING GLOBAL CRISES
The Financial Crisis and New Frontiers in Regional Governance

Kobena T. Hanson, Cristina D'Alessandro and Francis Owusu (*editors*)
MANAGING AFRICA'S NATURAL RESOURCES
Capacities for Development

Daniel Daianu, Carlo D'Adda, Giorgio Basevi and Rajeesh Kumar (*editors*)
THE EUROZONE CRISIS AND THE FUTURE OF EUROPE
The Political Economy of Further Integration and Governance

Karen E. Young
THE POLITICAL ECONOMY OF ENERGY, FINANCE AND SECURITY IN THE UNITED ARAB EMIRATES
Between the Majilis and the Market

Monique Taylor
THE CHINESE STATE, OIL AND ENERGY SECURITY

Benedicte Bull, Fulvio Castellacci and Yuri Kasahara
BUSINESS GROUPS AND TRANSNATIONAL CAPITALISM IN CENTRAL AMERICA
Economic and Political Strategies

Leila Simona Talani
THE ARAB SPRING IN THE GLOBAL POLITICAL ECONOMY

Andreas Nölke (*editor*)
MULTINATIONAL CORPORATIONS FROM EMERGING MARKETS
State Capitalism 3.0

Eoshen Hendrickson
PROMOTING U.S. INVESTMENT IN SUB-SAHARAN AFRICA

Bhumitra Chakma
SOUTH ASIA IN TRANSITION
Democracy, Political Economy and Security

Greig Charnock, Thomas Purcell and Ramon Ribera-Fumaz
THE LIMITS TO CAPITAL IN SPAIN
Crisis and Revolt in the European South

Felipe Amin Filomeno
MONSANTO AND INTELLECTUAL PROPERTY IN SOUTH AMERICA

Eirikur Bergmann
ICELAND AND THE INTERNATIONAL FINANCIAL CRISIS
Boom, Bust and Recovery

Yildiz Atasoy (*editor*)
GLOBAL ECONOMIC CRISIS AND THE POLITICS OF DIVERSITY

Gabriel Siles-Brügge
CONSTRUCTING EUROPEAN UNION TRADE POLICY
A Global Idea of Europe

Jewellord Singh and France Bourgouin (*editors*)
RESOURCE GOVERNANCE AND DEVELOPMENTAL STATES IN THE GLOBAL SOUTH
Critical International Political Economy Perspectives

Tan Tai Yong and Md Mizanur Rahman (*editors*)
DIASPORA ENGAGEMENT AND DEVELOPMENT IN SOUTH ASIA

International Political Economy Series
Series Standing Order ISBN 978–0–333–71708–0 hardcover
978–0–333–71110–1 paperback

You can receive future titles in this series as they are published by placing a standing order. Please contact your bookseller or, in case of difficulty, write to us at the address below with your name and address, the title of the series and one of the ISBNs quoted above.

Customer Services Department, Macmillan Distribution Ltd, Houndmills, Basingstoke, Hampshire RG21 6XS, England

The Financial Statecraft of Emerging Powers

Shield and Sword in Asia and Latin America

Edited by

Leslie Elliott Armijo
Visiting Scholar, Portland State University, USA

and

Saori N. Katada
Associate Professor, University of Southern California, USA

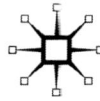

Editorial matter, selection, introduction and conclusion © Leslie Elliott Armijo and Saori N. Katada 2014
Individual chapters © Respective authors 2014
Foreword © Benjamin J. Cohen 2014

All rights reserved. No reproduction, copy or transmission of this publication may be made without written permission.

No portion of this publication may be reproduced, copied or transmitted save with written permission or in accordance with the provisions of the Copyright, Designs and Patents Act 1988, or under the terms of any licence permitting limited copying issued by the Copyright Licensing Agency, Saffron House, 6–10 Kirby Street, London EC1N 8TS.

Any person who does any unauthorized act in relation to this publication may be liable to criminal prosecution and civil claims for damages.

The authors have asserted their rights to be identified as the authors of this work in accordance with the Copyright, Designs and Patents Act 1988.

First published 2014 by
PALGRAVE MACMILLAN

Palgrave Macmillan in the UK is an imprint of Macmillan Publishers Limited, registered in England, company number 785998, of Houndmills, Basingstoke, Hampshire RG21 6XS.

Palgrave Macmillan in the US is a division of St Martin's Press LLC, 175 Fifth Avenue, New York, NY 10010.

Palgrave Macmillan is the global academic imprint of the above companies and has companies and representatives throughout the world.

Palgrave® and Macmillan® are registered trademarks in the United States, the United Kingdom, Europe and other countries

ISBN: 978–1–137–42937–7

This book is printed on paper suitable for recycling and made from fully managed and sustained forest sources. Logging, pulping and manufacturing processes are expected to conform to the environmental regulations of the country of origin.

A catalogue record for this book is available from the British Library.

A catalog record for this book is available from the Library of Congress.

Library
University of Texas
at San Antonio

To our loving families
Kaizad, Zubin, and Chitra
Satoshi and Kay

Contents

List of Figures	viii
List of Tables	ix
Foreword Benjamin J. Cohen	x
Acknowledgments	xii
Notes on Contributors	xiv
List of Abbreviations and Acronyms	xviii

1. New Kids on the Block: Rising Multipolarity, More Financial Statecraft — 1
   Leslie Elliott Armijo and Saori N. Katada

2. Who's Afraid of Reversing Neoliberal Reforms? Financial Statecraft in Argentina and Venezuela — 21
   Ignacio Labaqui

3. Brave New World? The Politics of International Finance in Brazil and India — 47
   Leslie Elliott Armijo and John Echeverri-Gent

4. The End of Monetary Mercantilism in Southeast Asia? — 77
   Natasha Hamilton-Hart

5. All Politics Is Local: The Renminbi's Prospects as a Future Global Currency — 103
   Ulrich Volz

6. Regionalism as Financial Statecraft: China and Japan's Pursuit of Counterweight Strategies — 138
   Saori N. Katada and Injoo Sohn

7. The Financial Statecraft of Emerging Powers: How, Why, and So What? — 162
   Saori N. Katada and Leslie Elliott Armijo

Index — 185

List of Figures

2.1	Argentina: public debt as a percentage of GDP	28
2.2	Argentina: international reserves (US$ billions)	31
2.3	Venezuela: international reserves (US$ billions)	36
2.4	International commodities, energy, and foodstuff price indexes, 1999–2010	40
2.5	Argentina and Venezuela: terms of trade with the world economy, 1999–2011	41
3.1	Brazil's policy interest rate (SELIC), 2000–2014	54
3.2	India's policy interest rate (Repo) and Cash Reserve Ratio, October 2005–June 2013	55
3.3	Brazil and India: merchandise trade balance, 1990–2011	65
3.4	Brazil and India: current account balance as percentage of GDP, 1990–2011	66
4.1	Southeast Asia: exchange rate trends	85

List of Tables

1.1	Emerging powers: modalities of financial statecraft	10
2.1	Argentina: debt ratios before default and after restructuring	29
2.2	Argentina: sources of financing 2005–2010 (US$ billions)	30
4.1	Southeast and Northeast Asia: foreign exchange reserves	82
4.2	Southeast Asia: current account balances as percentage of GDP	85
4.3	World: currency composition of foreign exchange reserves	91
5.1	China: framework of capital controls	109
5.2	China: major steps toward RMB internationalization	110
5.3	China: bilateral swap agreements with other central banks (as of December 2013)	113
7.1	Emerging powers in Asia and Latin America: modalities of FS, 2000–2013	168

Foreword

This book could not be more timely. Recent years have seen major shifts in the distribution of capabilities in global monetary affairs. Can anyone doubt that there really are, as the editors put it, "new kids on the block" – emergent powers eager to flex their newfound financial muscle? Yet we still know little about their policy priorities or perspectives. Serious comparative analysis of the financial statecraft of the "new kids" is long overdue.

Why have the "new kids" received so little attention until now? Mainly, I would suggest, it is because for decades students of international finance have been riveted by another shift in the balance of monetary capabilities, separate from the issue of state-to-state relations. That is the dramatic redistribution of power from states as a group to market actors – a trend that has persisted since soon after the Second World War, resulting from pressures of private competition as well as modish policies of financial liberalization. In the 1950s, capital markets everywhere (with the notable exception of the United States) were generally weak, insular, and strictly controlled, reduced from their previously central role in the world economy to offer little more than a negligible amount of trade financing. Starting in the 1960s, however, private lending and investment once again began to gather momentum, generating a phenomenal growth of cross-border financial flows and an increasingly close integration of national markets. By the end of the 20th century, the acceleration of capital mobility had proceeded to the point where the authority of sovereign governments seemed directly threatened. At minimum, states were thrown on the defensive, no longer able to enforce their will without constraint. At a maximum, states appeared on the verge of total emasculation, with monetary power moving inexorably from national governments to "stateless" markets. Scholars naturally concentrated their energies on studying the causes and consequences of this new world of "privatized" global finance.

By contrast, the balance of power among states seemed relatively stable once the post-World War II recoveries of Western Europe and Japan were well under way. Earlier, of course, the United States had enjoyed an overwhelming predominance in monetary affairs; challenges to U.S. hegemony over the course of the 1960s from the likes of West Germany, France, and Japan were hardly welcome to Washington and for a time were even actively resisted. But by the 1970s, with the creation of what came to be known as the Group of Seven (G7), an inner club was effectively established composed of Britain, Canada, France, Italy, Japan, the United States, and West Germany. The arrangement, which took the form of an informal negotiating forum, proved to be remarkably durable. In ensuing decades, by common assent, the G7 functioned as a kind of steering committee for global monetary affairs.

But then came the great financial crisis of 2008, triggered by the collapse of America's housing bubble. On the one hand, states now had every reason to seek to recapture some of the authority they had lost to market actors. More pro-active policy measures, including discretionary capital controls, came back into fashion; no longer would financial liberalization take overriding priority. On the other hand, it was now clear that the G7 could no longer manage events on its own. Newly emergent powers, led by China, had to be brought in as well. The transition was acknowledged with the passing of the baton from the Group of Seven to the Group of Twenty (G20), which in addition to the more mature economies includes the largest of the emergent powers. Henceforth, it was agreed, it would now be the G20 that would be empowered to provide some semblance of governance for the world economy. The importance of the "new kids" was affirmed.

Yet we still know relatively little about what to expect from them. What are their goals, and what are they prepared to do to achieve them? That is where *Financial Statecraft of Emerging Powers* comes in. The book does not pretend to provide definitive answers to these questions. That would be too much to expect of any single collection of essays. But it does break important new ground, adding much to our understanding of the motivations and preferences of a key group of states in Asia and Latin America. The authors are all acknowledged experts with keen insight and a strong command of the facts on the ground. The book should be read by anyone with an interest in the future of the global monetary system.

Benjamin J. Cohen
Louis G. Lancaster Professor of International Political Economy
University of California, Santa Barbara

Acknowledgments

Our book, *Financial Statecraft of Emerging Powers*, came out of the collaboration of three initiators, Carol Wise, Leslie Elliott Armijo, and Saori N. Katada, who were fortunate to receive generous funding from a grant jointly awarded by the Latin American Studies Association (LASA) and the Andrew W. Mellon Foundation in 2011. After we collectively steered the project through its initial workshop stage, two of us went on to edit this book. As scholars of international political economy focusing on East Asia and Latin America, we have been intrigued by the rise of emerging powers from these regions and the way they now use such newly gained economic powers to promote their foreign policy agendas. We feel very privileged that first-rate scholars in this field have joined us to advance this project in this collective book. We thank John Echeverri-Gent, Natasha Hamilton-Hart, Ignacio Labaqui, Injoo Sohn, and Ulrich Volz, not only for their brilliant chapters, but also for their patience and commitment as we have brought this project to fruition.

Scholarship is a product of intellect, imagination, and hard work, but it thrives largely because of the community that values and supports such efforts. We feel blessed to be living in such a community, fostered by generous funders, inspiring mentors, and exciting colleagues. In the process of producing this book, we have been particularly indebted to our common mentor and dear friend, Benjamin "Jerry" Cohen, who has kindly contributed a foreword to this book. His admirable scholarship and personal generosity has been an on-going inspiration to us both – not to mention his helpful role in originally introducing the two editors to one another!

We also owe significant debts to other scholars who helped us through this project, with their participation in two workshops, both held at University of Southern California. The participants and other colleagues provided us with pertinent criticisms and valuable suggestions that moved the project forward. We thank Joshua Aizenman, Mark Beeson, Shaun Breslin, Gregory Chin, Barbara Fritz, Ben Graham, Gerardo Esquivel Hernandez, Eric Hershberg, Heon Joo Jung, David Kang, Maria Antonieta Del Tedesco Lins, Kurt von Mettenheim, Laurissa Mühlich, Victor Shih, Barbara Stallings, Maria Lorca Sussino, and Andrew Walter. We also thank our very capable research assistants, Michael Perez, Will Kwon, Gloria Koo, Scott Wilbur, and Ming-min Yang. The Center for

International Studies, the School of International Relations, and the Korean Studies Institute at the University of Southern California have also provided us with generous funding that complemented the LASA-Mellon Grant and made these workshops possible.

Several of the chapters were presented at the Annual Congress of the Latin American Studies Association in San Francisco in May 2012. The project has also benefited significantly from inputs from Colin Hay, the editor of an academic journal, *New Political Economy*, who published a version of the theoretical discussion guiding this project earlier this year.

We consider ourselves lucky in our publisher for this book. Palgrave Macmillan's International Political Economy (IPE) series is superb, and the unreserved enthusiasm of its series editor, Tim Shaw, as well as the proficient and friendly support of its acquisitions editor, Christina Brian, has delighted us. We also acknowledge the helpful inputs and suggestions made by the manuscript's anonymous reviewer(s).

Finally, we thank our families for giving us space and support to work on research that we are passionate about. Juggling motherhood and work is always a challenge, but it has been very rewarding for both of us.

Notes on Contributors

Leslie Elliott Armijo is a visiting scholar at Portland State University and nonresident faculty fellow at American University. A former Fulbright scholar at the Pontifical Catholic University of Rio de Janeiro, fellow at the American Institute of Indian Studies in New Delhi, and fellow of the Desigualdades Project of the Freie Universität Berlin, Leslie studies the intersection of democratic politics and capitalist markets in emerging powers. Her books are *Financial Globalization and Democracy in Emerging Markets* (1999) and *Debating the Global Financial Architecture* (2001). She is completing two volumes, both coauthored with Sybil Rhodes, on researching public policymaking in nontraditional venues: "International Public Policy beyond the Advanced Industrial Countries: Contending Hemispheric Visions of the United States, Brazil, and Venezuela" and "Comparative Public Policy beyond the Advanced Industrial Countries: Voice and Money in India and Brazil." Leslie's recent articles have appeared in *New Political Economy* (2014), *Journal of Policy Modeling* (2013), *Latin American Politics and Society* (2013), *Polity* (2010), *Democratization* (2008, 2010), *Latin American Research Review* (2008), *Asian Perspective* (2007), and *Comparative Political Studies* (2006).

Benjamin J. Cohen is Louis G. Lancaster Professor of International Political Economy at the University of California, Santa Barbara, where he has been a member of the Political Science Department since 1991. He was educated at Columbia University, earning a PhD in Economics in 1963. He has worked as a research economist at the Federal Reserve Bank of New York (1962–1964) and previously taught at Princeton University (1964–1971) and the Fletcher School of Law and Diplomacy, Tufts University (1971–1991). A specialist in the political economy of international money and finance, he serves on the editorial boards of several leading academic journals and is the author of 14 books, including most recently *Advanced Introduction to International Political Economy* (2014). He has won numerous awards and in 2000 was named Distinguished Scholar of the year by the International Political Economy Section of the International Studies Association.

John Echeverri-Gent is an associate professor in the Department of Politics at the University of Virginia. His books include *The State and the*

Poor: Public Policy and Political Development in India and the United States (1993) and *Economic Reform in Three Giants: U.S. Foreign Policy and the USSR, China, and India* (1990) which he co-edited. His published articles focus on the political economy of development and comparative public policy. He is currently completing a book chapter entitled "Politics of Markets: Political Economy of India's Financial Market Development in Comparative Perspective." John serves as treasurer of the American Institute of Indian Studies and as a member of the editorial board of *Political Science Quarterly*. He has chaired the American Political Science Task Force on "Difference and Inequality in Developing Societies," and in 1983 won the Theodore J. Lowi Award of the Policy Studies Organization for the best article in the *Policy Studies Journal*. He has also served as MacArthur scholar in residence at the Overseas Development Council, senior fellow at the American Institute of Indian Studies, and Fulbright scholar.

Natasha Hamilton-Hart joined the Department of Management and International Business at the University of Auckland in January 2011. Prior to joining the University of Auckland, she held positions at the National University of Singapore and the Australian National University. She received her PhD from Cornell University in 1999 and BA (Hons) from the University of Otago in 1990. Natasha's research interests include monetary and financial issues in East Asia, business in Southeast Asia and business-government relations, particularly in the banking and natural resource sectors. She is the author of *Asian States, Asian Bankers: Central Banking in Southeast Asia* and *Hard Interests, Soft Illusions: Southeast Asia and American Power*.

Saori N. Katada is an associate professor at the School of International Relations and the Director of the Political Science and International Relations (POIR) Program at University of Southern California (USC). She is the author of *Banking on Stability: Japan and the Cross-Pacific Dynamics of International Financial Crisis Management* (2001), which was awarded Masayoshi Ohira Memorial Book Award in 2002. She has published four edited and co-edited books and numerous articles on the subject of trade, financial and monetary cooperation in East Asia as well as Japanese foreign aid. For her research on regionalism, she was recently awarded the Japan Foundation Research Grant and National Endowment for the Humanities Fellowship. Saori received her PhD from the University of North Carolina at Chapel Hill (Political Science) in 1994, and BA from Hitotsubashi University (Tokyo). Before joining USC, she served as a researcher at the World Bank in Washington DC, and as International Program officer at the UNDP in Mexico City.

Ignacio Labaqui teaches Latin American Politics and International Relations at the Institute of Political Sciences and International Relations at the Universidad Catolica Argentina. He is also a senior analyst for Latin America at Medley Global Advisors based in Buenos Aires. Ignacio has a master's degree from the London School of Economics and Political Science and holds a BA in Political Science from the Universidad Católica Argentina. He has published papers and book chapters on IMF-Argentina relations, U.S.-Latin American relations, regional trade integration in South America, and defense policy in Latin America. He has worked for FLACSO-Argentina as a researcher in the International Relations Department, and the Eurasia Group as an analyst for Argentina.

Injoo Sohn is an associate professor in the Politics and Public Administration Department at the University of Hong Kong. Prior to joining the University of Hong Kong, he was a postdoctoral fellow at the Princeton–Harvard China and the World Program and a visiting research fellow at the Princeton Institute for International and Regional Studies. He also consulted for the Intergovernmental Group of 24 (G-24) and the United Nations Conference on Trade and Development (UNCTAD), and was a commissioner of the Warwick Commission on International Financial Reform (2009). His work has appeared in *European Journal of International Relations*, *Review of International Political Economy*, *China Quarterly*, *Global Governance*, and *Pacific Review*.

Ulrich Volz is a senior lecturer (associate professor) at the Department of Economics, SOAS, University of London. He is also a senior research fellow at the German Development Institute/Deutsches Institut für Entwicklungspolitik (DIE). In 2012 he was a visiting professor at Peking University's School of Economics. Ulrich spent stints working at the European Central Bank and the European Bank for Reconstruction and Development and held adjunct or visiting positions at the University of Oxford, Hertie School of Governance, University of Birmingham, University of Leipzig, Freie Universität Berlin, European Central Bank, Bank Indonesia, and Aoyama Gakuin University in Tokyo. He was also a Fox International fellow and Max Kade scholar at Yale University. Ulrich holds a doctorate in Economics from Freie Universität Berlin. Ulrich's research interests include international finance, open economy macroeconomics, global economic governance, financial market development and stability, and green finance. Ulrich is the author of *Prospects for Monetary Cooperation and Integration in East Asia* (2010) and the editor or co-editor of several books, including *Towards Monetary and Financial*

Integration in East Asia (2009), *Regional and Global Liquidity Arrangements* (2010), *Regional Integration, Economic Development and Global Governance* (2011), and *Financial Stability in Emerging Markets: Dealing with Global Liquidity* (2012).

List of Abbreviations and Acronyms

ABMI	Asian Bond Market Initiative
ACCSF	Asian Currency Crisis Support Facility
ACU	Asian Currency Unit
AD	Democratic Action Party (Acción Democrática) (Venzuela)
AFC	Asian Financial Crisis
ALBA	Bolivarian Alternative for the Americas
AMF	Asian Monetary Fund
AMRO	ASEAN (+3) Macroeconomic Research Office
ANSES	National Social Security Agency (Argentina)
APEC	Asia-Pacific Economic Cooperation
BCB	Brazilian Central Bank
BCBS	Basel Committee on Banking Supervision
BNDES	National Economic and Social Development Bank (Brazil)
CADIVI	Commission for the Administration of Currency Exchange (Comisión Administradora de Divisas) (Venezuela)
CCI	Contemporary Capabilities Index
CCP	Chinese Communist Party
CEF	Federal Savings Bank (Brazil)
CLGFEA	Central Leading Group on Finance and Economic Affairs
CMI	Chiang Mai Initiative
CMIM	Chiang Mai Initiative Multilateralized
COPEI	Social Christian Party (Venezuela)
CPSS	Committee on Payment and Settlement Systems
CRA	Contingent Reserve Arrangement/Credit rating agency
CRR	Cash Reserve Ratio (India)
DIE	German Development Institute (Deutsches Institut für Entwicklungspolitik)
EFSF	European Financial Stability Facility
EMEs	Emerging Market Economies
ERIA	Economic Research Institute for ASEAN and East Asia
ESM	European Stability Mechanism
FCL	Flexible Credit Line
FDI	Foreign Direct Investment
FGS	Guarantee and Sustainability Funds (Argentina)

FONDEN	National Development Fund (El Fondo Nacional para el Desarrollo Nacional) (Venezuela)
FS	Financial Statecraft
FSB	Financial Stability Board
GATS	General Agreement on Trade in Services
GDP	Gross Domestic Product
GFC	Global Financial Crisis
GIC	Government of Singapore Investment Corporation
IFIs	International Financial Institutions
ILDIS	Latin-American Institute of Social Research (Instituto Latinoamericano de Investigaciones Sociales)
IMF	International Monetary Fund
IOF	Financial Operations Tax (Brazil)
IOSCO	International Organization of Securities Commissions
IPS	Interpress Service
ISI	Import Substitution Industrialization
IT	Inflation Targeting
MERCOSUR	Common Market of the South
MOF	Ministry of Finance
NDA	National Democratic Alliance
NDRC	National Development and Reform Commission
NEAT	Network of East Asian Think Tanks
NRIs	Non-resident Indians
PBOC	People's Bank of China
PDVSA	Venezuela Petroleum (Petróleos de Venezuela)
PLL	Precautionary and Liquidity Line
PSDB	Brazilian Social Democratic Party
PT	Workers' Party (Brazil)
QFII	Qualified Foreign Institutional Investors
RBI	Reserve Bank of India
RMB	Renminbi (China)
SDRs	Special Drawing Rights (IMF)
SELIC	Special System for Settlement and Custody (Brazil)
SLR	Statutory Liquidity Ratio (India)
SML	Local Currency Payments' System
SOEs	State-owned Enterprises
SUCRE	Unified Regional Clearing System (Sistema Único de Compensación Regional)

SWF	Sovereign Wealth Fund
UNASUR	Union of South American Nations
UPA	United Progressive Alliance (India)
USNIC	United States National Intelligence Council
WTO	World Trade Organization

1
New Kids on the Block: Rising Multipolarity, More Financial Statecraft

Leslie Elliott Armijo and Saori N. Katada

With a rise of emerging market economies such as China, India, and Brazil, the distribution of global capabilities is shifting. In 2011, a newly inaugurated World Bank annual report, *Global Development Horizons 2011*, began with the following bold assertions:

> The inaugural edition of GDH addresses the broad trend toward multipolarity in the global economy... By 2025, the most probable global currency scenario will be a multipolar one centered around the dollar, euro, and renminbi... [In the postwar era,] in exchange for the United States assuming the responsibilities of system maintenance, serving as the open market of last resort, and issuing the most widely used international reserve currency, its key partners, Western European countries and Japan, acquiesced to the special privileges enjoyed by the United States – seiniorage gains, domestic macroeconomic policy autonomy, and balance of payments flexibility... [Today] three conventional pillars [of global economic governance] need to be reappraised: the link between economic power concentration and stability, the North-South axis of capital flows, and the centrality of the U.S. dollar in the global monetary system. (World Bank 2011: xi–xii; 2)

This is quite striking language from the World Bank, suggesting as it does that global inequality might be a source of economic volatility, that major emerging powers might become senders rather than recipients of international investment, and that the U.S. dollar could gradually yield its position as the anchor currency for the world economy. Increasingly, such once controversial themes also figure prominently in the elite global business press. London's *Financial Times* observed that, "The old notion of rich countries funding poor countries is no longer appropriate, as emerging markets rise in economic clout and are as much sources of development cash as they are recipients" (Politi 2012).

This ongoing and underlying transition became particularly apparent following the global financial crisis (GFC) initiated in the housing finance markets of the United States in 2007, which intensified in the aftermath of the shock associated with the failure of Lehman Brothers investment bank in September of 2008, and was followed by a lingering European sovereign debt crisis from 2009 into 2013. The GFC has been a significant blow to the international influence of the neoliberal economic paradigm and of leading advanced capitalist democracies, exposing their underlying fiscal and banking fragilities, which have continued to roil markets and unseat incumbent governments. Governments of many of the larger emerging economies perceive in current conditions the opportunity to exert themselves more actively in international affairs, including via financial statecraft (FS).

"Financial statecraft" is defined as the intentional use, by national governments, of a country's monetary or financial capabilities or conditions for the purpose of achieving ongoing foreign policy goals, whether political, economic, or financial. In this book, which builds on earlier theoretical work by the editors (Armijo and Katada in press), we focus on the FS strategies of key emerging powers in Asia and Latin America. These countries have for several decades struggled to implement market-oriented economic reforms while experiencing their share of financial crises stemming from international borrowing or cross-border investment, crises that repeatedly disrupted development plans, temporarily halting or even reversing countries' economic growth. In the first decade of 21st century, however, we observe their comparative financial and economic rise, and associated with it, the use of their financial powers to protect their economies and assert their political and commercial objectives. The questions we ask in our collective study include these. Has the increase in the overall material capabilities of previously marginal players in Latin America and Asia translated into more active FS by these countries? What motivates the players? What tools do they use to engage global finance, and for what political purposes? To set the stage, this chapter introduces the main sources and instruments of FS around the Pacific Rim (defined broadly to encompass Brazil and India) and begins the inquiry into how they might be employed in the cause of global rebalancing, particularly in the post-GFC world.

The chapter's first section suggests that the underlying interstate distribution of capabilities is shifting, and that the governments of many emerging powers have taken this as their cue to engage more actively in the exercise of FS. Section two theorizes the concept of FS and sets out hypotheses about how it has evolved among the set of emerging powers. We conclude with brief summaries of the chapters to follow.

Shifting capabilities, rising aspirations

Are there indeed "new kids on the block" among the world's major financial powers? The discussion of the use of international financial statecraft by new global and regional players rests on the assumption that the distribution of capabilities among sovereign states itself is in flux. This shift eventually should transform global influence over international political and economic outcomes.

One way to conceptualize which states are significant in global politics is to look at national control over material resources. Taking a purely "realist" position (Waltz 1979; Mearsheimer 2001), "power" in international politics may be conceptualized as deriving from countries' relative positions in a notional global balance of capabilities, where each country's weight is measured as its share of world totals of such dimensions as total armaments (in practice, usually measured by their purchase value, admittedly a limited assessment tool), global population, and other scarce resources, from access to blue water ports to fossil fuel reserves. Besides the means to make the country secure from attack – still today dependent on geography, although much less so than historically was the case – the most significant material asset is size of the nation's economy, as money may be exchanged for most other goods and services desired.

In terms of the interstate distribution of material capabilities, the world is becoming more multipolar. There has been quite a dramatic shift in the shares of the global economy accounted for by the large emerging economies as compared to the major advanced industrial powers. According to the latest figures from the OECD, the combined gross domestic product (GDP) in 2005 of five major emerging and transitional economies (China, India, Indonesia, Russia, and South Africa) was about 42 percent of the size of that of the G7 group of major economies (Canada, France, Germany, Italy, Japan, United Kingdom, and United States). By 2012, the economies of these five nontraditional powers were almost 64 percent of the total of the advanced industrial powers – an increase of 22 percentage points in only seven years.[1]

Armijo, Muehlich, and Tirone (forthcoming) calculate a "Contemporary Capabilities Index" (CCI), that includes the mean of national shares in global totals of: national income (GDP at PPP rates), population, telephone subscriptions (both fixed and mobile), industrial value-added, foreign exchange reserves, and military spending. By the CCI, the share of the G7 in global totals declined from 47 to 36 percent between 1990 and 2007, while that of China, India, and Brazil doubled from 10 to 22 percent, most dramatically due to the growth of China. Similarly, the U.S. government's National Intelligence Council (USNIC 2012: v) identified as one of the five "tectonic shifts" expected between the present and 2030 the "definitive shift of economic power to the East and South." In general, virtually any possible index of relative material capabilities shows a smaller share for the major advanced industrial countries than was the case in the late 20th century.

Skeptics mock such crude measures of relative state capabilities, which admittedly are rousingly unsubtle, including only easily quantified dimensions while excluding national capabilities that fall into the realm of "soft power" (Nye 1990; 2004), such as having a dominant culture, a globally used language, a world-class educational system, attractive market and political institutions, and a strong international reputation more generally. Yet nontraditional players also are enhancing their soft power, albeit from a low base. For example, after being humbled by the series of financial crises that hit the emerging market economies of Latin America (1980s and 1990s) and Asia (1997–1998), these countries' governments became significantly more confident when they recovered quite swiftly from the GFC (Wise, Armijo, and Katada under review). The series of economic crises that have enmeshed the advanced economies since the late 2000s have cast dark shadows on the neoliberal economic paradigm preached by the leaders of these advanced economies. Their power of persuasion has been undermined.

Many contemporary scholars of course insist that "power" should be understood not as capabilities but instead as realized influence, as when State A persuades or coerces State B into taking actions that State B otherwise would not have chosen (Baldwin 2013; Barnett and Duvall 2005). The influence of emerging powers also has increased. The clearest example of the gradual yet perceptible shift of global influence from the major advanced industrial democracies toward nontraditional powers came in the initial G20 Summit, convened in Washington, DC following the September 2008 crash of Lehman Brothers investment bank. This was a visible indication of the inability on the part of the G7 major powers, accustomed to behind-the-scenes crisis management led (sometimes aggressively) by the United States, to cope with the global financial crisis. The G20 Summit emerged in the center stage of global financial governance as the finance ministers of the traditional powers, including U.S. Treasury Secretary Henry Paulson, realized it would be foolhardy to try to implement global countercyclical policies to stop global financial contagion without active participation from many of the world's largest emerging market economies. Following the second G20 Summit in April 2009 in London, British Prime Minister Gordon Brown announced a "New World Order" of unprecedented multilateral cooperation.

Since then, the large emerging powers have come to be seen as increasingly essential partners in foreign policymaking – although there also has been pushback by the major advanced industrial democracies, unused to consulting widely when taking diplomatic action. As recently as 2010, for example, an apparently well-intentioned effort by Turkey and Brazil to play the role of honest broker by suggesting a compromise solution to the nuclear inspection standoff between the major powers and the government of Iran was met by anger and derision in Washington, DC and other major Western capitals. Yet, the United States has had to accept Brazil's and India's somewhat independent stances with respect to nuclear nonproliferation, a goal that all three governments strongly claim to endorse. In late September 2013, U.S. President Obama's effort to punish or sanction Syria's government for alleged use of chemical weapons on civilians only remained alive due to the compromise proposals unexpectedly offered by Russian President Vladimir Putin. Meanwhile, U.S. President Obama reached out to telephone to new Iranian President Rouhani when he came to New York to visit the United Nations, marking one of the closest contacts to that point between leaders of the two countries since 1989 (Erdbrink 2013).

In sum, and within a relatively short period of time, there has been a clear shift in the distribution of interstate capabilities, with major emerging powers such as China, India, Russia, and Brazil accounting for an increasing share of overall global capabilities as measured by a variety of yardsticks. In addition, over the past three decades emerging powers have reformed and modernized their domestic financial sectors, which also has contributed to their gradually increasing range of options for engaging in FS.

Following the debt crisis of the 1980s, most Latin American countries implemented pro-market reforms, which aimed to make their domestic financial systems both more efficient and more stable (Nelson 1990). Their policy choices after 2000 were, however, more differentiated. Some countries such as Mexico, Chile, Peru, and Colombia have continued to move in a liberalizing direction, while others such as Venezuela and Argentina reversed neoliberal and pro-market reforms of the 1990s, becoming visibly interventionist in their financial regulation. In both the 1990s and 2000s, Brazil on the whole liberalized financially, but at a modest (and some would say insufficient) pace. In Asia, gradual financial liberalization in the 1990s arguably invited the Asian financial crisis (AFC) of 1997. The countries that accepted IMF conditions at the time of the AFC – including Korea, Thailand, and Indonesia – were obliged to further liberalize their domestic finance. Yet, the largest emerging powers of the region, India and China, took a slow road to domestic financial liberalization and still maintain relatively high levels of capital control and state-ownership of banks and other financial institutions.

One important challenge for these and other emerging market economies continues to be that of coping with massive and volatile inflows and outflows of foreign capital. These governments want to avoid erratic capital flows and exchange rate movements that exacerbate economic and political uncertainty. In the aftermath of the AFC, most Latin American economies began to utilize flexible exchange rates as a way of accommodating their domestic macroeconomic environments to global fluctuations, while most East Asian countries (with the notable exception of South Korea) maintained a loose and de facto currency peg with the U.S. dollar at depressed rates in order to maintain their export competitiveness.

In fact, many emerging market economies that experienced devastating financial crises in the last several decades managed to establish reasonably effective financial shields despite their concurrent adoption of pro-market macroeconomic stabilization. In several cases, their leaders also have concluded that activist financial policies, including efforts to influence global financial governance practices and beliefs, may have emerged as their best strategy options, both to avoid future crises and to project influence on a variety of topics.

The FS of emerging powers: shields, swords, and new possibilities for systemic influence

Governments long have used both military and financial might to achieve foreign policy goals (Viner 1948). In particular, FS is a part of "economic statecraft." Traditionally, "economic statecraft" has been defined as the employment by the state of economic levers as a means to achieve foreign policy ends. Thus, for example, trade sanctions may be imposed on a foreign country with the goals of pressuring its government to end human rights violations against its own citizens or cease construction of a nuclear weapon. Conversely, military or diplomatic allies may receive subsidized loans or trade preferences. Baldwin's (1985) seminal work on the use of economic means to achieve foreign security policy goals highlights how economic statecraft – particularly via trade and other economic sanctions – can be deployed in support of state security objectives. Multiple contemporary scholars have investigated economic sanctions both in terms of their domestic political foundations and the effectiveness of such sanction decisions.[2]

Consistent with this usage, "financial statecraft" (FS) would refer to a national government's use of monetary or financial regulations or policies to achieve foreign policy ends. Thus Steil and Litan (2006: 4) refer to FS as "those aspects of economic statecraft that are directed at influencing [international] capital flows." Their interest is in the use of these capital flows mainly for traditional security and foreign policy goals, and mainly against a specific foreign target state. Examples of FS instruments that may be implemented bilaterally include capital flow guarantees and restrictions, financial sanctions on state and nonstate actors (Crawford and Klotz 1999), and government decisions to underwrite foreign debt in a currency crisis, create currency unions, or opt for dollarization. Scholars also have examined the relations between financial power and FS through currency relations (Kirshner 1995; 2003; Helleiner and Kirshner 2009), or through the politics of finance (Maxfield 1990; Woo 1991; Walter 2008) or of financial crises (Aggarwal 1996; Wade 1998; Armijo 1999; Haggard 2000; Noble and Ravenhill 2000).

The present collective project sheds light on FS among emerging powers. As such, it contributes to an important new international relations literature that attempts to theorize the roles, preferences, and strategies of that group of countries referred to as rising, intermediate, middle, or emerging powers in global politics (Tammen et al. 2000; Hurrell 2009; Roberts 2010; Gilley 2013). But, in order to provide sufficient intellectual framing for such analysis, we need to go beyond existing work on FS. Standard definitions of FS – mostly focused around sanctions, and occasionally inducements, directed by strong states at much weaker target states – have been unnecessarily narrow (Armijo and Katada in press). Much of this work also has a strong large-country bias. Authors' research interests focus on the wealthy democracies, particularly the United States, the country which imposes most of the sanctions. For example, work by Hufbauer et al. (2009) on economic sanctions imposed between 1914 and 2006 statistically analyzes the characteristics of the home and target states of the sanctions, as well as indicators of success. These scholars propose that the size differential between the home state (which imposes the sanction) and the target state (the sanction's recipient) has to be at least 10 to 1 in order for the sanctions to be minimally feasible, and that the sanction deployed has to amount to at least 1 percent of the target's GNP for the sanction to be effective. By setting the bar for potential real-world significance so high, much previous research has discounted the use of FS by emerging economies, even of those in possession of substantial economic and financial capabilities.

Our goal in this volume is to understand the ways in which international politics is altered by the appearance of rising states, defined as countries that are as yet far from dominant, yet are acquiring increasingly higher financial capabilities. The changing balance among major powers presages eventual multipolarity, and it is important to expand our understanding of FS to shift the scholarly focus to where the action is. To achieve this analytical goal, we propose that FS strategies be sorted in terms of three dichotomies. Our framework explicitly builds on previous work by Andrews (2006) and his collaborators.

First, the aims of FS may be essentially "defensive" ("internally-oriented" in the terminology of Andrews 2006), and intended to shield the domestic economy (or polity) from external financial pressure. Weaker states deploy their defensive shield when, for example, they impose capital controls on cross-border financial flows or begin to construct a regional stabilization fund, utilizing mutual currency swap arrangements that potentially could aid neighbors confronting liquidity crises. Alternatively, the goal of FS may be "offensive" (Andrews 2006 would say "externally-oriented"). The goal of such offensive or assertive FS would be to alter the behavior of other states or conditions of the international environment through active engagement. Bilateral sovereign lending in which the creditor state exacts a political quid pro quo, such as voting with it in international organizations, constitutes use by the creditor state of its sword of financial power.

Second, a state's FS also divides between "bilateral" actions that target a particular rival, partner, or client state and "systemic" policies aimed at influencing global financial markets or governance institutions and practices. Traditionally, FS has been understood as exclusively direct and bilateral: State A coerces or induces State B to alter its behavior. Yet great and ongoing influence also accrues to those who can exercise structural or indirect power (Strange 1998; Barnett and Duvall 2005), as by altering the conditions of interaction within an international policy arena by means of controlling the content of procedural rules, organizing collective sanctions for deviants, or defining the agenda to be discussed in international organizations. For example, a country such as the U.S. that is able to dominate global financial markets by the size and capability of its transnational banks and investors also will be able to exercise great influence in forums for negotiating collaborative global financial regulation, such as the various multilateral committees in Basle considering bank capital adequacy and other risk-mitigation regulations. Systemic influence includes both global market dominance and decisive weight in the institutions of international financial governance. Countries whose national currencies voluntarily are held by other governments and private individuals as a store of value enjoy the "exorbitant," and systemic, "privilege" (Eichengreen 2011) of being a reserve currency country.

Finally, a third dichotomous dimension, also explored by Andrews (2006: 18–24), divides strictly "financial" types of FS, involving credit, investment, and other international flows, from the "monetary" dimension of FS, referring to matters of exchange rate levels, regimes, and international currency usage. Traditional financial sanctions or inducements revolve around withholding or providing international loans, access to offshore accounts, and other financial benefits. Monetary influence across borders is more subtle but immensely influential. Benjamin J. Cohen (1966; 2006) has suggested two types of monetary power. Both are rooted in the assumption that a bilateral trade imbalance cannot continue indefinitely: the default form of adjustment is that the deficit country either reduces economic activity, which also cuts the demand for imports, or it devalues its currency, thereby reducing imports by making them more expensive. However, an alternative is for a country to exercise its monetary power in order to export the problem, obliging another government to make adjustments, and in the process to absorb the domestic political costs of undoing its carefully constructed intersectoral bargains over macroeconomic policy. Thus, in Cohen's terminology, a reserve currency country may possess the "power to delay" adjustment, perhaps indefinitely, because other countries are willing to hold excess emissions of its currency. Any large economy, meanwhile, may possess the "power to deflect" currency or macroeconomic adjustment toward a smaller neighbor, for whom maintaining strong bilateral trading ties typically remains relatively more critical.[3] Large countries with high levels of liquidity and borrowing capacity, along with diversified economies, always have higher power to delay and deflect, while small countries typically lack both. Cohen (2006: 49–50) also observes that international monetary relations have tended to be hierarchical. Acknowledging that such hierarchy exists, our project focuses on the players who strive to ascend within international monetary hierarchies.

Table 1.1 shows the resulting major categories of contemporary FS, giving examples of instruments in each category that contemporary emerging powers either have used or reasonably might employ. The table's four major quadrants show variation across our first and second dichotomies, with the third dichotomy diagrammed within each major quadrant. Examples of *defensive and bilateral* FS (Table 1.1's upper left-hand quadrant) include policies designed to reduce a weak state's vulnerability to transnational banks or other major foreign lenders or investors, backed by powerful foreign governments. Historically, almost

Table 1.1 Emerging powers: modalities of financial statecraft

	Defensive (State A employs a financial shield)	**Offensive** (State A wields a financial sword)
Bilateral (State A directs its action toward State B)	*Financial* * Default * Nationalize FDI * Diversify sources or modalities of foreign sovereign borrowing *Monetary* * Diversify reserve currency holdings	*Financial* * Use credit or aid to exert control over smaller neighbor *Monetary* * Encourage local currency trade invoicing with smaller neighbor * Manipulate bilateral exchange rate
Systemic (State A directs its action toward structures and processes of global markets or governance institutions)	*Financial* * Capital controls * State banks *Monetary* * Accumulate reserves * Lobby for expansion of SDRs * Regional swap arrangements	*Financial* * Promote preferred changes in international regulation – e.g., global bankruptcy legislation * Become regional or global financial hub *Monetary* * Actively participate in global monetary governance * Promote norm of adjustment by both surplus and deficit states

the only option for developing country debtor states was such defensive bilateral statecraft. When they encountered payment difficulties they simply defaulted, or unilaterally rescheduled – as waves of Latin American countries did in the 1820s, the 1880s, the 1930s, and the 1980s. As a financial shield, however, default, like nationalizations of foreign direct investments, is a strategy of the weak, and not often successful. In earlier decades, private foreign creditors routinely called upon their home governments for military assistance in foreign debt collection. Today, the equivalent sanction is likely to be exclusion from future borrowing in global private markets, which has powerfully negative implications for a country's trade, access to new technology, and its public finances.

Alternatively and more proactively, the government of the emerging economy explicitly may seek to spread its sovereign borrowing (or that of its private banks and nonfinancial businesses) over lenders and investors from multiple foreign countries, rendering inter-creditor cooperation more difficult in case of a debt crisis. A similar monetary strategy – reserve currency diversification – could help a country to defend against the possibility of external monetary coercion, although it can only work if there is, in fact, a real choice among alternative reserve currencies. Moreover, the country's trading patterns normally dictate its appropriate reserve currency. For Mexico or Canada, 70–80 percent of whose trade is with the United States, expanding holdings of the euro would be of little help.

Offensive and bilateral FS (Table 1.1's upper right-hand quadrant) by emerging economies typically would refer to larger countries acting as regional hegemons, dispensing loans or foreign aid to weaker neighbors in exchange for political support or other forms of quid pro quo, including securing guaranteed future access to natural resources. This is an important strategy pursued by China today. North–South financial ties are already in some measure being replaced by South–South ones, including significant Chinese loans to Latin America (which have gone especially to countries with left-leaning governments distrusted by private international banks and investors), and both Chinese and Brazilian investments in sub-Saharan Africa (Gallagher, Irwin, and Koleski 2012; Brautigam 2010; Frayssinet 2013). Larger emerging powers, especially but not only China, also may anticipate wielding the sword of currency power in their regions. Thus the many contemporary proposals for local currency invoicing of trade championed by Russia, China, India, South Africa, and other members of the financial G20 that are *not* advanced industrial countries surely come with a savings in direct transaction costs – after all, why should the Ukraine, for example, need to purchase or earn U.S. dollars in order to buy natural gas from Russia? Yet, apparently cheaper ruble-denominated debt obligations in time could bring an unexpectedly high level of political vulnerability later. For example, Russia's recent history of economic relations with its regional periphery has been quite aggressive (Hancock 2009). Countries may also manipulate their exchange rates to improve their bilateral trade balances, a strategy termed "monetary mercantilism" (see Hamilton-Hart, Chapter 4).

The FS of emerging powers also may be *defensive and systemic*, as in the table's lower left-hand quadrant. Systemic FS is not directed against a particular foreign state or states, but rather is intended to influence the country's interactions with the international political economy in general. It includes capital controls, intended to reduce the volatility of cross-border flows, which may be responding to "push" conditions in global markets, such as the level of interest rates prevailing within the major advanced industrial countries, rather than to the "pull" of attractive investment conditions within the receiving economy. Thus the low interest rates maintained in the United States and Western Europe in the wake of the 2008–2009 GFC have sent capital chasing higher returns in countries from Brazil to India to South Africa. In this context, the mere hint in August 2013 by U.S. Federal Reserve Bank Chairman Ben Bernanke of his intent to taper off on the Fed's $85 billion in monthly asset purchases caused both the currencies and stock markets of many emerging economies to sink rapidly. Capital controls are intended to mute this too-sympathetic tuning of developing country economies to the highly variable music of global markets.

The use of state-owned banks to implement countercyclical policies in a sudden credit downturn is another shielding policy that is directed against systemic danger originating in global markets, rather than toward a specific foreign partner or rival state. On the monetary side, defensive and systemic FS includes the intentional accumulation of foreign exchange reserves as a preemptive war chest against pressure on one's home currency, as well as other strategies, including lobbying in global financial governance institutions for an expansion of reserve assets, such as the Special Drawing Rights (SDRs) of the IMF, that are not controlled by a single national government. Regional currency swap strategies also are systemic and defensive.

Finally, we reserve the label *offensive and systemic* FS, shown in the lower right-hand quadrant of Table 1.1, for a state's financial initiatives that are directed toward gaining global market power or rewriting the rules of international financial regulations and governance. We assume that, in all such cases, incumbent national governments will prefer processes, rules, and institutions that tend to advantage their citizens, banks, and government coffers. Most economists acknowledge that, when it comes to general principles of global financial regulation, there are no truly neutral rules for deciding, for example, how much risk-weighted capital systemically consequential banks ought to hold, or what types of discretion the international financial institutions should exercise when deciding on the domestic economic (and sometimes social or political) reforms a country needs to implement in order to be eligible for multilateral official credits. Any possible reform generates relative winners and losers.

In principle, the most assertive thrust of a rising power's financial sword comes when its leaders demand that they be included in the central councils of international economic governance. It is for precisely this reason that the BRICS countries at their leaders' summits in 2009 and after linked their decisions to contribute additional funds to the IMF and World Bank (arguably necessary to prevent destruction of the eurozone) to reallocation of voting shares at these institutions in their favor. South–South cooperation is more difficult than it sounds, however, as developing countries themselves have increasingly diverse substantive financial preferences. Thus, most finance ministers of emerging powers rhetorically support the notion that chronically surplus as well as deficit states should participate in adjustment. Meanwhile, they are in practice no more willing than their peers in advanced industrial countries to volunteer for painful domestic policy changes.

Having experienced severe dollar shortages and global financial instability in the aftermath of the Lehman shock, emerging market governments are demanding reforms of the global currency structure to protect their economies. Now that these emerging powers have seats at the table of global financial governance in the form of the G20 leaders' summits, they are willing to raise issues important to themselves – even when their active participation is perceived in the United States and other traditional powers as unhelpful or as an aggressive attack on the existing system. For example, officials of emerging economies such as Brazil and China have questioned the legitimacy of the continuing dominance of the U.S. dollar as the key currency for global economic exchange. At the G20 Summit in Seoul in 2010, the South Korean government put forward the "Seoul Development Consensus for Shared Growth," which explicitly incorporates the development agenda into the international economic governance discussion, thus linking topics that many in the advanced industrial countries would prefer to address separately. Although the history of the emerging powers engaging in offensive and systemic FS is not very long, we see clear signs of these governments starting to utilize these instruments to achieve their economic and political goals.

In some cases, we admit, the line between defensive shield and offensive sword in systemic FS becomes blurred. Of course, this is a common phenomenon in international relations: the well-known concept of the "security dilemma" suggests that an arms buildup genuinely perceived by State A as prudent, restrained, and defensive will almost inevitably appear to neighboring State B as dangerous, provocative, and potentially offensive (Jervis 1978). A good example of this ambiguity in FS comes from the realm of international monetary policy. At least three radically different interpretations of the political economy of China's exchange rate policies coexist in the scholarly and policy literature. From outside the country, and particularly in major Western capitals, it appears obvious that the renminbi (RMB) is vastly and presumably intentionally undervalued, leading to the conclusion that China's export-led growth has come at the expense of the United States and other trading partners (Goldstein and Lardy 2008). That is, China's exchange rate policy constitutes offensive FS. In contrast, Chin (2008) summarizes the arguments of most Chinese leaders and scholars, who perceive their country's currency policies as essentially defensive: the RMB–USD exchange rate is pegged for reasons of predictability, not predation, and the accumulation of official reserves constitutes both necessary insurance for China's economy and a benefit for foreign governments and consumers. Moreover, promotion of the RMB as an alternate reserve currency is a global systemic benefit, as it expands the options available to third-party countries (Chin 2010). Yet a third view considers China's international and domestic monetary policies to be rooted in the rent-seeking behavior of politically powerful domestic factions or special interests, such as state-owned firms (Shih 2008; Vermeiren 2013; and Volz in this volume). In this last interpretation, the foreign policy implications of Chinese exchange rate and reserve accumulation policies are almost incidental, as the real story is domestic.

The preceding example of contending interpretations of Chinese currency levels suggests that, as is the case with many theoretical models of political economy, the empirical identification of the different varieties of FS is not always straightforward, particularly when the material interests of different parties to an interpretive debate would benefit from reaching dissimilar conclusions. Hence, it is quite likely that the RMB exchange rate is overdetermined, as well as being undervalued. Nonetheless, a more nuanced understanding of the alternative main varieties of FS strategies will assist scholars in mapping the international political economy of states' financial and monetary policy choices.

In this volume, the framing of our discussion in terms of four main types of FS, each of which also exists in two subtypes (financial and monetary), allows us to make predictions linking categories of countries with characteristic forms of FS. Earlier, we noted that the most often implied meaning for FS in the existing foreign policy literature refers to what we here term "offensive and bilateral statecraft," as in the use by leaders of a powerful country of the threat of sudden withdrawal of international credits (a financial sanction) to bring a weaker country's government to heel. Meanwhile, developing countries frequently have used defensive and bilateral FS to protect their economies. As the relative capabilities and influence of emerging economies change over time, these countries will begin to address systemic-level challenges using their financial power. Identification of different modalities of FS allows us to develop hypotheses linking a country's overall position in the global interstate distribution of capabilities to the types of FS that we expect its leaders to pursue.

Thus, we anticipate the following evolution of patterns of FS. Initially, the traditional forays of developing or relatively weaker countries into financial and monetary statecraft should be purely bilateral and defensive, with shielding actions directed against a stronger rival or neighbor country perceived as threatening and dangerous. Subsequently, as certain emerging or transitional economies become relatively more capable, they should begin to employ bilateral financial swords themselves – yet typically against still smaller developing countries, not vis-à-vis major powers. Later still, many intermediate or middle powers may become sufficiently confident to enact systemically oriented policies that their governments perceive as necessary to shield the domestic economy or polity from global financial storms. These powers will hope to defy global pressure (whether from international financial markets or global governance institutions, such as the IMF) through such defensive and systemic FS. Finally, only the largest and most capable emerging powers – notably the four original BRICs countries, and particularly China – reasonably can aspire to engage in systemic and offensive (and constitutive) FS at the global level.

Plan of the book

In recent decades, governments around the Pacific Rim have developed increasingly sophisticated uses of financial shields, and in some cases financial swords. This collaborative project has explored the efforts of incumbent governments of several of the larger economies in Latin America and Asia to increase their overall ranges of national and foreign policy autonomy by employing a variety of financial, and occasionally also monetary, levers and options.

The book contains six additional chapters. Five discuss the dynamics of early 21st century FS of the countries and regions of the Pacific Rim (here defined expansively so as to include India and Brazil), while a final chapter concludes the volume. The countries analyzed in greatest depth are those larger countries whose financial policies have been more overtly interventionist, both nationally and globally, including Brazil, Argentina, and Venezuela in Latin America, as well as China, India, Malaysia, and Indonesia in Asia. Although Japan is an advanced industrial country and longtime member of the G7, it has recently elaborated important regional financial initiatives in East Asia with major emerging economies, and thus figures prominently in Chapter 6's discussion of Asian monetary regionalism.

In Chapter 2, Ignacio Labaqui compares the contemporary financial policies of Argentina and Venezuela. During the first decade of the 21st century, both countries largely reversed the neoliberal reforms of the 1990s, and reduced their dependency on international capital markets and international financial institutions. In late December 2001, Argentina halted payment on $82 billion in foreign debt, at the time the largest sovereign default ever. Venezuela's government repudiated existing contracts with transnational investors, while President Chávez repeatedly blamed his country's domestic economic problems on the United States. Contrary to the expectations of most observers, at least in the medium run, both Argentina and Venezuela apparently enhanced their autonomy in the realm of economic policy. However, the background condition enabling these outcomes was the windfall of financial resources generated by the international commodity boom of the 2000s. In analytical terms, both of these countries have employed classic forms of defensive and bilateral FS. In addition, Venezuela has sought regional political influence through offensive bilateral FS, mainly by extending loans to smaller or cash-strapped neighbors including Argentina.

In Chapter 3, Leslie Elliott Armijo and John Echeverri-Gent compare the different styles of Brazil and India as each seeks to engage with the global financial system, employing both shield and sword. The authors observe that Brazil's rhetorical attacks on systemic international monetary conditions have been sharper than India's, a difference they account for principally by reference to India's greater balance of payments vulnerability, along with its more dangerous international security circumstances, both of which render India more risk-averse. Brazilian leaders also have more confidence in their ability to engage in regional financial leadership. Yet the governments of both countries appear to have concluded that only genuine engagement in global financial governance at a high level, a quintessentially offensive and systemic orientation to FS, will be likely to ease the problems of periodic financial crises that both countries have experienced.

Next the discussion moves to Southeast Asia. In Chapter 4, Natasha Hamilton-Hart reviews the pros and cons for major governments of the region – including Indonesia, Malaysia, and Thailand – of "monetary mercantilism," or the efforts by these leaders to stockpile official reserves as a system-level defensive financial strategy. Her chapter emphasizes the domestic costs of this reserve accumulation strategy, which are both economic (in terms of foregone growth) and political (as entrenched export sectors prosper, often at the expense of consumers and more balanced growth, as well as more open policy debates).

The remaining two empirical chapters provide two different windows into the financial and monetary statecraft of China, the world's second largest economy. In Chapter 5, Ulrich Volz digs into China's somewhat conflicted and inconsistent efforts to promote the renminbi as an alternate reserve currency, observing that such a shift, while economically rational, would necessarily imply a redistribution of domestic political power that powerful interests will resist as long as possible. Then, in Chapter 6, Saori N. Katada and Injoo Sohn argue that those who dismiss the regional monetary cooperation framework initiated at Chiang Mai in 2000 as trivial because it has thus far never been utilized by distressed borrowers misunderstand its true uses for both China and Japan. East Asian regional monetary cooperation serves both as a systemic financial shield in the form of additional insurance, and as an initial foray by both these now-major Asian powers into more systemic and offensive FS, ultimately aimed at reformulating the international political economy of finance in directions more congenial to themselves.

Our concluding chapter returns once again to the larger themes of global rebalancing and our expectations of how these and other emerging powers may in future deploy their increasingly significant financial and monetary capabilities as an important credential in their drive to become global middle – or major – powers.

Notes

1. Author calculation based on data available at www.oecd.org for GDP in U.S. dollars, at currency prices and purchasing power parity, update of September 9, 2013.
2. On economic statecraft, see Mastanduno (1998), Drury (1998), Pape (1997), Drezner (1999, 2003), Hufbauer, Schott, Elliott, and Oegg (2009), and Cortright and Lopez (2002). Blanchard and Ripsman (2008) critique this literature.
3. Thus, for example, in an era of mostly fixed exchange rates, a small country whose trade was heavily oriented toward a larger neighbor might need to float or devalue its currency. This choice solves the problem for the small country's export sector but raises costs for its importers, thus upsetting previous political economy bargains among domestic interests in the smaller economy.

References

Aggarwal, Vinod. 1996. *Debt Games: Strategic Interaction in International Debt Rescheduling*. Cambridge: Cambridge University Press.

Andrews, David M. 2006. "Monetary Power and Monetary Statecraft," in David M. Andrews (ed.) *International Monetary Power*. Ithaca: Cornell University Press, pp. 7–28.

Armijo, Leslie Elliott. (ed.) 1999. *Financial Globalization and Democracy in Emerging Markets*. New York: Palgrave/St. Martins.

Armijo, Leslie Elliott, and Saori N. Katada. "Theorizing the Financial Statecraft of Emerging Powers," *New Political Economy*. Online publication January 13, 2014. DOI: 10.1080/13563467.2013.866082 (in press).

Armijo, Leslie Elliott, Laurissa Muehlich, and Daniel Tirone. "The Systemic Financial Importance of Emerging Powers." For Special Issue "Measuring and Modeling Regional Powers," ed. Philippe De Lombaerde, *Journal of Policy Modeling*, Online publication November 2013, DOI: 10.1016/j.jpolmod.2013.10.009 (in press).

Baldwin, David A. 1985. *Economic Statecraft*. Princeton: Princeton University Press.

Baldwin, David A. 2013. "Power and International Relations," in W. Carlsnaes, T. Risse, and B.A. Simmons (eds) *Handbook of International Relations* 2nd ed. Thousand Oaks, CA: SAGE Publications, pp. 273–297.

Barnett, Michael, and Raymond Duvall. 2005. "Power in International Politics," *International Organization* 59, Winter, 39–75.

Blanchard, Jean-Marc F., and Norrin M. Ripsman. 2008. "A Political Theory of Economic Statecraft," *Foreign Policy Analysis* 4, 371–398.

Brautigam, Deborah. 2010. *The Dragon's Gift: The Real Story of China in Africa*. Oxford: Oxford University Press.

Chin, Gregory T. 2010. "Remaking the Architecture: The Emerging Powers, Self-ensuring and Regional Insulation," *International Affairs* 86(3), 693–715.

Chin, Gregory T. 2013. "Understanding Currency Policy and Central Banking in China," *Journal of Asian Studies*, June. DOI: 10.1017/S002191181300051X.

Cohen, Benjamin J. 1966. "Adjustment Costs and the Distribution of New Reserves," *Princeton Studies in International Finance*, No. 18. Princeton, NJ: Princeton University, Department of Economics, International Finance Section.

Cohen, Benjamin J. 2006. "The Macrofoundations of Monetary Power," in David M. Andrews (ed.) *International Monetary Power*. Ithaca: Cornell University Press, pp. 31–50.

Cortright, David, and George A. Lopez. (eds) 2002. *In Smart Sanctions Targeting Economic Statecraft*. Lanham, Maryland: Rowman & Littlefield Publishers.

Crawford, Neta and Audie Klotz. (eds) 1999. *How Sanctions Work: Lessons from South Africa*. New York: Palgrave/St. Martins.

Drezner, Daniel W. 1999. *The Sanctions Paradox: Economic Statecraft and International Relations*. Cambridge: Cambridge University Press.

Drezner, Daniel W. 2003. "The Hidden Hand of Economic Coercion," *International Organization* 57, 643–659.

Drury, A. Cooper. 1998. "Revisiting Economic Sanctions Reconsidered," *Journal of Peace Research* 35(4), July, 497–509.

Eichengreen, Barry. 2011. *Exorbitant Privilege: The Rise and Fall of the Dollar and the Future of the International Monetary System*. New York: Oxford University Press.

Erdbrink, Thomas. 2013. "Enigmatic Leader of Iran Backs Overture, for Now," *New York Times*, September 23. [Note: this is headline from September 24 print edition. Check.]

Frayssinet, Fabiana. 2013. "Africa in Debt to Brazil: Forgiveness Isn't Always Free," Interpress Service (IPS), September 10. <www.ipsnews.net>

Gallagher, Kevin P., Amos Irwin, and Katherine Koleski. 2012. "The New Banks in Town: Chinese Finance in Latin America," *Inter-American Dialogue Report*, February.

Gilley, Bruce, and Andrew O'Neil. (eds) 2013. *Seeing Beyond Hegemony: Middle Powers and the Rise of China*. Book manuscript, under review.

Goldstein, Morris, and Nicholas R. Lardy (eds) 2008. *Debating China's Exchange Rate Policy*. Washington, DC: Peterson Institute for International Economics.

Haggard, S. 2000. *The Political Economy of the Asian Financial Crisis*. Washington, DC: Institute for International Economics.

Hancock, Kathleen J. 2009. *Regional Integration: Choosing Plutocracy*. New York: Palgrave Macmillan.

Helleiner, Eric and Jonathan Kirshner. (eds) 2009. *The Future of the Dollar*. Ithaca: Cornell University Press.

Hufbauer, Gary C., Jeffrey J. Schott, Kimberly A. Elliott, and Barbara Oegg. 2009. *Economic Sanctions Reconsidered* (3rd edition). Washington DC: Petersons Institute for International Economics.

Hurrell, Andrew. 2009. "Rising Powers and the Question of Status in International Society," Paper presented at Annual Meeting of the International Studies Association, New York City, February 15–18.

Jervis, Robert. 1978. "Cooperation under the Security Dilemma," *World Politics*, 30(2), January, 167–214.

Kirshner, Jonathan. 1995. *Currency and Coercion*. Princeton: Princeton University Press.

Kirshner, Jonathan. (ed.). 2003. *Monetary Orders: Ambiguous Economics, Ubiquitous Politics*. Ithaca: Cornell University Press.

Mastanduno, Michael. 1998. "Economics and Security in Statecraft and Scholarship," *International Organization*, 52(4), 121–154.

Maxfield, Sylvia. 1990. *Governing Capital: International Finance and Mexican Politics*. Ithaca: Cornell University Press.

Mearsheimer, John. 2001. *The Tragedy of Great Power Politics*. New York: W.W. Norton.

Nelson. Joan. 1990, "Introduction: The Politics of Economic Adjustment in Developing Nations," in Joan Nelson (ed.) *Economic Crisis and Policy Choice: The Politics of Adjustment in the Third World*. Princeton: Princeton University Press, pp. 3–32.

Noble, Gregory W. and John Ravenhill. (eds) 2000. *The Asian Financial Crisis and the Architecture of Global Finance*. Cambridge: Cambridge University Press.

Nye, Joseph. 2004. *Soft Power: The Means to Success in World Politics*. New York: Public Affairs Press.

Nye, Joseph. 1990. *Bound to Lead: The Changing Nature of American Power*. New York: Basic Books.

Pape, Robert. 1997. "Why Economic Sanctions do not Work," *International Security* 22, 90–136.

Politi, James. 2012. "New World Order Sets a Double Goal," *Financial Times*, November 23, 2012. www.ft.com/development-banks-2012.

Roberts, Cynthia. 2010. "'Introduction' to 'Polity Forum: Challengers or Stakeholders? BRICs and the Liberal World Order,'" *Polity* 42(1), January, 1–13.

Shih, Victor. 2008. *Factions and Finance: Elite Conflict and Inflation*. Cambridge: Cambridge University Press.

Steil, Benn, and Robert E. Litan. 2006. *Financial Statecraft: The Role of Financial Markets in American Foreign Policy*. New Haven, CT: Yale University Press.

Strange, Susan. 1998. *States and Markets*. London: Bloomsbury Academic.

Tammen, Ronald L., Jacek Kugler, Douglas Lemke, Allan C. Stam III, Carole Asharabati, Mark Andrew Abdollahian, Brian Efird, and A.F.K. Organski (2000) *Power Transitions: Strategies for the 21st Century*. New York: Chatham House Publishers of Seven Bridges Press.

US National Intelligence Council (USNIC). 2012. *Global Trends 2030: Alternative Worlds*. Washington, DC, US Government Printing Office.

Vermeiren, Mattias. 2013. "Foreign Exchange Accumulation and the Entrapment of Chinese Monetary Power: Toward a Balanced Growth Regime?," *New Political Economy*, January. DOI:10.1080/13563467.2013.736958.

Viner, Jacob. 1948. "Power versus Plenty as Objectives of Foreign Policy in the Seventeenth and Eighteenth Centuries," *World Politics*, 1(1), 1–28.

Wade, Robert. 1998. "The Asian Debt-and-development Crisis of 1997–?: Causes and Consequences," *World Development*, 26(8), 1535–1553.

Walter, Andrew. 2008. *Governing Finance: East Asia's Adoption of International Standards*. Ithaca: Cornell University Press.

Waltz, Kenneth N. 1979. *Theory of International Politics*. New York: McGraw-Hill.

Wise, Carol, Leslie Elliott Armijo, and Saori N. Katada (eds). Under review. *Unexpected Outcomes: How Emerging Markets Survived the Global Financial Crisis*. Book manuscript.

Woo, Jung-en. 1991. *Race to the Swift: State and Finance in Korean Industrialization*. New York: Columbia University Press.

World Bank. 2011. *Global Development Horizons 2011*. Washington DC: World Bank.

2
Who's Afraid of Reversing Neoliberal Reforms? Financial Statecraft in Argentina and Venezuela

Ignacio Labaqui

Early in the first decade of the 21st-first century, leftist governments in both Argentina and Venezuela reversed neoliberal economic reforms that were implemented in the 1990s. Shortly thereafter, both countries reduced their dependence on private international capital markets and ceased borrowing from the international financial institutions (IFIs). Popular political leaders argued that these steps were necessary to defend their domestic economies. Contrary to the dire predictions of the political opposition in both countries as well as academic theorists, however, their national economies did not collapse during the subsequent decade, nor did voters repudiate political incumbents. If their policies prove sustainable, Argentina and Venezuela will have reinvigorated the option of the blunt and confrontational forms of defensive bilateral financial statecraft (FS), similar to tactics employed by distressed sovereign borrowers prior to the 1980s in an attempt to create national financial autonomy. Furthermore, the Chávez government in Venezuela began to employ systemic FS to criticize the existing global financial governance structure and establish regional alternatives. The success of their strategies, even if it proves temporary, has been surprising. Most scholars and analysts had expected that, after the dramatic neoliberal reforms in the late 1990s and early 2000s, greater financial integration and economic liberalization had made it too costly, both economically and politically, for Latin American governments to reverse such reforms. In contrast, I argue that the Chávez administration in Venezuela and the two Kirchner administrations in Argentina managed to implement unorthodox economic policies and to reduce the power of global capital and IFIs not only due to the good fortune that they found in high commodity prices, but also thanks to domestic political support from those feeling marginalized under neoliberal economic policies.

The argument develops through five sections. The first section offers reasons to compare Argentina and Venezuela. The chapter's second and third sections detail the two countries' recent employment of uncompromising FS. Fourth section analyzes the unusual conjuncture of conditions that has enabled the apparent success of these techniques, while the final section's conclusions pose open questions for the future.

Reasons to compare Argentina and Venezuela

Argentina and Venezuela make an intriguing comparative pair because they share notable similarities in both initial structural conditions and historical experiences leading into the most recent decade. Both are among the larger states in Latin America and the Caribbean, with Argentina third in economic size (after Brazil and Mexico) and fourth (following Brazil, Mexico, and Colombia) in population, while Venezuela is fourth and sixth (after Peru) in these dimensions. In the 1980s, both Argentina and Venezuela, in common with the majority of their neighbors, experienced international debt crises and almost a decade of low or negative growth, with Argentina falling on average by 1 percent annually and Venezuela growing on average by 0.01 percent (CEPAL database). Just as the debt crisis hit in the early 1980s, Argentina returned to democratic rule, joining Venezuela among the ranks of imperfect yet functioning electoral regimes in South America. In another important similarity, in the 1990s political leaders in both countries long identified with left-leaning rhetoric and populist spending made abrupt policy shifts and began to implement neoliberal reforms. Nonetheless, during the transition to the 21st century, both countries experienced deep economic and political crises.

Argentina's military rulers yielded control of the state to civilians in 1983, following the failed attempt to reclaim the Malvinas (Falklands) Islands from Britain. In 1989, President Carlos Menem of the Justicialist Party (Peronist and historically nationalistic, populist, and statist) won the election, assuming office six months early when the government of his Radical (center-left) predecessor, President Raul Alfonsín, collapsed amid hyperinflation. Shortly after taking office, Menem unexpectedly swept Argentina onto the neoliberal reformist path. His administration not only privatized the bulk of state-owned enterprises, including public utilities, energy plants, and even the state-owned oil firm YPF, but also conducted radical trade liberalization, and lifted barriers to foreign direct investment and international capital flows. In 1991, Argentina adopted the Convertibility Act, a currency board scheme that pegged the local currency to the U.S. dollar.

The currency board became the cornerstone of Argentina's economy in the 1990s (Dammill, Frenkel, and Maurizio 2002). Argentina's central bank pegged the local currency to the US dollar and contracted to hold the total domestic money supply to no more than 100 percent of the country's mainly U.S. dollar reserves. The resultant sharp decline in inflation and resumption of growth allowed Menem to reform Argentina's constitution, lift the ban on presidential reelection, and secure a second term in office in 1995. For most of the decade, Argentina was heralded as the de facto poster child for the mix of pro-market economic reforms preferred by the International Monetary Fund (IMF) and other IFIs (Mussa 2002; Pastor and Wise 2001). However, by the end of the 1990s, an increasingly overvalued exchange rate for the Argentine peso had slowed growth and decimated exports. On the eve of the Asian financial crisis of 1997–1999, and its knock-on financial crises around the world, the excessively rigid Argentine development model already was in trouble. For example, in January 1999, Brazil, one of Argentina's major trading partners, was forced to devalue and then float its currency. At this juncture, Argentina could have abrogated the Convertibility Act, abandoning the currency board scheme it had adopted in 1991, and let the Argentine *peso* float. That option, however, implied significant domestic economic and political costs, and so was rejected both by the Menem (Peronist) and the De la Rúa (Radical Party) administrations until it was too late.

Venezuela had become a democracy in 1958 through a set of pacts, sometimes implicit yet, in many cases, the product of explicitly negotiated deals between the major political parties and the main pressure groups including the Catholic Church, the Armed Forces, business elites, and labor unions. The *Pacto de Punto Fijo* was a carefully designed arrangement for explicit alternation in high offices between the two parties that long had dominated Venezuelan politics: the center left *Acción Democrática* (AD) and the center-right Social Christian Party (COPEI). This power-sharing scheme allowed Venezuela to enjoy two decades of reasonable democratic stability. The oil boom of the 1970s made possible a continuous expansion of both government expenditures and indebtedness, as foreign lenders saw government-controlled petroleum reserves as sufficient indication of good credit.

Venezuela's credit was so good, in fact, that initially the country was hardly hit by the 1982 debt crisis. Both the Herrera Campíns (1979–1984) and Lusinchi (1984–1989) administrations resisted making any structural economic reforms, worsening public debt, deficits, and inflation. Hoping for a return to boom years of the 1970s, Venezuelans in 1989 reelected former President Carlos Andres Pérez, politically located on the center left, who in his first term in office (1974–1979, as the candidate of AD) had engaged in populist politics and expansionary fiscal policies.

Like Menem in Argentina, when Pérez took office in 1989, he surprised many of his supporters by embarking on the Venezuela's first serious attempt to adopt neoliberal economic reforms, including reductions in public deficits and modest privatizations of state-owned firms. However, Pérez's reforms, the so-called "great turnabout," met with strong popular resistance. After surviving two failed military coup attempts – one led by then Lieutenant Colonel Hugo Chávez – President Pérez was impeached by the Venezuelan Congress (Levine and Crisp 1999). Pérez's failure conforms to a common pattern in Venezuela: every attempt to initiate structural economic reforms since the 1980s has been abandoned in the midst of a profound economic crisis (Corrales 2001). Pérez's center-right successor, President Rafael Caldera (1994–1999), fared no better, so by the end of the 1990s the reformist agenda had at its best been partially completed. In Latin America as a whole, the outcome of the mostly neoliberal decade of the 1990s was deeply disappointing when compared with the relatively rapid expansion of the 1950s through the 1970s, yet certainly marked an improvement with regard to the 1980s, the so-called "lost decade." However, in the case of Venezuela, the continuous stop-and-go reform cycles turned the 1990s into a second lost decade.

By the late 1990s, pundits and ordinary citizens in both countries perceived their economies to be in serious trouble. Political and economic crises in both Argentina and Venezuela at the turn of the Millennium led their publics to elect left-leaning politicians who ran on antiestablishment platforms. Such public support enticed them to use international FS to defy the pressure of international capital markets and investors. In Argentina, the contours of the economic crisis itself initially pushed President Eduardo Duhalde (January 2002–May 2003) into adopting emergency policies, including a currency devaluation, which followed the huge foreign debt default of December 2001. Although both the default and the Argentina peso devaluation were viewed as confrontational by international creditors, only later did Dulhade's successors

Nestor Kirchner (May 2003–December 2007) and Cristina Fernández de Kirchner (December 2007–present) explicitly embrace antiglobalization and anticapitalist rhetoric and policies as a main theme of Argentina's defensive FS. In Venezuela, the record of abrupt economic policy shifts had combined with popular frustration at the failures of the two traditional and elitist ruling parties, AD and COPEI, to the point that Hugo Chávez Frías, a firebrand army officer of lower-class origins, jailed for two years in the early 1990s for attempting a military coup, could win an election in December 1998 with a mandate for radical policy change, including via the exercise of defensive, and later offensive and systemic, international FS.

Crisis and the assertion of sovereignty: Argentina's international FS after the Millennium

Argentina's deep and often-admired neoliberal structural reforms of the 1990s did not prevent a major economic crisis that culminated in 2001–2002 (Chudnovsky, Lopez, and Pupato 2003; Armijo and Faucher 2004). A succession of exogenous shocks starting with the Asian and then the 1998 Russian and Brazilian financial crises had worsened the rigidities of the convertibility scheme's hard currency peg, leading the country into recession and banking crisis by the second half of 1998. This was followed by rioting, the resignation of President Fernando de la Rúa (December 1999–December 2001), and a spectacular sovereign default on foreign debt worth $82 billion (over half the total public debt of $144 billion) in December 2001. The currency board, an exchange rate system that had pegged one peso to one U.S. dollar, and which the government for years had pledged never to remove, collapsed in January 2002, when the exchange rate abruptly floated.

The Argentine economy, whose growth rate had been declining steadily since the third quarter of 1998, shrank by fully 10.9 percent in 2002, suffering from both the foreign debt default and the dramatic exchange rate collapse. President Eduardo Duhalde (January 2002–May 2003), elected by the legislature to complete de la Rua's term, stabilized the economy and laid the basis for the resumption of growth. However, he had very few resources and options for responding to the needs of his own citizens, much less foreign creditors, who included both the IFIs and private creditors. Consequently, Duhalde's administration did not resolve most of the outstanding and serious legal conflicts with foreign investors resulting from the December 2001 default, despite strong pressures from creditors and especially the IMF (Dammill, Frenkel, and

Rapetti 2005). When Duhalde's brief presidency ended, the domestic economy had stabilized, but relations with foreign creditors were at an impasse, leaving Argentina entirely shut out of from both private and multilateral sources of international borrowing.

It was against this backdrop that Nestor Kirchner was elected President in April 2003. The Peronist governor of the Patagonian province of Santa Cruz, Kirchner, had been handpicked by Duhalde to prevent the return of former President Carlos Menem (also a Peronist, but representing a different wing of the Party). Kirchner, who in the 1990s had been supportive of neoliberal reforms, in 2003 adopted a discourse highly critical of the Washington Consensus and the policies prescribed by the IFIs. Although Carlos Menem won the first round of the April elections, polling suggested that he would lose badly to Kirchner in the second round, as other defeated candidates threw their support to whomever could prevent Menem's reelection. Menem withdrew from the second round, allowing Kirchner, who had received a mere 22 percent of the vote in the initial balloting, to become president, but without the full legitimacy for bold policies that a decisive win could have provided.

Although the economy was already growing when Nestor Kirchner took office in May 2003, Argentina still depended on IMF assistance and had to negotiate a solution for the 2001 debt default. Furthermore, Kirchner's political standing was weak. His administration's economic policy initially was fairly orthodox from a fiscal viewpoint. The preservation of a competitive exchange rate, as well as twin fiscal and external sector surpluses, became the main underpinnings of the government's economic policy (Dammil and Frenkel 2009; Albrieu and Fanelli 2008). Later President Nestor Kirchner's administration moved away from economic orthodoxy and resorted to populist spending, eventually opting for outright manipulation of the inflation statistic as its basic response to the acceleration in inflationary pressures (*La Nación*, February 1, 2007). Nonetheless, his government's policies, combined with the boost to industry resulting from the substantial real devaluation, delivered economic growth averaging 9 percent over 2003–2007.

These good economic results allowed Kirchner to nominate his wife, Senator Cristina Fernández de Kirchner, as presidential candidate. She was elected in 2007 with 45 percent of the vote. The first Cristina Fernández de Kirchner administration (2007–2011) marked a gradual departure from her husband's generally more moderate domestic economic policy framework. Under President Fernández, economic policies became notably more populist (Dammil and Frenkel 2009). Fiscal policy become overtly expansive, and an increasingly overvalued nominal exchange rate turned into the administration's main tool to prevent the acceleration of inflation. The fiscal and external sector balances deteriorated. But because the economy continued to grow, both Kirchners remained popular.

In sum, both the Nestor Kirchner and Cristina Fernández administrations made extensive use of mostly heterodox measures of defensive FS. Their purpose was to, as Argentina's leaders saw it, defend Argentina from international capital markets, whose rules of engagement, both in the private global markets and even in the IFIs, were consistently biased against them.

Argentina's defensive FS, bilateral and systemic

Although the complaints of Argentina's incumbent leaders focused on systemic problems, many of their defensive policy actions were aimed at specific foreign partners, and thus may be categorized as bilateral. Measures of defensive FS employed in Argentina in the 2000s under both Kirchners included taking an extremely tough stand in debt restructuring negotiations, as well as various measures to reduce the state's international borrowing by substituting domestic for foreign sovereign debt.

As compared to his predecessor, President Duhalde, President Nestor Kirchner's stance toward Argentina's international creditors hardened. Faced with the task of negotiating with Argentina's creditors, Kirchner made an offer that global markets quickly valued at 35 percent (a 65 percent write-down) of the defaulted debt (Helleiner 2005; Dammill, Frenkel, and Rapetti 2005; Cooper and Mosmani 2005). Despite rejection by several bondholders' associations and the IMF, by early 2005 the owners of about 76 percent of the government's sovereign bond debt had accepted the deal. Thereafter, the state borrowed from the local private sector, as well as from foreign investors willing to exchange hard currency for pesos to invest in Argentina. Whereas in the 1990s Argentine government bonds had been traded on key global exchanges, legal proceedings brought by those bondholders who had refused the 2005 package meant that it was too risky for the Argentine government to issue new debt in international markets. Between 2005 and 2008, local market financing in the form of public debt denominated in Argentine pesos played a significant role in the administration's financial policy. The Venezuelan government also made loans to the Argentine government by purchasing Argentine public bonds – which was simultaneously an instance of defensive bilateral FS by Argentina and of offensive/assertive bilateral FS by Venezuela.

These measures of defensive FS under President Nestor Kirchner quickly yielded dramatically improved numbers. For example, as shown in Figure 2.1, Argentina's gross public debt/GDP ratio dropped from 113 to 73 percent, comparing the situation immediately prior to the default (late 2001) to that after the restructuring was declared a success in 2005. As shown in Table 2.1, other debt measures improved similarly. The default itself and the restructuring, which was carried out directly between Argentina and its private creditors and not blessed by the IMF, came to be understood in Argentine policy circles as successful instances of FS. By this volume's coding scheme, they were "defensive," yet they represented novel and assertive policies by a developing country debtor, making Argentina something of a hero among left-leaning economists worldwide.

Subsequently, the Cristina Fernández de Kirchner administration employed two additional defensive measures to enhance Argentina's autonomy vis-à-vis international capital markets and the IFIs: nationalization of the private pension fund system in 2008 and an increase in the use of intra-public-sector lending as a key component of its domestic financial and fiscal policy (Labaqui 2012). Each of these strategies constituted a government decision to engage in domestic financial repression (in effect offering Argentine savers a lower return than they would have received in a freer domestic financial market) for the sake

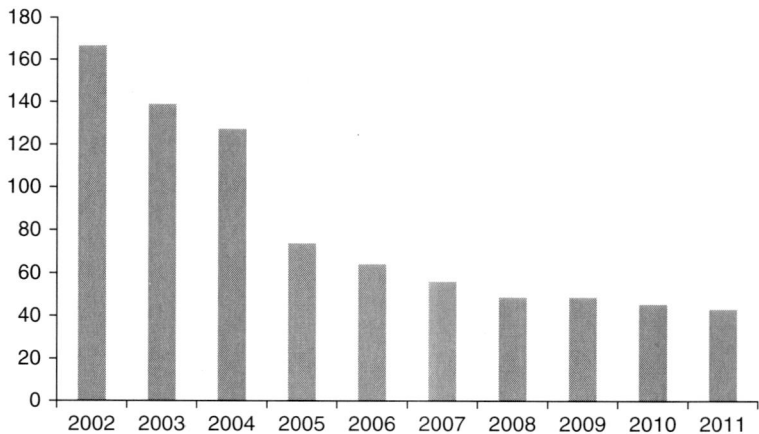

Figure 2.1 Argentina: public debt as a percentage of GDP
Source: Government of Argentina, Ministry of Economy.

Table 2.1 Argentina: debt ratios before default and after restructuring

	December 2001 (%)	March 2005 (%)
Interest payments/Exports	38	9
Gross public debt/Exports	544	367
Foreign currency-denominated gross public debt /Exports	527	230
Interest payments/Central Bank reserves	70	16
Interest payments/Government revenues	22	10
Gross debt/GDP	113	73
Amortizations falling in the following five years/Total debt	88	53

Source: Government of Argentina, Ministry of Economy (2005).

of enabling the federal government to fund itself domestically, thus defending against the need to borrow internationally. In October 2008, the government nationalized the private pension system on the questionable grounds that this was necessary to safeguard pensioners savings (*La Nación*, October 23, 2008). Not only did the government benefit from the flow of social security contributions, but it also seized the stock of assets previously managed by these funds, which was transferred to the Guarantee and Sustainability Fund (FGS), a state fund managed by the government's National Social Security Agency (ANSES). These assets amounted to $31 billion at that time, of which nearly 60 percent were public debt instruments (ANSES 2009). As a consequence of this asset transfer, the government came to hold a large share of its own debt.

However, even local capital markets became skeptical about the Argentine government as a reliable creditor following concerns about the manipulation of government statistics beginning in January 2007, and related doubts about the sustainability of the government's economic policy. Thereafter, the government resorted to different intra-public-sector sources of financing. These included temporary cash advances from the Central Bank, short-term loans from state-owned *Banco Nación*, the rollover of debt payments falling to the public sector agencies, and the placement of debt with decentralized public sector agencies. This policy was reinforced in 2010 when the government again used Central Bank reserves to prepay foreign debt obligations (Labaqui 2012).

Table 2.2 depicts these changes in the sources of financing during the administrations of the two Kirchners through 2010. Between 2005

Table 2.2 Argentina: sources of financing 2005–2010 (US$ billions)

Sources of funds (US$ bns)	2005	2006	2007	2008	2009	2010
Market operations, domestic	2.3	2.5	3.1	0.3		
Venezuela	1.5	2.3	2	2.8		
IFIs*					1	0.22
Central Bank**	0.9	0.5	0.9	1.6	1.4	8.6
Intra-public sector loans***	0.05	3.1	2.5	3.1	7.8	7.2
Primary budget surplus	6.7	7.5	8.2	10.3	4.6	6.4
Total	*21.25*	*15.9*	*16.7*	*18.1*	*14.8*	*22.42*

Notes: * Net flows from International Financial Institutions.
** Includes both the Central Bank's temporary cash advances and use of Central Bank reserves.
*** Includes placements of bonds and treasury notes to public sector agencies and loans granted by state-owned *Banco Nación*.

Source: Ministry of Economy, Argentina.

and 2007, debt issuance in domestic financial market represented a significant source of public financing, as did Venezuela's direct acquisition of Argentine government bonds. After 2008, both these avenues of financing became increasingly expensive, forcing the government to rely almost exclusively on intra-public sector transfers and its own resources (see Table 2.2). By the end of 2011, public sector holdings of government debt (including the government's debt with the Central Bank) represented about 52 percent of the total public debt, while private creditors held only about 33 percent of the debt.

In addition to aggressive foreign debt restructuring and dramatic increases in domestic financial repression, both Kirchners publically battled the heads of Argentina's monetary authority, the *Banco Central de la República Argentina* (Central Bank), over the disposition of the country's foreign exchange reserves (see Figure 2.2). The Central Bank wanted to retain a substantial war chest of foreign exchange reserves – which had accumulated following the dramatic end of the currency board in early 2002 and subsequent improvement in the external accounts – in order to protect the country from future financial contagion, while the Kirchners placed higher value on using the reserves to pay down foreign debts, in order to enhance the government's autonomy and eliminate dependence on either market financing or IFIs loans. In early 2006, just after the government declared that its foreign debt negotiations with unhappy private creditors were over, and bondholders could either accept or reject the existing deal, Argentina repaid the IMF in full, employing $9.8 billion of international reserves (*Ministério de Economía*

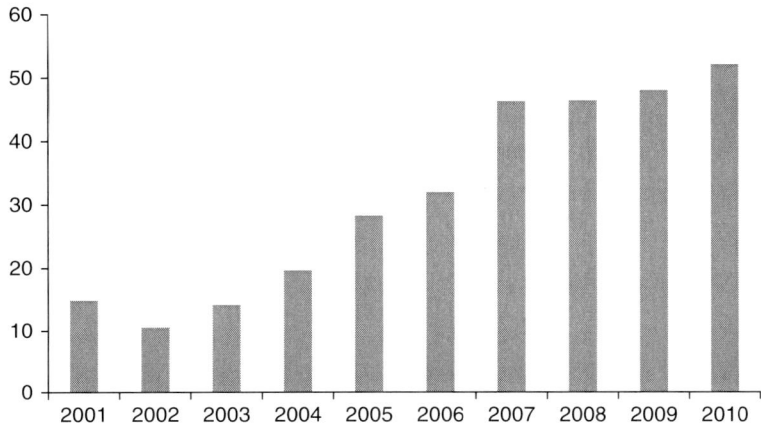

Figure 2.2 Argentina: international reserves (US$ billions)
Source: Banco Central de la República Argentina.

2006). In 2010, the government also began using reserves for the cancellation of debt owed to private creditors (*La Nación* December 14, 2009). This decision was surrounded by controversy, resulting in the removal of the Central Bank president who had opposed this use of the country's foreign exchange reserves. Overall, from 2006 through 2012, the Argentine government borrowed $32 billion from Central Bank reserves (*Banco Central de la República Argentina* 2012).

The final category of defensive FS used by Argentina in the 2000s was that of increasingly stringent capital controls. The adoption of exchange rate controls as a defensive device passed through two different stages in Argentina. Following the early 2002 devaluation and float, the country ran a large current account surplus, allowing the Central Bank to accumulate reserves but at the same time forcing significant interventions in foreign exchange markets to prevent a nominal appreciation of the exchange rate. Initially capital controls – a 30 percent reserve requirement on short-term inflows – were intended to discourage speculative inflows and to prevent appreciation (*Banco Central de la República Argentina* 2006). At least until 2008, the maintenance of a competitive real exchange rate remained a central government priority.

Subsequently, however, investor worries about the administration's increasingly statist economic policy provoked rampant capital flight. So long as the economy enjoyed a large current account surplus, capital flight was hardly a problem for the government. But by the end of 2011, inflation had significantly eroded Argentina's external competitiveness – to the extent that the current account surplus had nearly disappeared. At this point, the problem was controlling capital outflows and nominal depreciation of the currency, rather than preventing short-term capital inflows and an appreciation of the exchange rate. Capital flight totaled some $67 billion between 2007 and 2011 (*Banco Central de la República Argentina* 2011). By 2012, the Central Bank had severely restricted individuals and firms' access to foreign exchange, limiting foreign currency to government approved uses in an attempt to preserve a steep decline in Argentina's Central Bank reserves and prevent a dramatic depreciation of the Argentine peso.

Criticizing global neoliberalism

Argentina's offensive FS, which is aimed at reconstituting the rules and institutions of international financial governance, has been much more limited than its resort to defensive measures. Both Presidents Nestor Kirchner and Cristina Fernández de Kirchner were highly critical of the existing global financial architecture, particularly the IMF, and took advantage of Argentina's presence in both the leading economies' G20 and the United Nations' General Assembly, to voice those criticisms. Argentina has advocated reform of the IFIs, including the elimination of ex ante conditionality at the Fund, and has also proposed that G20 members apply tighter surveillance over hedge funds and credit-rating agencies. Under the Kirchners, Argentina has actively supported new issuances of IMF's own quasi-currency, the Special Drawing Rights (SDRs), based on a basket of multiple currencies. One benefit of a shift toward greater SDR use, in the view of recent Argentine governments, would be a lesser global role for the U.S. dollar. The Cristina Kirchner administration has also advocated greater control over the activities of credit-rating agencies and penalties for fiscal paradises (Abeles and Kiper 2010).

Furthermore, both Kirchners were enthusiastic supporters of regional initiatives such as the *Banco del Sur* (Bank of the South) and more recently the proposal for creation of a pool of reserves within the framework of the new multilateral political grouping, UNASUR (Union of South American Nations), to shield its members from an external shock (*La Nación* August 12, 2011). Argentina has also engaged in some attempts to replace the U.S. dollar as a trade transactions currency. Thus in 2008, Argentina and Brazil created the Local Currency Payments' System (SML) for bilateral trade, although its use thus far has been limited (Pasin 2010). Similarly, in April 2009, Argentina and China signed a three-year currency swap agreement, allowing for the exchange of up to 70 billion yuan for 38 billion Argentine pesos (*Banco Central de la República Argentina* 2010).

Crisis and the hope of regional leadership: Venezuela's international FS in the 21st century

The inability of Venezuela's traditional parties to deal adequately with the collapse of the inward looking import substitution industrialization (ISI) model in the context of the 1980s debt crisis resulted in a major crisis of governmental legitimacy that paved the way for the ascent to power of Hugo Chávez, the former military officer who had staged a failed coup in 1992. Chávez ran as an outsider and won the 1998 presidential elections with 56 percent of the vote, defeating the candidate backed by the economic establishment and both traditional parties. During the campaign, Chávez maintained a discourse critical of neoliberalism during a period in which Venezuela was going through another of its reform-bust cycles (Corrales 2001; Corrales and Penfold 2011). After assuming office, Chávez's high level of popular political support allowed his administration to rewrite Venezuela's Constitution in 2000 and reduce the power of the political opposition in the legislature. Yet from an economic standpoint, his government's situation was far from comfortable. International oil prices were at an historic low in the early 2000s, and the Venezuelan economy was growing sluggishly and suffering from high inflation (Corrales and Penfold 2011). Consequently, despite his highly charged anticapitalist rhetoric, until at least 2003 Chávez was unwilling to take the risk of radical economic reforms, instead maintaining an essentially moderate economic program that prioritized macroeconomic stability (Lander and Navarrete 2007).

However, growing political polarization led to a failed coup against Chávez in April 2002, and later that year the political opposition staged a three-month general strike that virtually paralyzed the state-controlled petroleum company, *Petróleos de Venezuela* (PDVSA), and hit at both Chávez's authority and public revenues. Not surprisingly, the economy shrunk by 8.9 in 2002 and another 7.8 percent the following year. Following the general strike, President Chávez retaliated by firing 17,000 PDVSA employees and abandoning the moderate economic policy stance he had held to up to that point. He had the tremendous good fortune that his turn toward an increasingly interventionist economic approach coincided with peak international oil prices.

Chávez's new policies included overtly expansionary fiscal and monetary policies buttressed by exchange and price controls, and a clearly statist orientation in economic regulation, including a series of nationalizations and other antibusiness measures that smothered private investment (Guerra 2008; Corrales and Penfold 2011). Yet between 2004 and 2008, the second five years of Chávez's presidency, Venezuela experienced an unprecedented oil boom, allowing the economy to expand over 10 percent annually. During those years, the average international price in constant dollars for Venezuelan production was more than double the average during Chávez's initial five years from 1999 to 2003 (Corrales and Penfold 2011: 47–54). Yet subsequently, another downturn in world petroleum prices resulting from the expanding global financial crisis in 2008 once again hit Venezuela hard, causing large contractions in both 2009 and 2010. Overall, growth during the decade averaged only 3.5 percent. After the administration established price and exchange rate controls in 2003, disguised inflationary pressures began to build, averaging 28 percent between 2008 and 2011. Despite the negative toll of the 2008–2009 global crisis, Chávez won a referendum overturning constitutional term limits and enabling him to continue in office.

Venezuela's defensive FS

Beginning in 2003, the Chávez administration adopted a variety of defensive FS policies, intended to reduce Venezuela's vulnerability to the whims of global investors – and also to support the "Bolivarian" project at home. The oil boom of 2004–2008 was the necessary condition allowing those economic policies. In a country where petroleum exports supply about 80 percent of foreign exchange earnings, tighter control over the state-owned oil company, PDVSA, and of foreign investment in the extractive sector enhanced the government's margin of maneuver in the realm of economic policy, as well as endowing it with a highly powerful political instrument. Reserve accumulation and exchange rate controls during the oil boom years stand also among the financial shield strategies deployed by the Chávez administration.

The passing of the 2001 Hydrocarbons Act was the first step to increase control over the company. This not only reduced PDVSA's autonomy from the Executive Branch but also enabled the subsequent reversal of the *Apertura Petrolera* law enacted in the 1990s, which had liberalized foreign direct investment in hydrocarbons (Domingo et al. 1996; Wainberg 2003). Henceforth, all new projects would require a 51 percent PDVSA participation. Furthermore, the new law increased royalties for all projects, including those that had been previously negotiated with foreign investors, and pledged to employ the oil wealth in social projects (Orhaganzi 2011; Corrales and Penfold 2011). The reversal of the

Apertura Petrolera approved by the National Assembly in 2006, completed the control of the oil sector. Thereafter, firms had to form new consortiums in which PDVSA had a majority. Most foreign companies accepted the new rules of the game (Lander and Navarrete 2007; Corrales and Penfold 2011; Orhaganzi 2011). A second step in the conquest of PDVSA was the removal of the highly professional company's top management. The 2002–2003 strike provided Chávez with the political opportunity to purge PDVSA's staff of officials opposed to the President's plans.

Finally, modification of the Central Bank's charter in 2005 allowed Chávez to seize a larger share of PDVSA's earnings. According to the new procedure, PDVSA would only sell to the Central Bank the foreign currency required for its operational expenditures and its fiscal obligations. The remainder would be transferred to the National Development Fund (Fonden) (*Banco Central de Venezuela* 2005; Gracia Hernández and Rodríguez Aveldaño 2008), a state-owned fund managed directly by President Hugo Chávez. Created in 2005, its goals are the financing of investment projects, health spending, the improvement of the debt profile, and improving emergency responses. Between 2005 and 2010, Fonden received nearly US$29 billion from PDVSA (*Banco Central de Venezuela* 2005–2010). In essence, the president has since 2005 managed a parallel budget through Fonden, which became a key instrument for financing social policy initiatives, purchasing other countries' debt instruments, and Venezuelan government liability management operations (Guerra 2008; *Banco Central de Venezuela* 2006).

Exchange rate controls were also a fundamental part of Chávez's FS toolkit. From the late 1990s, the government maintained exchange rate bands, replaced in 2002 by a free-floating scheme (CEPAL 2003). However, due to rampant capital flight prompted by the rising political conflict and the PDVSA strike, the government reimplemented tight exchange rate control in February 2003, fixing the foreign exchange parity at a rate of US$1 to 1600 Bolivars. Access to foreign exchange by individuals and firms required permission from the *Comisión Administradora de Divisas* (CADIVI) which allocates foreign exchange according to import, debt payments, and travel requirements, and depending on the availability of foreign exchange. The Bs$1600 parity was adjusted upwards by 20 percent in 2004 and by a further 12 percent in 2005, representing a devaluation of the Venezuelan currency.

The consequences of this exchange rate system were twofold. In the first place, exchange rate controls and rationing of foreign exchange led to the emergence of a parallel foreign exchange market, with a much higher parity as the Bolivar weakened against the U.S. dollar. Second, the mix of a fixed exchange rate and double digit inflation rates resulted in a significant real exchange rate appreciation in the official rate which, against the backdrop of the economic boom fueled by the oil prices between 2004 and 2007, led to a dramatic increase in imports. Using the excuse of volatile oil prices and the gathering global financial crisis, the government in January 2008 dropped three zeros from the currency, and in February 2010 took the opportunity to devalue. Venezuela also introduced a dual exchange rate scheme with a Bs$2.6 parity for basic goods' imports and a Bs$4.3 parity for other imports (Vera 2010; Balza Guanipa 2010). In 2011, the government unified the exchange rate at the Bs$4.3 parity, eliminating the lower tier of the dual exchange rate scheme (CEPAL 2011).

As in Argentina, the combination of capital controls and careful exchange rate management (or manipulation, depending on one's viewpoint), in the context of the 2004–2008 oil price bonanza, allowed Venezuela to run a large current account surplus during these years, and to accumulate substantial foreign exchange reserves, which peaked in 2008 at US$43 billion. Also as in Argentina, the incumbent government found uses for some of these official reserves. Between 2005 and 2010, the Central Bank transferred $35.8 billion to Fonden (*Banco Central de Venezuela*). By 2011, reserves had fallen to only $30 billion, due to both the decline in oil prices and the transfer of reserves to Fonden (see Figure 2.3).

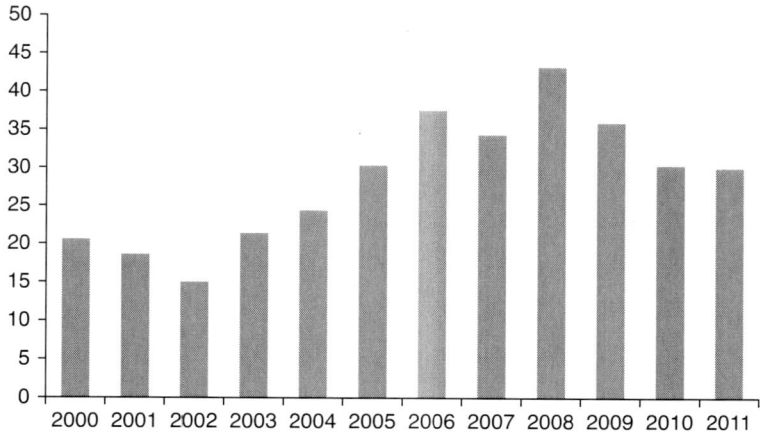

Figure 2.3 Venezuela: international reserves (US$ billions)
Source: Central Bank of Venezuela.

The role of finance in Venezuela's challenge to U.S. hegemony

The use of offensive and systemic FS was more extensive in Venezuela than in Argentina. While both countries were vocally critical of the existing global economic order in the 2000s, Chávez formulated an explicit systemic challenge with his attempt to create a set of regional financial institutions aimed at reducing the influence of the IFIs based in, and presumably beholden to, Washington, DC. His government also extended financial aid and loans to other Latin American countries with the goal of curtailing US influence in the Western Hemisphere. In fact, since assuming office in 1999, Chávez had made repeated explicit references to multipolarity and regional integration processes, signaling very clearly his intentions of balancing U.S. power in the Western Hemisphere (Lander and Navarrete 2007). The tighter grip over PDVSA and the oil price boom of the 2000s facilitated the enactment of an ambitious foreign policy. By the same token, some of Chávez's policies lost momentum after 2008 as a consequence of global financial crisis.

The creation of a regional financial institution, *Banco del Sur* (Bank of the South), the setting up of the *Sistema Único de Compensación Regional* (Unified Regional Compensation System, SUCRE), a trading system in local currency, and the loans to other countries in the region stand among the main initiatives launched by Chávez. *Banco del Sur*, envisioned by the Venezuelan government as an alternative to traditional IFIs, was launched by presidents Chávez and Kirchner in February 2007 (Rosales 2010; Lustig 2009). This initiative had a positive reception among regional countries from both the left-leaning Bolivarian Alternative for the Americas (ALBA) and the more politically moderate Mercosur (the Common Market of the South). As a result, during the UNASUR Summit of December 2007, Argentina, Bolivia, Brazil, Ecuador, Paraguay, Uruguay, and Venezuela signed the foundational act of the *Banco del Sur*, and in September 2009 the signatory countries subscribed the Bank's Constitutive Agreement. However, the bank's actual design now best fits Brazil's view of the *Banco del Sur* as a regional development bank rather than Chávez's intention of directly challenging the existing multilateral and regional IFIs: the IMF, the World Bank, and the Inter-American Development Bank. Despite the enthusiasm shown by signatory countries, negotiations for the effective launching of the Bank have proceeded at a slow pace (Rosales 2010). As of late 2013, the project remained stalled.

Venezuela has also sought to challenge the role of the U.S. dollar by promoting trade in other currencies with some of its trading partners. An alternative currency, the SUCRE, was launched in April 2009 by

Cuba, Bolivia, Honduras, Nicaragua, and Venezuela, all members of the Venezuela-led ALBA (Bolivarian Alliance). SUCRE's goals are to replace the US dollar in regional trade transactions and promote regional monetary integration (Rosales, Cerezal, and Molero 2011). In practice, neither the *Banco del Sur* nor the SUCRE has yet materialized in any meaningful fashion.

In contrast, the granting of loans and aid around Latin America and the Caribbean became in the 2000s a concrete element in Venezuela's foreign policy. The oil boom allowed the Venezuelan government to practice "check diplomacy" – a form of bilateral and offensive FS – by providing financial assistance to other countries in the region in order to promote Venezuela's regional leadership. This policy peaked between 2004 and 2008, when the Venezuelan government enjoyed plentiful of resources to grant unconditional – albeit neither free nor cheap – financial assistance. Argentina was the largest recipient of Venezuela's financing during those years. Between 2005 and 2008, Venezuela provided $8.6 billion in financing to the Argentine government by underwriting its sovereign bonds (Labaqui 2012). These Argentine bonds were later off-loaded to the Venezuelan private sector through the three *Bono del Sur* (Bond of the South) joint issuances. According to the Central Bank of Venezuela (2007), the goal of these joint issuances was to promote regional financial integration. Meanwhile, the appeal of joint issuances for private Venezuelan firms and individuals is hardly surprising: *Bono del Sur* issuances provided access to hard currency (the instruments that were part of *Bono del Sur* were all U.S. dollar-denominated securities) in the context of tight exchange rate controls and foreign currency rationing.

From a purely political perspective, *Bono del Sur* was all gain for both the Venezuelan and Argentine governments. The Kirchner administration, which used some of the money to pay off its debt to the IMF, had access to an alternative and unconditional source of financing. And as for Chávez, financial assistance to his neighbors (which was in the end by no means cheaper for them than market financing) provided him with a powerful diplomatic instrument to cement his regional political leadership (Labaqui 2012). However, against the backdrop of Argentina's higher sovereign spreads and a less comfortable fiscal situation in Venezuela, there were no more purchases of Argentina's debt by the Chávez administration after 2008. Venezuela also purchased, although on a much smaller scale, US$300 million in Ecuadorean sovereign bonds in 2005 (*El Universo* 2005) and US$100 million in Paraguayan debt in 2007 (*ABC 2006*).

Accounting for the "success" of heterodox FS in South America

For many outside observers, the surprise has been the apparently high degree of success the Argentine and Venezuelan governments have obtained from the highly confrontational and heterodox measures of both defensive and offensive FS adopted since the turn of the Millennium. This is success as measured in terms of obtaining acceptable, if not stellar, outcomes in such measures as GDP growth and employment, plus the political approval of their populations. Both Hugo Chávez and Cristina Fernández de Kirchner have been successful in the ballot box. Chávez was reelected in 2006 and again in 2012, while Cristina Kirchner secured a second term in office in 2011. Moreover, Venezuela's "check diplomacy" clearly won friends for the Bolivarian movement and its leader around Latin America and the Caribbean.

This was not what either most foreign observers or the domestic political opposition in the two countries expected to occur. By the end of the 1990s and early 2000s, following more than a decade dominated by the Washington Consensus agenda, the scholarly consensus was that reforms had made Latin American countries not only more fiscally responsible, but also more vulnerable to volatility in international capital flows, thus effectively curtailing their ability to pursue any domestic policies judged as unsound by international capital markets. The main consequence of the greater financial integration resulting from neoliberal reforms was the limited room for reversing those reforms due to the high economic and political costs assumed to be attached to such a course of action (Weyland 2004; Remmer 2003). However, as this chapter demonstrates, this was not the case in either Argentina or Venezuela in the 2000s. Although private financial markets did not reward Argentina and Venezuela's populist macroeconomic policies, both countries were able to achieve growth and their heads of state enjoyed a remarkable success with voters. Both the Chávez and the two Kirchner administrations succeeded in reducing the leverage of international capital markets and IFIs, carving out for themselves greater space for implementing unorthodox economic policies.

I close by asking whether this model really has worked as well as it looks to have done, or whether other fortuitous factors intervened, which may explain much of the apparently good performance of this highly heterodox model and bold use of international FS. Both countries' ability to achieve higher growth rates than in the past (at least through 2011) and at the same time challenge the prescriptions of

IFI's and the markets suggests that populist macroeconomic policies in some circumstances may be sustainable, at least in the medium term. However, as noted by Ocampo (2010), high commodity prices explain most of the story of Latin American, and especially South American, economies in the 2000s. Argentina and Venezuela were no exception. Both countries benefitted from the remarkable improvement in their terms of trade during the 2000s. This improvement was much higher in Venezuela than in Argentina. Figures 2.4 and 2.5 compare the evolution of energy prices (relevant for Venezuela) and foodstuff prices (beneficial to Argentina) during the 2000s, as well as the evolution of both countries' terms of trade.

The greater margin of maneuver enjoyed by both countries vis-à-vis international capital markets and the IFIs in the 2000s is consistent with previous findings. As Maxfield and Haggard (1996) observe, financial integration turns governments into hostages of foreign exchange and capital markets, obliging them to higher levels of fiscal and monetary discipline. Presumably, then, politicians will avoid pursuing the policies

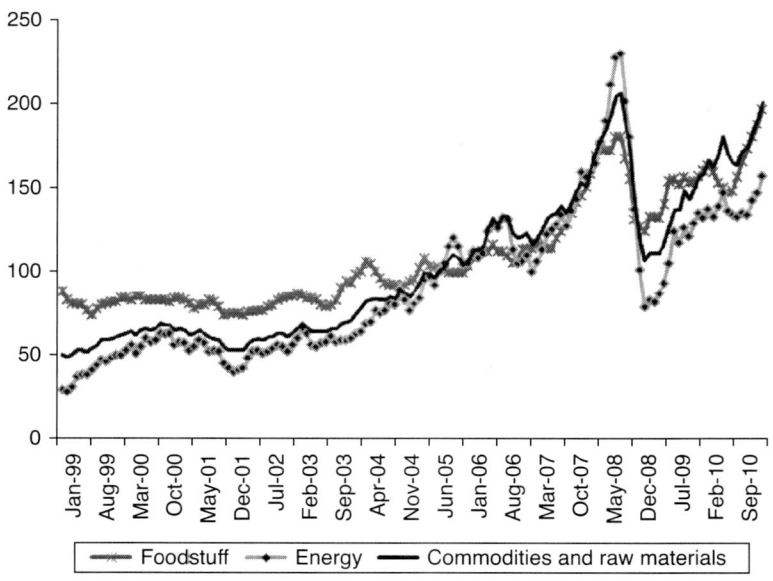

Figure 2.4 International commodities, energy, and foodstuff price indexes, 1999–2010 (2005=100)

Source: Economic Commission for Latin America and the Caribbean (CEPAL).

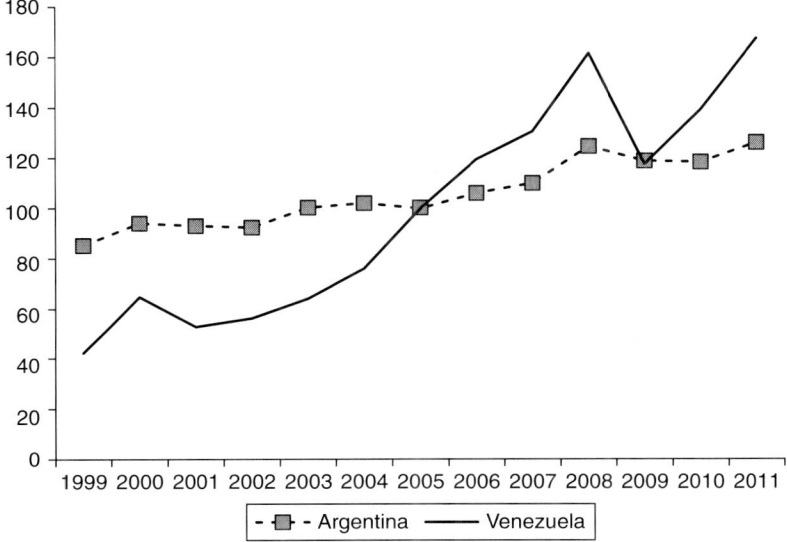

Figure 2.5 Argentina and Venezuela: terms of trade with the world economy, 1999–2011 (2005=100)
Source: CEPAL.

demanded by international capital markets, unless the cost of violating their prescriptions becomes a threat to their incumbency. During the 1990s, as predicted, the need to attract foreign investors led politicians to liberalize capital movements and to increase central bank independence with the goal of signaling investors, effectively reducing their margin of maneuver in the realm of economic policy (Maxfield 1997). However, in the face of favorable conditions granting an easy access to foreign exchange, either because of abundant international liquidity or because of an export boom, many governments will opt to set up exchange rate controls and enhance their bargaining power vis-à-vis international investors (Maxfield and Haggard 1996). If they also benefit from other sources of good fortune – such as high prices for what they export – so much the better.

Conclusions

During the past decade, both Argentina and Venezuela adopted economic policies that departed significantly from the prescriptions of IFIs and the preferences of international capital markets. While the scholarly literature from the late 1990s and early 2000s argued that engaging in such policies would entail high political and economic costs that would make a reversal of neoliberal reforms almost impossible, both the Argentine and Venezuelan experiences suggest that this is not always the case. Defensive bilateral and systemic FS strategies allowed both countries to regain degrees of freedom with respect to the IFIs and international investors. In both cases, a highly favorable international economic environment characterized by a significant improvement in their terms of trade provided the condition necessary to set in motion economic policies judged as unsound by international capital markets and IFIs.

Still, there is some variation in the resort to the defensive FS between these two cases. The debt restructuring of 2005 was crucial for the enhancement of Argentina's autonomy in the field of economic policy. The commodity boom, in turn, allowed the Argentine government to accumulate central bank reserves which were used first to bring to an end the long-standing and conflictive relationship with the IMF, and later as an alternative to market financing. In the case of Venezuela, the takeover of the national petroleum firm and major earner of foreign exchange, PDVSA, which until the 2002–2003 strike had enjoyed considerable autonomy from the executive branch, was a crucial enabling condition for Chávez's "twenty-first century socialism." This was especially true in the context of a global boom in energy prices that persisted through 2008.

Offensive FS, or the attempt by incumbent national governments to employ financial resources to alter the international environment, was much more evident in Venezuelan than in Argentina, whether we consider bilateral inducements to create or solidify friendly relations with neighbors or original systemic initiatives to remake the institutions of international financial governance,. The magnitude of the oil boom, the weight of the oil sector in terms of both exports and revenues, and Chávez's personal ambitions for regional leadership together provide a tentative explanation for Venezuela's more extensive use of offensive FS particularly at the regional level. Argentina has cheered Venezuela's initiatives and more importantly has taken its criticisms toward the existing global financial governance to the G20 (of which Venezuela is not a member) and other international forums, but overall has been less active than Venezuela in the international arena. Nonetheless, Venezuela's offensive FS initiatives such as the *Banco del Sur*, SUCRE, and the joint issuance of debt instruments seem to have had only limited success when compared to its use of defensive FS.

This said, the long-term efficacy of these assertive and heterodox instruments of defensive FS in terms of their ability to shield the domestic economy from exogenous shocks is debatable. Both Argentina and Venezuela were hard hit by the global economic downturn of 2009 despite their defensive measures. In terms of growth, both Argentina and Venezuela accelerated their growth rates during the 2000s, albeit against the backdrop of a double digit inflation rate that is rarely found in other countries in the region, much less the larger world. Still it is difficult to contend that defensive FS, rather than highly favorable international economic conditions – particularly between about 2003 and 2008 – was the main explanation for either country's economic performance. The leaders' political calculations vis-à-vis their domestic audiences have dominated their agenda, and they have thus far managed to succeed electorally. It remains an open question whether the populist macroeconomic road taken by both countries is actually an adequate strategy to protect their economies from an exogenous shock in the present international financial context of rising uncertainty.

Note

I am grateful to Leslie Elliott Armijo for her comments on this chapter. The errors are entirely mine.

References

Abeles, Martín, and Esteban Kiper. 2010. "El G20 y el rol de la Argentina." Serie Aportes N9, Fundación Friedrich Ebert, Buenos Aires, Argentina. Available from: http://library.fes.de/pdf-files/bueros/argentinien/07653.pdf (accessed January 12, 2012).

Armijo, Leslie, and Philippe Faucher. 2004. "Crises cambiais e estrutura decisória: a política de recuperação econômica na Argentina e no Brasil," *Dados* 47(2), Rio de Janeiro, 297–334.

Balza Guanipa, Ronald. 2010. "La Tercera Devaluación de Hugo Chávez." ARI No. 24/2010. Real Instituto Elcano, Madrid. Available from: http://www.realinstitutoelcano.org/wps/wcm/connect/3c36ff004137d584976af76d616c2160/ARI24-2010_Balza_devaluacion_Venezuela.pdf?MOD=AJPERES&CACHEID=3c36ff004137d584976af76d616c2160 (accessed January 31, 2012).

Banco Central de la República Argentina. 2006. "Informe al Honorable Congreso de la Nación." Buenos Aires: Banco Central de la República Argentina. Available from: www.bcra.gov.ar (accessed January 10, 2012).

Banco Central de la República Argentina. 2010. "Informe al Honorable Congreso de la Nación." Buenos Aires: Banco Central de la República Argentina. Available from: www.bcra.gov.ar (accessed January 10, 2012).

Banco Central de la República Bolivariana de Venezuela. 1999–2010. "Informe Económico (various editions)." Caracas: Banco Central de la República de

Venezuela. Available from: http://www.bcv.org.ve/c1/Publicaciones.asp?Codigo=122&Operacion=2&Sec=True (accessed February 7–March 1, 2012).

Chudnovsky, Daniel, Andrés López, and Germán Pupato. 2003. *Las recientes crisis sistémicas en países emergentes: las peculiaridades del caso argentino*. Buenos Aires: Siglo XXI Editores.

Comisión Económica para América Latina y el Caribe. 2000–2011. "Estudio Económico de América Latina y el Caribe (various editions)." Santiago de Chile: CEPAL. Available from http://www.eclac.org/cgi-bin/getProd.asp?xml=/de/agrupadores_xml/aes252.xml&xsl=/publicaciones/agrupa_listado.xsl&base=/publicaciones/top_publicaciones.xsl (accessed February 7–March 10, 2012).

Cooper, Andrew F., and Bessma Mosmani. 2005. "Negotiating Out of Argentina's Financial Crisis: Segmenting the International Creditors," *New Political Economy*, 10(3), 305–302.

Corrales, Javier. 2001. "Estados Rezagados en las Reformas y la Cuestión de la Devaluación: La Respuesta de Venezuela a las Conmociones Exógenas de 1997–98," in Wise, Carol, and Riordan Roett (eds) *Políticas de Tasa de Cambio en América Latina*. Buenos Aires: Editorial Nuevo Hacer, pp. 157–197.

Corrales, Javier, and Michael Penfold. 2011. *Dragon in the Tropics: Hugo Chávez and the Political Economy of Revolution in Venezuela*. Washington, DC: Brookings Institution Press.

Damill, Mario and Roberto Frenkel. 2009."Las políticas macroeconómicas en la evolución reciente argentina." Nuevos Documentos CEDES N65. Buenos Aires: Centro de Estudios de Estado y Sociedad.

Damill, Mario, Roberto Frenkel, and Roxana Maurizio. 2002. Argentina: Una década de convertibilidad, Oficina Internacional del Trabajo (OIT), Santiago de Chile.

Domingo, Carlos, Maruja Fargier, Jesús Mora, Vicente Ramírez, Andrés Rojas y Giorgio Tonella 1996. "La Apertura Petrolera en el Capitalismo Rentístico Venezolano: un intento de explicación," *Comercio Exterior*, 46(11), November.

Gracia Hernández, Maximiliano, and Raquel Reyes Avendaño. 2008. "Análisis de la Política Económica en Venezuela 1998–2006," *Revista Oikos*, 26, 25–47.

Guerra, José Ángel. 2008. "El endeudamiento público en Venezuela: Situación actual e implicaciones futuras." Instituto Latinoamericano de Investigaciones Sociales (ILDIS), Caracas. Available from: http://www.ildis.org.ve/website/p_index.php?ids=7&tipo=P&vermas=130 (accessed February 11, 2012).

Haggard, Stephand, and Sylvia Maxfield. 1996. "The Political Economy of Financial Internationalization in the Developing World," *International Organization*, 50(1), 35–68.

Helleiner, Eric. 2005. "The Strange Story of Bush and the Argentine Debt Crisis," *Third World Quarterly*, 26(6), 951–969.

Labaqui, Ignacio. 2012. "Living with Our Own Means: The Role of Financial Policy in the Néstor and Cristina Fernández de Kirchner Administrations," paper prepared for the XXX International Congress of the Latin American Studies Association, San Francisco, May 23–26.

Lander, Edgardo, and Pablo Navarrete. 2007. "The Economic Policy of the Latin American Left in Government: Venezuela." Briefing 2007/02, Havens Center-Rosa Luxemburg Stiftung Transnational Institute, Amsterdam.

Levine, D. H., and Crisp, Brian. 1999. "Venezuela," in Diamond, Larry, Hartlyn, Jonathan, Lipset, Seymour Martin, and Linz, Juan (eds) *Democracy in Developing Countries*, 2nd ed. Lynne Rienner, Boulder Colorado.

Lustig, Carola. 2009. "Banco del Sur, ¿Un modelo a seguir para la construcción de instituciones regionales en el marco de la nueva agenda de América del Sur?." Ponencia presentada en las Jornadas del Área de Relaciones Internacionales de FLACSO-Argentina "Las relaciones internacionales, una disciplina en constante movimiento," Buenos Aires, October 1–3, 2009.

Maxfield, Sylvia. 1997. Gatekeepers of Growth. *The Political Economy of Central Banking in Developing Countries*. Princeton: Princeton University Press.

Mussa, Michael. 2002. *Argentina y el FMI. Del triunfo a la tragedia*. Buenos Aires, Argentina: Planeta.

Ocampo, José Antonio. 2010. "How Well has Latin America Fared during the Global Financial crisis." Policy Brief 56, Iniciativa para la Transparencia Financiera. Available from: http://www.itf.org.ar/pdf/lecturas/lectura56.pdf

Orhaganzi Özgür. 2011. "Contours of Alternative Policy Making in Venezuela," *Political Economy Research Institute*, University of Amherst, Massachusetts. Available from: http://www.peri.umass.edu/236/hash/ae52c887aef80a167a95 2b2d23f58447/publication/487/ (accessed February 12, 2012).

Pasin, María Cristina. 2010. "Sistema de Pagos en Moneda Local (SML) Argentina-Brasil," presentation at the Reunión Regional: Reforma de la Arquitectura Financiera Internacional y Cooperación Monetaria y Financiera en América Latina y el Caribe, Caracas, Venezuela, April 9–10th.

Remmer, Karen. 2003. "Elections and Economics in Contemporary Latin America," in Wise, Carol and Riordan Roett (eds) *Post-stabilization politics in Latin America. Competition, Transition, Collapse*. Washington, DC: Brookings Institution, pp. 31–55.

Rosales, Antulio. 2010. "El Banco del Sur y el Sucre: (Des)Acuerdos sobre una arquitectura financiera alternativa." Available from: http://www.rosalux.org. ec/es/analisis/bolivia/itemlist/tag/Banco%20del%20Sur.html (accessed March 20, 2012).

Rosales, Antulio, Manuel Cerezal, and Ricardo Molero. 2011. "Sucre: A Monetary Tool Toward Economic Complementarity." *Research on Money and Finance Discussion Paper N11*. Available from: http://researchonmoneyandfinance.org/ media/papers/RMF-31-Rosales-Cerezal-Molero.pdf (accessed March 22, 2012).

Vera, Leonardo. 2010. "Venezuela: anatomía de una recesión profunda y prolongada," *Nueva Sociedad*, 228, 14–25.

Weyland, Kurt. 2004. "Neoliberalism and Democracy in Latin America: A Mixed Record," *Latin American Politics and Society*, 46(1), 135–157.

Wise, Carol, and Pastor, Manuel. 2001. "From Poster Child to Basket Case," *Foreign Affairs*, 80(6) 60–72.

Statisitical websites (consulted August 2013)

Banco Central de la República Argentina: www.bcra.gov.ar
Banco Central de la República Bolivariana de Venezuela: www.bcv.org.ve
Casa Rosada (Argentina) www.casarosada.gov.ar [Official website for the Presidency and Executive Branch of the government.]
Comisión Económica para América Latina y el Caribe (CEPAL): www.eclac.org
Instituto Nacional de Estadísticas y Censos: www.indec.gov.ar [Argentine National Statistical Institute]

Government of Argentina, Ministry of Economy www.mecon.gov.ar
Government of Venezuela, Public Credit Bureau. *Oficina de Crédito Público de la República Bolivariana de Venezuela*: www.oncp.gob.ve
Ministerio de Economía y Finanzas Públicas de la República Argentina. 2005–2010. *Cuenta de Inversión* (various editions) Available from http://www.mecon.gov.ar/hacienda/cgn/cuenta/ (accessed January 15, 2012).
Ministerio de Economía y Finanzas Públicas de la República Argentina. 2011. *Informe de Deuda Pública al 30/09/2011*. Available from: http://www.mecon.gov.ar/finanzas/sfinan/deuda_ultimo.htm (accessed January 15, 2012).

Periodicals

Diario ABC Color (Paraguay): www.abc.com.py
Diario La Nación (Argentina): www.lanacion.com.ar
El Universo (Ecuador): www.eluniverso.com

3
Brave New World? The Politics of International Finance in Brazil and India

Leslie Elliott Armijo and John Echeverri-Gent

The financial reputations of Brazil and India have undergone remarkable transitions since the early 1990s. At that time, Brazilian inflation soared beyond a thousand percent annually, following a decade of increasingly desperate, and ultimately failed, emergency stabilization plans. In 1991, India suffered its worst monetary crisis in decades. Panicked investors tried to take money out of the country, very tight capital controls notwithstanding, while the government was forced to devalue the rupee by almost 19 percent. Only 20 years later, much had changed. By the time of the global financial crisis (GFC) of 2008–2009, both countries were acknowledged as significant global economic and political players, and in November 2008 Brazilian President Lula da Silva and Indian Prime Minister Manmohan Singh joined a select group of other senior world leaders at the first G20 Summit.

This chapter inquires into the ways in which Brazil and India have sought to employ financial statecraft (FS) amidst the momentous global – and national – changes since the second millennium. As the world gradually evolves toward a more decentralized distribution of power and resources, the two provide a particularly apt comparison. Among the rising economies, only China clearly is likely to join the United States as a superpower. At the same time, an emerging tier of countries, including Brazil and India, will become increasingly consequential. This chapter asks how their relative, if incremental, ascendance has been reflected in the FS choices of these two intermediate powers. This volume's introductory chapter hypothesizes that global rebalancing will be reflected in the emergence of different types of FS. Do we see the expected patterns reflected in the financial policy choices of the governments of Brazil and India?

We argue that systemic, rather than bilateral, FS is now the dominant modus operandi of leaders in both countries, and that Brazil and India each engage with global markets and financial governance institutions and practices both defensively and offensively. However the style – and to some extent also the substance – of recent Brazilian forays into FS has been notably more assertive and challenging to the status quo global financial powers than has been the case with India's rather circumspect and polite waving of its international financial sword.

The chapter's first section details our reasons for comparing the two large emerging economies. Section two considers bilateral FS, today much less important to either country than it was during earlier eras. Sections three and four consider, respectively, defensive/systemic and then offensive/systemic FS. Our penultimate section accounts for the differences between Brazilian and Indian international financial and monetary policymaking by reference to three factors: their relative international economic vulnerability, regional geopolitics, and domestic politics. The conclusion addresses this volume's larger themes.

Brazil and India: structural parallels suggest similar strategies

Through the 1980s, state-promoted industrialization was the dominant development strategy in both countries, accompanied in each by pervasive government intervention in banks and financial markets. Both Brazil and India significantly liberalized trade and finance in the 1990s. Subsequently, growth accelerated in each, becoming steady in Brazil and positively exuberant in India. By 2007, on the eve of the GFC, each had become a large emerging market of roughly similar size, Brazil with a GDP of $1.4 trillion and India with a GDP of $1.2 trillion, both calculated at market rates. When measured at purchasing power parity, India's GDP exceeded Brazil's.[1]

The two countries' financial structures also were similar by 2007, on at least four different dimensions. First, both nations had widely respected, although not formally independent, central banks and recent histories of stable, single-digit inflation, although Brazil had finally tamed its chronic hyperinflation only in the mid-1990s (Armijo 2005). After its currency, the real, floated in 1999, the Brazilian Central Bank (BCB) instituted inflation-targeting. By the late 2000s, BCB officials, typically drawn from the private financial sector or academia, regularly received kudos from their peers worldwide. The BCB's most important policy instrument has been the policy interest rate, which the open market committee of the central bank announces directly and manages via SELIC (Special System for Settlement and Custody), its open market trading system.

India's central bank, the Reserve Bank of India (RBI), was founded in 1935 under the British. Historically committed to holding inflation to single digits and maintaining exchange rate stability, the RBI usually has been led by career civil servants with financial expertise, appointed by the Ministry of Finance. Until 2000, the RBI targeted the banking sector's reserve money – composed of the Cash Reserve Ratio (CRR), which requires banks to maintain at least 5 percent of their demand liabilities in noninterest bearing accounts, and also the statutory liquidity ratio (SLR), which long required banks to hold not less than 20 percent of their demand and time liabilities in cash, gold, or government securities – as its primary monetary policy instrument. In times of stress, such as the balance of payments crisis of 1990–1991, the RBI would raise total reserve requirements to over 50 percent of deposits. India's central bank reduced its reliance on these cruder instruments during the 1990s, and in 2000 it introduced the Liquidity Adjustment Facility which enabled it to use the treasury securities' repurchase rate as a policy interest rate.

Second, both countries have a mixture of public- and private-sector domestic banks, and each maintains both de jure and de facto barriers against foreign banks, although to a lesser degree in Brazil than in India. In the 1990s, Brazil was forced to modernize and privatize its banking sector in a hurry, as inflation's demise revealed waves of illiquid and insolvent banks (Stallings and Studart 2006). Two giant public sector development banks, the BNDES (National Economic and Social Development Bank) and CEF (Federal Savings Bank), remain Brazil's primary sources of long-term finance but are not direct competitors with commercial banks, which focus on working capital loans and financial services. Brazil's commercial banks, now fewer and larger than in the early 1990s, top the list of Latin America's largest. Today's big four display the gamut of ownership structures, ranging from majority public-sector *Banco do Brasil*, to private sector *Itaú* and *Bradesco*, to majority Spanish-owned *Santander Brasil*.

In India, nationalizations of British and other foreign banks immediately following independence, and then again of large Indian-owned banks in 1969 and 1980, brought all of the country's large banks into the public sector. Incremental banking reforms that began in the 1990s have enabled private sector banks to have a limited but growing presence. Nonetheless, as of 2007, over 70 percent of Indian banking assets remained with public sector banks, and financial products, rates, and lending practices remained tightly regulated.

Third, both countries have significant securities markets. Brazil's equity market capitalization, only 5 percent of GDP in 1980, had soared to 113 percent by 2009, while India's jumped from 3 to an astonishing 173 percent of GDP during the same period. However, Brazil's corporate debt market, 19 percent of GDP in 2009, outpaces India's, which is only 4 percent of GDP. Overall, in the decade of the 2000's total financial assets (bank deposits, insurance assets, stocks, and bonds) rose from 164 to 302 percent in Brazil and from 142 to 334 percent in India (Beck and Levine 2000).[2] Among the set of larger emerging economies, both Brazil and India fall somewhere between the thoroughly privatized and liberalized banking and financial sectors of Mexico or South Korea – and China's state monopoly of banking.

A final structural financial similarity inheres in the size, although not necessarily the composition, of the two countries' links to global financial markets. In 2009, Brazil's total stock of external financial liabilities was 68 percent of GDP – while India's was closely equivalent at 66 percent (Lane and Milesi-Ferretti 2007).[3] Brazil's more liberal inward foreign direct investment (FDI) regime meant that a larger share of its international liabilities were FDI in plants and equipment, while the Indian authorities have preferred to attract portfolio investments, often in assets marketed to the diaspora community. Both countries also built up their foreign exchange reserves following the emerging markets' crises of the 1990s. By 2007, Brazil's were $180 billion, while India's totaled $276 billion.[4]

In sum, in recent years both countries have liberalized notably, while yet retaining a vigorous state financial presence. On one index of financial policy liberalization (ranging from 0 to 100, representing least to most neoliberal), Brazil's score in 2007 was 54.2 and India's 49.1. For comparison, the U.S.' score was 81.3.[5] Both countries floated their exchange rates around the turn of the millennium, Brazil under market duress in January 1999 and India more gradually in mid-2007. All in all, their significant structural financial parallels suggest the possibility of similar choices when it comes to FS.

Bilateral FS: fading or merely transforming?

Until quite recently, neither Brazil nor India expected to be able to compete in international financial markets, nor did their governments expect to shape global financial rules. Their efforts at FS were almost entirely defensive. Financial defense also was typically bilateral, as the threats came from specific creditors and not from systemic contagion.

Prior to World War II, Brazil's major creditors were Britain, from the early 19th century to the mid-1930s, and thereafter the United States. Successive Brazilian governments negotiated cleverly with these dominant powers over debts, and occasionally direct investments, sometimes quite intentionally playing one foreign creditor off against the other. For example, President Getúlio Vargas in the late 1930s flirted with cooperating with the Axis powers in order to secure more generous aid from the United States as a quid pro quo for providing submarine refueling bases on the northeast Brazilian coast and sending a Brazilian division to fight with the Allies in Italy. In contrast, because India's major creditor, Britain, was also the imperial ruling power, overt bilateral and defensive FS by India only first came into play during the negotiations over Indian independence in 1946–1947. Britain had purchased extensive supplies from India and other Commonwealth nations during the war, but made payment only into the government of India's sterling account in London, which was frozen until the war's end. At that time, Britain and the soon-to-be independent government of India disagreed over the appropriate sterling–rupee conversion rate for these debts, with each insisting on the rate more favorable to it. India prevailed only when the United States took its side.

Bilateral and defensive FS became less important in both countries in the postwar era, as the protective efforts of the Brazilian and Indian governments were increasingly directed toward monitoring systemic interactions, not bilateral exchanges. For Brazil, the major recent period of bilateral, defensive FS was during the 1980s debt crisis. Brazil took several unilateral steps that its policymakers considered necessary, including a moratorium on debt principal (but not interest) repayments declared in 1987. India's Prime Minister Indira Gandhi engaged in bilateral and defensive FS when she signed the Indo-Soviet Treaty of Friendship and cooperation in 1971 and began accepting foreign aid and political advice from Moscow. In both of these high-profile incidents, the developing country successfully resisted foreign pressure in the short to medium term, although incurring some monetary and reputational costs.[6]

With respect to bilateral and offensive FS, we note that both Brazil's and India's neighbors occasionally have believed that these regionally dominant powers were exercising financial and monetary power aggressively. Brazil in particular has become active as a direct investor in its smaller neighbors, leading to charges of Brazilian imperialism whenever there are conflicts. Nonetheless, Brazilian leaders have tried hard to soft-pedal their dominant position in South America. For instance, when the government of Bolivia in 2008 decided to seize a natural gas field for which Brazil's state petroleum firm, *Petrobras*, had a long-term development lease, Brazil could have exerted compelling financial pressure had it chosen to do so. After all Brazil offered a unique mix of capital, technology, and political acceptability as a foreign investor to the left-leaning Bolivian government – besides being a major market for Bolivian gas. Instead, President Lula da Silva's government decided to take a conciliatory attitude, so much so that Lula received scathing criticism within Brazil. More recently, Brazil's growing bilateral investment and aid ties with sub-Saharan Africa are often noticed, and may well have contributed to Brazil's strong showing in recent international popularity contests, such as the case in 2013 that resulted in the election of Brazilian Roberto Azevêdo as the new head of the World Trade Organization (WTO). However, any specific demands for bilateral reciprocity are very difficult to demonstrate. India has had fewer opportunities for employing its financial sword in a bilateral conflict, as India's strategy for entering global financial markets has focused less on South–South ties and more on becoming a provider of niche financial services in advanced industrial country markets.

We conclude that, at this point in their histories, both Brazil and India are too large to need to defend themselves against aggressive FS from others, but too small to be able to project significant power on a bilateral basis in the international financial sphere. Their involvement in bilateral FS, whether defensive or offensive, is thus limited.

Systemic defense: between economic liberalism and interventionism

In the 1950s through the 1980s, FS in these two sleepy giants was dominated by defensive and systemic measures to limit and control interactions with global capital markets, including multiple exchange rates (in Brazil through the mid-1960s), an extensive and restrictive licensing system for access to foreign exchange (which in India lasted into the early 1990s), and pervasive capital controls, particularly in India. By the 1990s, many of these long-term systemic financial defenses were looking increasingly outmoded and were slowly dismantled in both countries. Through the 1990s and 2000s, policymakers in both countries promoted incremental domestic financial deregulation and external capital account liberalization, sometimes out of a conviction that freer financial markets would stimulate growth, and other times from a simple need to attract foreign capital. Thus, on the eve of the crisis that began in U.S. financial markets in 2007, financial policies in both Brazil and India had been moving in a liberalizing direction.

More recently, the turmoil generated by the global crisis impressed many policymakers and intellectuals in both Brazil and India with the need for state intervention in the short run while also increasing concerns about the long-term goal of dramatic international financial opening. During the main periods of international contagion in 2008–2009, both governments employed FS to defend against systemic dangers, while nonetheless maintaining their domestic policy autonomy.

Monetary policy during the GFC

The first line of defense against the GFC was monetary policy, which the central banks in each country de facto reoriented from a focus on domestic to an emphasis on international conditions. Although our main interest in this volume lies with interventionist policies that fall outside the standard neoclassical macroeconomic repertoire, domestic monetary policy provides the essential backdrop. As theorists of the "impossibility trinity" point out, maintaining autonomous monetary policy is problematic in a world of globalized capital markets with high capital mobility and floating exchange rates. The disruption caused by the GFC placed a premium on the capacity for flexible monetary responses.

The two big emerging economies were at opposite stages in their respective domestic monetary policy cycles when the crisis hit, with Brazilian central bankers trying to loosen and their Indian counterparts trying to tighten. The crisis forced both countries to reverse course. In the case of Brazil, the government had been attempting to lower the policy interest rate (SELIC rate) ever since its spike when the exchange rate floated in early 1999. Since then Brazil's nominal and real interest rates had been among the world's highest, as shown in Figure 3.1. High rates not only had historical causes, but also resulted from Brazil's inflation-targeting regime in the context of often expansionary fiscal policy. The ongoing GFC repeatedly forced the BCB to tighten, as in mid-2008 through early 2009, and again from about March 2010 through mid-2011, in order to stem panicked investors' "flight to quality." Nonetheless, the peaks were significantly lower than those earlier in the decade, especially the spike in late 2002 just prior to the presidential elections that brought to power an historic leftist, Luiz Inácio ("Lula") da Silva of the Workers' Party (PT).[7] Following the January 2011 inauguration of President Dilma

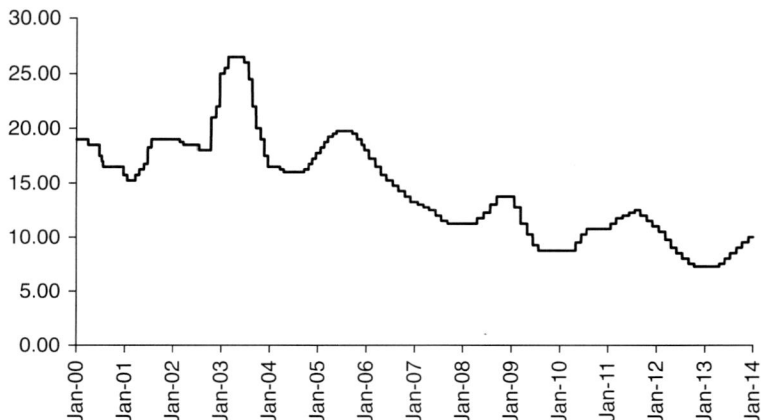

Figure 3.1 Brazil's policy interest rate (SELIC), 2000–2014
Source: www.ipeadata.gov.br.

Rouseff, her government began a concerted push to take advantage of low interest rates in major markets in order to return to the long-term goal of bringing Brazil's policy rate down (without risking massive capital flight), while also pressuring banks to reduce their deposit-loan spreads. Yet with worries about the U.S. Fed's intended monetary taper, Brazilian rates again began rising in 2013.

When Lehman Brothers crashed in 2008, India's RBI had been in a period of tightening. As a result of the crash, there was a brief but frightening run on ICICI Bank, India's largest private bank and second largest commercial bank overall, because some observers worried that its U.K. subsidiary might have exposure to subprime assets in the United States. The fears dissolved only when the Reserve Bank announced its unqualified support for all of ICICI's depositors. The ICICI incident was an example of how, despite Indian capital controls, the Indian domestic financial sector was affected by the GFC. Prior to the GFC, many Indian firms had increasingly accessed less expensive foreign markets to fund their short-term capital needs. When the crisis hit and foreign markets froze, these firms were unable to roll over their trade credits and external commercial borrowings. In desperate need of liquidity, the firms began borrowing from the Indian money market. Investors' declining risk appetite deflated equity and real estate prices and put additional pressure on India's financial institutions. The resultant liquidity crisis contributed to a collapse in the index of industrial production from an average growth rate of 8.5 percent in 2007 to 0.5 percent in the final quarter of 2008 (Reserve Bank of India 2010: 283). This triggered the RBI's switch to an expansionary monetary regime. Overall, the effective policy interest rate dropped from 9.00 percent in September 2008 to 3.25 percent in April 2009, with similar cuts in the CRR and SLR (see Figure 3.2). Together, these measures injected liquidity estimated at about 3.6 percent of GDP in the initial year of the crisis. From the second quarter of 2010 onwards, the RBI was able to return to its previous policy of gradual tightening of the policy interest rate, while the CRR remained low.

Although the GFC complicated monetary policymaking in Brazil and India, on the whole policymakers in both countries acquitted themselves well, engaging in reasonably successful fire-fighting related to international pressures, eventually enabling them to return to focusing on their domestic priorities.

Capital controls during the GFC

Senior policymakers in both countries also believed that they needed capital controls in order for their monetary policy interventions to work. Brazil's most important capital control in the 2000s was a tax on all cross-border operations, the IOF (financial operations tax).[8] In

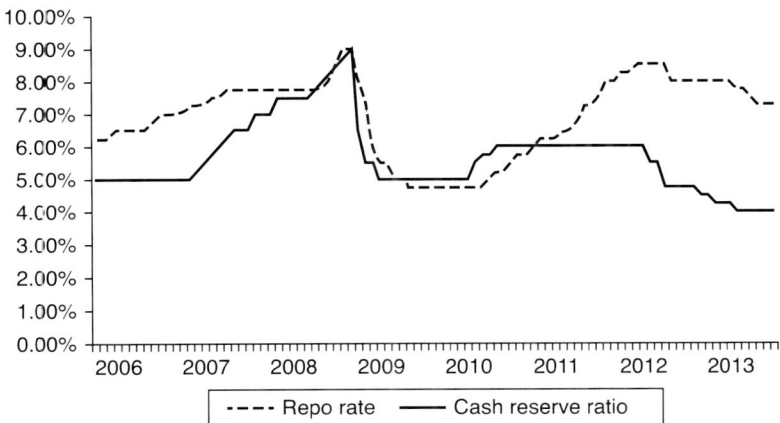

Figure 3.2 India's policy interest rate (Repo) and Cash Reserve Ratio, October 2005–June 2013

Source: Reserve Bank of India, *Handbook of Statistics on Indian Economy 2012–13*, Table 46. Available from: http://www.rbi.org.in/scripts/AnnualPublications.aspx?head=Handbook%20 of%20Statistics%20on%20Indian%20Economy (accessed on January 17, 2013).

general, Brazilian policymakers treated the capital controls regime as an instrument for monetary policy fine-tuning – similar to their frequent adjustments to the policy interest rate, the SELIC rate. Occasionally, policymakers became so frustrated with short-term capital inflows pushing up the exchange rate that they raised taxes on capital inflows to prohibitive levels – as when in late 2010 the IOF on Brazilian government bonds briefly reached 98 percent for foreign portfolio investors holding the bonds only 24 hours! Brazilian policymakers under the left-leaning Lula da Silva and Rousseff governments also remained committed to certain financial regulations that were not directly relevant to the management of short-term capital movements, but which arguably contributed to national economic independence. For example, foreign banks were required to constitute themselves as subsidiaries of the parent (a legal form that obliged them to raise much of their initial capital locally), rather than as bank branches. *Financial Times* columnist Gillian Tett (2009) concluded that this requirement in fact had encouraged foreign banks to identify more with the host rather than the home economy during the recent crisis.

India also implemented inward capital and investment controls, although many market participants found them clumsy. In general and historically, India's capital controls had often been categorical or quota-driven, rather than incentive and market-based (if rather changeable) as in Brazil. The essence of India's system has been the distinction among three types of private investors, each with decreasing privileges: local citizens, the Indian diaspora (known as nonresident Indians, or NRIs), and other foreigners.[9] In 2004 the RBI, which is both central bank and the main financial regulator, had created a five-year plan for gradual liberalization as part of India's commitments in the services trade (GATS) negotiations through the WTO. The RBI's principal response to the GFC was easy – it simply postponed the previously agreed financial services liberalization plan. This was particularly infuriating for NRI investors (*inter alia*, owners of about three-quarters of the common stock in India's two largest private banks, ICICI and HFDC), who were still smarting from a 2007 incident in which the RBI's deputy governor, alarmed at the speed of financial opening, had suggested that NRIs in the financial sector perhaps ought to be considered as ordinary "foreigners," which would have retroactively reduced some of the privileges associated with their intermediate status.[10]

In both countries, then, many incumbent senior financial policymakers clearly believed that the country's legacy of inherited capital controls had aided in its ability to absorb the international shocks of

2008–2009. At the same time, other economists concerned with slowing growth and crumbling or simply absent industrial infrastructure found these same barriers to free capital movements intensely frustrating.

Discretionary funds, state banks, and international reserves

How much financial discretion do national governments in a globalized economy need? Another variety of defensive and systemic FS includes state-controlled banks and discretionary financial resources that executive branch policymakers can grab and redeploy in a crisis. In the view of many senior economic policymakers in emerging economies, this is a capability that major powers routinely have enjoyed, but which the IMF and other "Washington Consensus" reformers would deny peripheral countries on the grounds that it is incompatible with free market precepts. For example, in late 1994, the Clinton administration's Treasury Department extended emergency financing to Mexico as the peso/tequila crisis was breaking. The emergency bailout money actually came from the Exchange Stabilization Fund, intended to protect the U.S. economy in the event of an attack on the dollar – which was not exactly the situation. Instead, the U.S. Treasury and Federal Reserve Bank deployed these as discretionary funds, not requiring lengthy approval from Congress, for short-term financial firefighting in a neighboring economy. Similarly, the U.S. Federal Reserve Bank in late 2008 made available emergency swap lines of up to $30 billion each to Brazil, Mexico, Singapore, and South Korea. Emerging economy finance ministers have asked why their governments should not also control discretionary funds to be deployed in emergencies.

When the international financial crisis hit in mid-2008, both Brazil's and India's governments had two types of state-controlled financial resources potentially at their disposal: large foreign exchange reserves, and the assets and institutional capabilities of public sector banks. The Brazilian Central Bank (BCB) employed its ample foreign exchange reserves to assume the foreign currency component of debts of Brazilian firms and banks abroad whose falling exports had suddenly rendered these loans hard to service, while the Finance Ministry turned to Brazil's major public banks to implement emergency support and expansionary policies. The National Economic and Social Development Bank (BNDES), an industrial development bank hitherto specialized in long-term support for Brazilian firms, began offering trade credit and working capital to Brazilian transnational firms operating abroad whose normal (foreign) sources of financing had dried up due to the global crisis (Armijo, in press). The bulk of Brazil's domestic fiscal stimulus also was channeled through the BNDES, which received $58 billion in direct transfers from the Treasury in 2008–2009, which the BNDES then channeled to larger business borrowers. About a third of these funds were on-loaned to Brazilian banks to serve smaller firms (Bevins 2010).

India's government acted similarly. In addition to switching from restrictive to expansionary monetary policy described above, the RBI spent nearly $63 billion of its foreign reserves to stabilize the value of the rupee and help Indian corporations keep current on their foreign debt payments (*Economist* 2008b). In addition, the government used fiscal policy to stimulate the economy. India's fiscal deficit increased from 2.7 percent of GDP in 2007–2008 to 6.0 percent in 2008–2009 and 6.5 percent in 2009–2010.[11]

This quick review of defensive and systemic FS suggests that, as compared to the 1980s and before, both Brazil and India were less financially interventionist in the 1990s and 2000s. However, the GFC shocked policymakers and opinion leaders in both countries, and their leaders' financial policy responses became more activist during 2008–2010, at least in the interim. Policymakers not only employed conventional monetary policy, but also manipulated capital controls and used state banks to support private sector banks and firms with foreign currency debts. Also interesting is the dog that did not bark – that is, the lack of any involvement by either Brazil or India in any regional monetary cooperation, swap, or stabilization schemes, either during the crisis or in response to it – a sharp contrast to the situation in East Asia, as discussed by Katada and Sohn in Chapter 6 of this volume.[12] At the end of this chapter, we speculate briefly about the likely effects of the GFC on future financial policymaking in the two countries.

Systemic financial swashbuckling: Brazilian bravado, Indian circumspection

This volume's fourth major analytical category is that of "offensive and systemic" FS. This label refers to the national government's use of the country's financial capabilities in an assertive fashion with the intent of influencing a range of international outcomes. Following a brief look at international aid to their private sectors, we look at both the substance and style of new efforts by the two countries' governments to become players in global financial governance.

Brazil and India's possession of nontrivial national financial capabilities led to their invitation into coveted international political power circles, first and most notably into the financial G20 and then to the regular leaders' summits initiated in November 2008, as well as into the Financial Stability Board and the Basle banking committees, where they became full members in 2009. Moreover, expanding South–South diplomatic links have some potential to enhance the systemic financial capabilities of both Brazil and India, as for example via the large emerging markets' club: the BRICS, which held its first official leaders' summit in April 2009 in Russia. Here, the choices made by recent Brazilian and Indian leaders diverged somewhat more than we saw in the previous section's comparison of their uses of defensive and systemic FS such as capital controls, channeling emergency funds through state banks, and employing foreign exchange reserves for crisis-related fire-fighting.

In all of the major advanced industrial democracies, one accepted task of national ministries of finance and trade (such as the U.S. Departments of Treasury and Commerce) long has been that of assisting home country firms and banks to compete abroad, including through financial support for their activities, as with favorable access to credit through export–import banks. While this type of assistance is not normally conceptualized as state financial interventionism, it clearly is. Many emerging market countries, including Brazil and India, have begun to see active support for their multinational firms and banks abroad as a crucial component of foreign policy. As of mid-2009, Brazil's public sector development bank, the BNDES, had a portfolio of $15.6 billion in credits to support exports of both goods and services such as heavy construction and engineering throughout South America.[13] Brazil has also targeted sub-Saharan Africa as an important destination for both exports and FDI.

India's external financial strategy centers on increasing global financial service exports. Extensive diasporic networks, expertise in business process outsourcing, and the experience gained from its relatively sophisticated equity market infrastructure have enabled India to become the sixth largest exporter of financial services in the world, albeit with only a little more than 2 percent of all global exports in financial services.[14] India's government has articulated plans to expand its share of financial service exports and become a major international player in this sector (Ministry of Finance of India 2007). Ragunathan Rajan, who in September 2013 was appointed Governor of the RBI, had in 2009 chaired a committee that drafted a key government report outlining the critical steps in a strategy to liberalize the financial sector and enhance its integration with the global economy (India Planning Commission 2009).

While their strategies to support their transnational firms were similar, the two countries differed in their willingness to express themselves publicly on issues of global financial governance. Under the center-right administrations of President Fernando Henrique Cardoso (1995–1998, 1999–2002), Brazil actively engaged with most of the world, traveling frequently to Europe and the United States, as well as around Latin America and Lusophone Africa. Cardoso strengthened MERCOSUR (the Common Market of the South, including Argentina, Uruguay, and Paraguay) and subsequently promoted a regional political cooperation process for all of South America formalized in 2006 as UNASUR (Union of South American Nations). Under the center-left administrations of his successor, President Lula da Silva, Brazilian leaders sharpened their focus on forming "South–South" alliances with other developing countries, including its South American neighbors, East Asia, Africa, and the Middle East. Under Lula, Brazil provided both rhetorical support and the promise of a substantial monetary contribution for Venezuela's proposal to create a multilateral *Banco del Sur* as an alternative to the IMF for South American countries. The *Banco del Sur* project, however, remained stalled as of late 2013.

During the international financial turmoil, President Lula and senior policymakers became quite bold in some of their public pronouncements, in some cases embarrassing more traditional Brazilian diplomats and politicians. Thus, in July 2008, President Lula da Silva bragged that the "financial tsunami" that had hit the United States and other developed nations was only a "*marelinha*" (small wave too small to surf on) in Brazil. In mid-March 2009, Finance Minister Mantega boldly promoted Brazilian public debt securities as a "safer alternative" to U.S. Treasury bonds. Later that month, during a state visit to Brazil by the ardent multilateralist, British Prime Minister Gordon Brown, President Lula publicly blamed the financial crisis that had punished "black and brown people" on the mistakes committed by "white people with blue eyes who before the crisis appeared to know everything and now demonstrate that they know nothing" (Wheatley 2009). After the IMF announced in April 2009 that it would issue its first international bond offering, the Chinese, Brazilians, and Indians all pointedly subscribed for large amounts: $30 billion, $10 billion, and $10 billion, respectively, allowing President Lula numerous opportunities at home to point out proudly that Brazil had, under his watch, been transformed from an international debtor to a creditor. In June 2009, Foreign Minister Celso Amorím imprudently declared that the G8 was "dead," leading to a subsequent rebuke by Brazil's partner in the BRICs' club, Russia – which was also a G8 member.

In September 2010, Mantega was the first senior policymaker publicly to name the rising tension over global imbalances – either caused by or reflected in "weak" and "strong" currencies – a "currency war." Encouraged by Brazil's vocal criticism of countries that manipulated their exchange rates to generate a trade advantage, U.S. Treasury Secretary Timothy Geithner journeyed to Brazil in hopes of securing a joint U.S.–Brazil statement censuring countries (implicitly China) that intervened to keep their currencies undervalued. But joint statements with the United States aimed at China did not fit with official Brazil's new self-image. Mantega instead let it be known that, in Brazil's view, the United States was equally guilty of contributing to global imbalances by implementing loose monetary policy, which generated low interest rates and put pressure on countries, like Brazil, fighting excessive capital inflows. Later Brazil's finance minister went further, declining to criticize BRICS[15] partner China at all, while complaining persistently about the United States as a source of global imbalances. This stance was somewhat disingenuous, since a coordinated stimulus sufficient to rescue the global economy surely required a major effort by the United States.

In contrast to the bold statements and independent positions that its leaders had taken during the 1970s heyday of the nonaligned movement, contemporary Indian leaders have been much more circumspect in the recent era of India's economic ascendance. Indian political leaders and senior economic policymakers have participated enthusiastically in global economic fora, from the G20 and BRICs groupings, to high-profile transnational gatherings such as the World Economic Forum at Davos. But their public pronouncements have been more modest than Brazil's. In fact, Indian business leaders, rather than politicians or senior economic policymakers, have been the main source of self-confident statements about India's role in the 21st-century world. Thus in 2008 Lakshmi Mittal, CEO of Arcelor Mittal, wrote in the *Economist* that the global economy was at the point of a major power shift toward emerging economies, noting that, "The developed world should be thankful for this trend. As consumers in the advanced economies retrench from unsustainable levels – American consumer spending alone accounts for 21 percent of global GDP – shoppers in the BRICs will take up the slack" (Economist 2008a).

Indian politicians have not entirely refrained from international pontificating. In the context of U.S.–China trade disputes that clouded the September 2009 meeting of the G20 in Pittsburgh, Prime Minister Manmohan Singh lectured India's G20 partners on the evils of protectionism. In April 2010, Finance Minister Pranab Mukherjee flatly rejected British Prime Minister Gordon Brown's proposal for a tax on all financial transactions worldwide (a version of the "Tobin tax") at the

G20 meeting. Brown's idea had been to use the monies raised to "reform the global financial system," which many of those present understood as code for providing additional resources for compensating Western European governments for the money they had spent and would spend on rescuing their troubled banks. Mukherjee made clear that any extra taxes on Indian banks would not be used to rescue wealthy Europeans, but would need to go toward extending basic financial services to the millions of unbanked poor in India. In November 2011, India joined China in a formal statement critical of the advanced economies for their sins of macroeconomic mismanagement.

Nonetheless, as compared to Brazilian leaders during these same years, Indian politicians were less publicly assertive in demanding changes to the institutions of international finance and more willing to settle for marginal changes within the status quo. Thus at the Cannes G20 meeting in November 2011, Prime Minister Manmohan Singh applauded the signing of the Convention of Mutual Assistance in Tax Matters and declared that "[t]he era of bank secrecy is over" (*Financial Express* 2011). At subsequent G20 meetings, India again has given high priority to its initiative to encourage countries to share tax information in an effort to curb tax evasion and the funding of terrorism. Hence, India is pushing for the improvement of financial transparency, a reform theme popular among the G7 countries, but decidedly less so among many emerging economies, including both China and Russia.

India also has been an enthusiastic participant in various incremental financial collaboration projects advanced at meetings of the BRICS. One such emerged in late 2011 as the leaders announced that the five countries would begin listing stock index futures and other basic derivatives on one another's stock exchanges. As a country in great need of investment in infrastructural projects, India formally proposed that the BRICS establish a development bank in February 2012. Unfortunately, a conflict quickly broke out over India's preference for a rotating chairmanship versus China's insistence that, as the likely major source of funds, its nationals should permanently head such an institution. In the New Delhi BRICS meeting at the end of March 2012, India's concerns about the "BRICS bank" delayed the advance of the project, and Manmohan Singh, prime minister of the largest recipient of World Bank assistance, expressed a preference to reform the World Bank rather than create a new institution (Bagchi 2012).

One sees, thus, a not so subtle contrast between Brazil and India in the degree to which each has sought to employ its newfound international financial prominence to promote itself assertively as a global player with an agenda to transform global finance. Brazil is more obviously enthusiastic about playing such a role. Nonetheless, the members of the BRICS share a common goal of "international financial reform," the core definition of which is greater influence for themselves in multilateral financial governance. Thus the BRICS have sometimes been an effective lobby within the G20 (Armijo and Roberts 2014). In 2009, for example, they made it clear that they would not agree to raise additional resources for the IMF to use in responding to the GFC until the other members of the G20 acceded to their request for greater developing country representation in the Fund. In early 2012, once again, Fund Managing Director Christine Lagarde requested an increase of $600 billion in IMF capital subscription, much of it to be used in support of Western European rescue. The BRICS again made their assent conditional on a further increment to their voting power within the Fund – which has been promised, although not yet implemented.[16]

At each of their biannual meetings, the BRICs have signaled their disapproval of the global dominance of the U.S. dollar. In March 2012, the five formally pledged to move, albeit incrementally, from dollar to local currency invoicing for bilateral trade and investment. Of course, China, with its $3.2 trillion in foreign reserves, has larger financial capabilities than its BRICS partners. Both Brazil and India worry over their structural trade deficits with China, the country which in 2009 displaced the United States as the principal trading partner of both countries. Sometimes, as in the case of the BRICS development bank, China's superior economic power impedes the group's deeper cooperation.

Accounting for similarity and divergence in FS

Our investigation has found both similar and divergent FS in our two cases. In recent years, both countries have used many of the same tools of *defensive and systemic* FS. The major difference between the two on the eve of the GFC was that the underlying national financial policy framework in Brazil was somewhat more liberalized. The medium-term trend in both countries is toward greater financial liberalization – but only up to a certain limit. Neither in Brazil nor in India are policymakers inclined to yield the tools that give them potential defensive and systemic FS capabilities for the future, particularly since many senior policymakers in both countries believe that certain kinds of state intervention were critical in allowing them to defend their respective countries with relatively ease during the recent period of global turmoil. With respect to *offensive and systemic* FS, however, the differences between Brazil and

India are larger. While both have been happy to employ their greater global prominence to lobby for enhanced participation in multilateral economic governance, Brazil has been more willing to publicly criticize U.S. global financial leadership. Plausible reasons for Brazil's more assertive FS and India's relatively more cautious approach since 2007 are rooted in their different political economies. We begin below with economic differences, and then move to political factors.

Despite the parallels deriving from Brazil and India's status as large emerging markets that liberalized their financial sectors after years of state-led development and financial repression, Brazil is less vulnerable than India to disruption caused by international economic markets. The variation plausibly spawns differences in their strategies of economic statecraft. To begin with, India is poorer. Although India has grown faster than Brazil since 1990, with India's per capita income increasing 4.2 times to 2011 compared to Brazil's 2.3 times in the same period, Brazil is a more developed emerging market. In 2011, Brazil's per capita income of $11,500 (in terms of purchasing power parity) was more than three times greater than India's per capita income of $3,620. The share of each country's population with daily incomes less than $1.25 is an instructive indicator of the sheer number of citizens that lack the financial resources to participate in growth, and that also have been excluded from most of the benefits of growth. In 2009, only 6 percent of Brazil's population lay below this poverty line as compared to a third of all Indians.[17]

India's growth is more tightly linked to that of the world economy. Despite the enduring image of India as a relatively closed economy, India's trade in goods and services amounted to 54 percent of GDP in India in 2012 in comparison to only 25 percent in Brazil. This divergence in the share of trade in the economy is quite recent, reflecting India's slow but steady trade liberalization since 1991. According to the Heritage Foundation's index of "trade freedom," which measures policy indicators on a scale of 0 to 100 (low to high), India increased its trade openness from less than 20 in 2000 to 51 in 2009, a period during which Brazil moved from 51 to 72.[18] That is, Brazil's trade regime was and remains more liberal, but India has opened more rapidly and trade is now more important for its national income. For India, trade has not only generated rapid growth – it also has introduced greater vulnerability to trade disruption and price volatility.

As Figure 3.3 demonstrates, Brazil's merchandise trade usually is either balanced or in surplus, and the country has benefitted from the commodity boom since the early 2000s. India suffers from a structural deficit in merchandise trade that has grown substantially since 2001. A

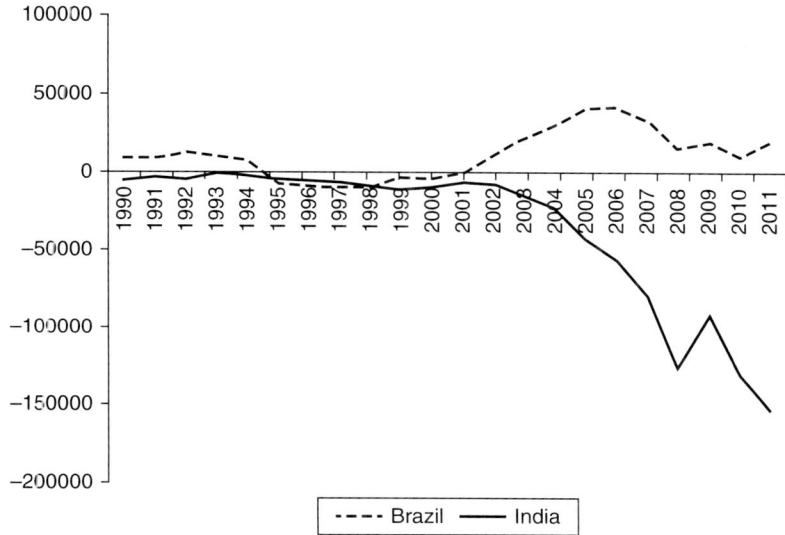

Figure 3.3 Brazil and India: merchandise trade balance, 1990–2011 (U.S.$ millions)
Source: World Trade Organization, statistical database.

key factor in India's structural deficit is that it imports three-fourths of its crude oil needs. While fuel accounts for about 36 percent of Indian merchandise imports, the 17 percent of Brazil's imports that are fuel are roughly balanced by Brazil's energy exports. Although India's merchandise trade deficit is almost always reduced by its surplus in invisibles, including financial services exports and remittances,[19] its current account usually remains in deficit. India's overall balance of payments deficits since 2003 have been substantially larger than Brazil's, as shown in Figure 3.4.

As discussed above, the two countries have accumulated similarly sized stocks of financial inflows. Nonetheless, Indian policymakers have felt more anxious about capital account volatility than have Brazilian policymakers. Policymakers in Brazil may be counting on their home financial markets being more developed, in the belief that greater domestic financial depth and breadth enables countries to better cope with the economic volatility that accompanies integration with global financial markets (Kose et al. 2007). India's equity market is at least as sophisticated as Brazil's, but Brazil has various advantages over India.[20]

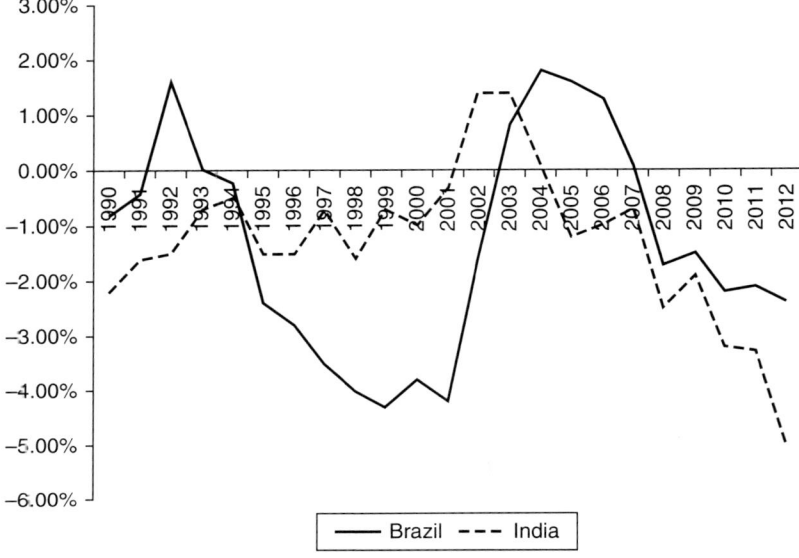

Figure 3.4 Brazil and India: current account balance as percentage of GDP, 1990–2011
Source: World Bank, world development indicators.

Brazil's debt, commodities, and derivatives markets are more advanced; Brazilian banks operate in a more competitive and generally better regulated market; and, as noted above, Brazil's capital controls regime has been more flexible. One recent study suggests that greater integration with global financial markets reduces economic volatility – but only when countries have flexible exchange rates, which Brazil has had since 1999, while India has tentatively floated the rupee only since 2007 (Adler and Tovar 2012). Overall, Brazilian policymakers can be more confident of their economic position vis-à-vis global markets – which likely gives them confidence to speak out.

Important variations in the political circumstances of Brazil and India also contribute to the somewhat different approaches to FS that the two countries have followed. The differences occur at both the international and domestic levels. The countries' *different geopolitical positions* are an important factor. Both countries are regionally dominant states. Brazil, as illustrated by its leadership in the MERCOSUR and UNASUR processes, is capable of helping to coordinate collective action among the countries of the region.[21] Enhanced regional political cooperation since the early 1990s has enabled both Brazilian state financial officials and private sector financial actors to pursue a regional and South-South strategy of international financial expansion (Armijo 2013). Brazil's largest commercial banks, as well as its securities exchange, BM&FBovespa, which is in the top five worldwide by market capitalization, plausibly intend to become the dominant foreign financial players throughout South America.

In contrast, India is bordered by Pakistan, its arch enemy; by China, the global power and Asian rival with which it has festering disputes along its 2000 mile border; and by smaller countries such as Sri Lanka and Nepal that bear long-standing historical resentments against their behemoth neighbor. Although in recent years India has taken measures to improve its relations with its neighbors, it still glaringly lacks the capacity to lead coordinated action in the region, as is highlighted by the difficulties in initiating cooperative endeavors through the South Asian Association for Regional Cooperation. The enmity that has historically characterized India's relations with its neighbors has until now closed the door on a possible strategy to expand into regional financial markets.

Differences in Brazil and India's *relations with the United States* also affect their respective strategies for international FS. Brazilian leaders today believe that the United States needs Brazil's help in Latin America more than the reverse. Brazil, since even before the discovery of vast oil deposits along its southeastern coast, is energy independent, and its long relationship with the United States gives it room to challenge the hemispheric (and global) hegemon while still remaining a close and inevitable ally. In contrast, India feels less able to take its newly developed closer relations with the United States for granted. It was partly due to India's energy needs and partly because of its desire to balance China with the United States that Indian Prime Minister Manmohan Singh signed the 2008 Civilian Nuclear Agreement with the United States. These new and relatively fragile links diminish any impulse for assertive FS against U.S. wishes.

Domestic financial regulatory politics also facilitate more assertive statecraft in Brazil than in India. Brazil has arrived at a rough domestic consensus on pursuing measured financial liberalization and regional financial expansion, a strategic mix that suits both the government's foreign policy goals and the interests of large Brazilian banks, both private and public, as well as the major actors in Brazil's active capital markets. This does not mean controversy over national financial policies is lacking – for example, the recent enormous expansion of public resources funneled through the BNDES, originally crisis-related but continued since then, has been much criticized as inefficient (Armijo, in press). Yet the rough contours of the current mix of private national, state, and foreign financial players are accepted by most participants. The privatization (and internationalization) of Brazil's banking sector is unlikely to go farther, and there is little domestic opposition to the state's financial role in supporting the regional expansion of Brazilian firms.

In India, though few involved in financial sector policymaking oppose continued liberalization per se, considerable controversy exists over the pace of reforms (Echeverri-Gent 2004, 2007, and under review). The dispute complicates India's FS. Relentless liberalizers with an institutional base in the Finance Ministry push for privatizing India's public sector banks, limiting the RBI's role to inflation targeting, enabling a larger role for foreign financial institutions in Indian markets and the formation of closer links between foreign and Indian firms. Meanwhile calibrating conservatives, often associated with the RBI, defend the role of public sector banks, praise the RBI's regulatory role as essential to preserving financial stability, and are cautious about opening Indian markets to foreign firms. The liberalizers' approach is to accept global financial norms and link India with foreign firms and global markets in a way that limits the use of the "sword" of external FS to advancing India's interests within the global financial system. The financial conservatives, especially the dwindling few who defend Indian institutions as they were prior to the 1990s reforms, are more inclined to use the shield of FS to insulate India's financial institutions from the volatility of global financial markets. Even though the conservatives' strength is in decline, the controversy that they have created has increased India's use of the shield and made its use of the sword less decisive.

Finally, the circumstances of *domestic partisan competition* also help to explain recent divergence in Brazil and India's FS. While each country has a highly fragmented party system, the domestic ideological placement of incumbent ruling coalitions from the turn of the century through this writing, about five years after the GFC, differed. In Brazil, the WP ascended to power from the left of the political spectrum when Lula da Silva won the office of the President in 2002. In India, partisan competition since the 1990s has seen the rise of two centrist coalitions – the United Progressive Alliance (UPA) led by the Congress Party and the National Democratic Alliance (NDA) led by the Bharatiya Janata Party (BJP).

The Workers' Party (PT) has ruled Brazil since January 2003. From 1989, when Lula lost presidential elections to Fernando Collor, to late

2002 when he defeated Jose Serra, the PT leadership underwent a significant transformation from an ideologically-committed, programmatic party to a more centrist, catch-all party. The change was in part a pragmatic response to pressures stemming from the international political economy that made certain pro-market policy positions essential for electoral and governing success for Lula, but also reflected incentives created by political competition in the context of Brazil's democratic political institutions (Hunter 2007). Under the leadership of President Fernando Henrique Cardoso (1995–2002), the modest rightward shift of the Brazilian Social Democratic Party (PSDB) from its center-left origins facilitated the WP transition to that center-left ideological space. The lack of a serious electoral rival on its left also reduced the costs of the centrist drift of the WP. Nonetheless, there remains considerable internal opposition to the change from key constituencies within the party, especially from members of white collar unions in the public sector. Some groups have broken their alliances with the PT, including the Landless Movement (*Movemiento dos sem Terra*) and Brazil's Green Party (Kingstone and Ponce 2010). During the summer and fall of 2013, moreover, there were a series of protests demonstrating mounting discontent with the PT government. Neither Lula nor his PT successor, Dilma Rousseff, who assumed the presidency in January 2011, has made many concessions to the left in domestic economic policy, but a modestly confrontational international rhetoric is popular with many PT voters – as well as with many nationalist Brazilians spanning the political spectrum. Were the PSDB-led center-right coalition to return to power, our expectation would be for modest softening in the rhetoric of Brazil's externally oriented FS, but little alteration in its substance, which reflects broadly held views that Brazil should participate more actively in global governance.

In contrast, India's domestic party politics has inclined its external FS in a more cautious direction. Despite the Congress Party's historic identification with nonalignment, ever since the end of the Cold War it had been reorienting its foreign policy to be closer to the United States (Ganguly and Mukherji 2011, 41–52; Mukherji 2010). After the Congress-led UPA came to power in 2004, further movement toward the United States was restricted by the reliance of the UPA coalition on outside support from India's Communist Party of India-Marxist, CPI(M). However, in 2008, in response to Prime Minister Manmohan Singh's resolute commitment to the Civilian Nuclear Agreement with the United States, the CPI(M) withdrew its support from the government. When the UPA cobbled together enough support to win a vote of no-confidence and later gained victory in the 2009 general elections, it freed itself to promote more friendly relations with the United States. Though there has been disappointment on both sides that the momentum achieved during the George W. Bush years has not been sustained, during the 2010 summit with U.S. President Barak Obama, Prime Minister Manmohan Singh declared that "I attach great importance to strengthening in every possible way India's cooperation with the United States. This is truly a relationship which can become a defining relationship for this 21st blessed century of ours."[22] Singh's statement underscores the willingness of the Congress Party leadership to stake out a pro-American position despite continuing powerful currents of anti-Americanism in India's domestic politics. Its commitment to building a positive relationship with the United States contributes to its reluctance to engage in FS openly challenging the United States.

While the BJP's Hindu nationalism could lead India toward a more muscular foreign policy, as it did when India conducted nuclear tests in 1998, there are good reasons to suppose that the BJP-led NDA, were it to lead India again, would hesitate to challenge the United States, even rhetorically, through its externally oriented FS. First, the BJP's more explicitly critical stance toward China would hinder efforts to cooperate with this leading Asian power. For instance, when BJP Prime Minister Atal Behari Vajpayee sent a letter to President Clinton explaining India's nuclear test, he invoked a nuclear China as India's main security threat. Second, the BJP does not carry the baggage of nonalignment. On the contrary, the BJP-led coalition historically has differentiated itself from the Congress Party's foreign policy by being explicitly pro-American. Ties with Americans improved during the 1977–1979 tenure of the Janata Party government in which the BJP was an important constituent and also during the rule of the BJP-led NDA from 1998 to 2004. The BJP's close ties to wealthy NRIs in the United States also help to ensure a nonassertive FS, because the Hindu nationalists would be loath to alienate these American citizens who are both major contributors to Hindu nationalist organizations and sizable investors in India. Finally, when in power 1998–2004 the NDA implemented a number of reforms, such as the Insurance Regulatory and Development Act and more liberal ceilings on FDI, which integrated the Indian economy with investors from the industrial core economies.

In sum, roughly similar levels of financial development and broadly equivalent positions in the international political economy likely account for the many similarities in Brazil's and India's international FS. The observable differences are more about style than substance, and reflect the greater willingness of contemporary Brazilian leaders to criticize the

United States openly. Brazilian bravado and Indian circumspection are probably overdetermined, reflecting India's somewhat greater international economic and international political vulnerability, while recent Brazilian governments have been keen to retain their leftist credentials by staking out positions independent of the United States.

Conclusions: strengths, vulnerabilities, and cautions going forward

As countries become progressively more integrated into global financial markets, they are increasingly likely to use the tools of systemic FS. But when are countries likely to use the shield in a defensive mode and when are they likely to wield the sword assertively to advance their interests? The scope of this study, covering two emerging economies with a number of structural and economic similarities, affords only speculative, preliminary observations. Nonetheless, we offer some suggestive hypotheses. We began with the relatively common sense observation that countries whose economies are more vulnerable to disruption by volatile global financial flows are more likely to be cautious in wielding the sword of FS. In our study, India with its chronic trade deficit and recent large current account deficits was more circumspect in its public pronouncements while Brazil, enjoying a trade surplus and manageable current account deficits during the period, took public positions more critical of the "old guard" global financial powers.

Regional geopolitics also influences the selection of strategies for financial development. Brazil has over the years developed cooperative relations with its neighbors, particularly since widespread democratization in Latin America in the 1980s. This facilitates its regional strategy for financial development, and inclines it more toward a South–South strategy of financial expansion. India's relations with its neighbors, on the other hand, are characterized by resentment, and in the case of Pakistan, intense enmity. India's problematic regional relations, in addition to the general low level of economic development in South Asia, make a regional strategy less viable. At the same time, its connections through diasporic networks and business process outsourcing direct it toward a strategy of financial service exports in advanced industrial countries. Pursuit of this financial growth strategy, we contend, makes India more circumspect in its criticisms of global financial powers.

Finally, we have noted that the circumstances characterizing domestic partisan competition have contributed to the differences in Brazil and

India's FS. Brazil's WP ascended to power from the left. As it pragmatically moderated its economic policy, its modestly confrontational international rhetoric helped to placate leftist critics within the PT and social movements outside. Partisan competition in India is characterized by two centrist coalitions – the Congress-led UPA on the center-left and the Bharatiya Janata Party on the center-right. Since 2008, each of these leading parties has taken pro-American positions in defiance of India's left. This position, in combination with India's strategy for financial sector development, has made India less inclined to utilize confrontational rhetoric as part of its FS.

Brazil and India's choices of FS strategies have broader consequences for global financial governance. As these large countries have become more affluent, their actions, along with those of other emerging economies, become more consequential for the future of global financial markets and financial governance.

Three challenges confront Brazil and India if they are to succeed in reforming global financial institutions and policies that support their long-term developmental goals. First, can they overcome their differences and work with each other and other developing countries to achieve their joint objectives? Their inability to resolve their disagreements during the Doha round of negotiations at the WTO – or even to unite around a common 'Southern' candidate for the heads of the IMF or World Bank in 2011 and 2012 – highlights the formidable challenges that they face. Second, will they overreach in their demands for reform? Brazil has shown periodic bravado that exceeds its ability to deliver outcomes on the international level. India has been more circumspect as its vulnerabilities, including rivalry with China, limit its ability to achieve its objectives. Finally, while Brazil and India have achieved remarkable economic success in the last 20 years, exercising influence at the global level requires reaching agreements with the still powerful countries of Europe and with the United States. If their ascendance leads to refusal to compromise with Europe and the United States, Brazil and India's overreach may lead to a stalemate that would prevent international negotiations from achieving needed reforms.

We end our analysis on a somewhat ambivalent note. It would be comforting to conclude that, if countries like Brazil and India play their cards right, it is plausible that they could negotiate to reshape global financial market in ways that are somewhat more efficient and equitable for all than what we find now. But also plausible is the more pessimistic assessment that the governments of Brazil and India, along with those of their fellow BRICS countries, are playing with fire in their attempts to dethrone the central, nay the hegemonic, role played by the U.S. currency, U.S. financial markets, and more or less collaborative financial governance by the advanced economies since the mid-20th century. It is safe to say that neither Brazil nor India – nor of course the larger international political economy – would be well-served by heightened international financial turmoil. Our own hope, therefore, is for continued incremental change.

Notes

1. Per capita income tells a rather different story. In 2007, Brazil's per capita income was $7194 in current US dollars and $9560 in PPP. Comparable figures for India were $1069 and $2760. (World Development Indicators, <data/wpr;dbamld/prgtp[ocecpmp,oc=[p;ocu-and-external-debt> accessed November 10, 2013.)
2. The figures rely on an updated version of dataset, dated May 2009, which is available from the World Bank. Note that "total financial assets" is the second of two "total" figures included in the dataset, reported in column AM.
3. Updated figures through 2010 were made available by the dataset's authors.
4. These figures are for total reserves, including gold. They are provided in current US dollars as reported in the *World Development Indicators 2012*.
5. We calculated "financial policy liberalization" as the mean of each country's scores for monetary, investor, and financial freedom as assessed in the Heritage Foundation's *Index of Economic Freedom 2012*. www.heritage.org/index/ That same year, relatively illiberal China received a score of 45.2, and South Korea and Mexico, among the most open of emerging economies, received scores of 66.3 and 62.3, respectively.
6. Of course, in international politics, a reputation for being assertive or intransigent is not necessarily always a cost, as this may benefit one in a future negotiation.
7. At that time, candidate Lula da Silva, remembered by the business community for having waved a hammer and sickle flag and calling for foreign debt repudiation at union rallies in the early 1980s, was forced to issue his "Letter to the Brazilian people." This was statement reprinted in newspapers nationwide in which Lula promised, if elected, to continue the prudent macroeconomic and international financial policies of his predecessor, President Fernando Henrique Cardoso. At the urging of the United States, the IMF responded by extending to Brazil an emergency loan of $30 billion, which ended the exchange rate crisis.
8. Brazil's IOF was similar to a domestically oriented tax, the CPMF (temporary tax on financial transactions, ended in 2007), that had been used to encourage both particular investment behaviors and as a revenue measure.
9. Indians residing abroad have been an important source of foreign capital inflows in recent years: their remittances in 2009 summed to 1.9 percent of GDP, as compared to only 0.3 percent in Brazil (Beck and Levine 2000, as augmented by recent dataset updates).

10. "As foreign banks detour, public banks forge ahead," Knowledge at Wharton, at http://knowledge.wharton.upenn.edu/india/article.cfm?articleid=4376
11. For a more comprehensive account of India's response to the GFC see Echeverri-Gent, forthcoming.
12. Brazil's government reliably gives lip service to regional financial cooperation in South America, but in practice has done relatively little to promote this goal (Armijo 2013).
13. "Carteira do BNDES na América do Sul soma US$ 15,6 bilhões," *Valor Econômico*, August 27, 2009.
14. Government of India, Ministry of Finance, *Economic Survey 2011–12*, p. 343. Available at http://indiabudget.nic.in/survey.asp (accessed on April 4, 2012).
15. In late 2009 the BRICs (Brazil, Russia, India, and China) added South Africa, becoming the BRICS.
16. IMF members agreed on a capital increase, along with a quota readjustment in favor of emerging economies in 2010, but through the end of 2013 the Republican majority in the U.S. Congress had refused to ratify the agreement.
17. All figures from World Bank, *World Development Indicators 2012*, consulted online.
18. At www.heritage.org/index
19. India's remittances, at $56 billion in 2010, more than double those for the next highest country, Mexico at $19 billion. India also enjoys a consistent and usually substantial positive balance in service trade.
20. On the politics of Indian equity market reforms, see Echeverri-Gent (2004, 2007).
21. Some observers such as Malamud (2011) emphasize the relatively low level of regional cooperation in South America as compared to Western Europe. We choose to see the glass as half full.
22. "Remarks by President Obama and Prime Minister Singh in Joint Press Conference in New Delhi, India" (November 8, 2010) available from http://www.whitehouse.gov/the-press-office/2010/11/08/remarks-president-obama-and-prime-minister-singh-joint-press-conference- (accessed on September 18, 2012).

References

Adler, Gustavo, and Camilo E. Tovar. 2012. "Riding Global Financial Waves: The Economic Impact of Global Financial Shocks on Emerging Market Economies," Washington, DC: IMF Working Paper wp/12/188.

Armijo, Leslie Elliott. 2005. "Mass Democracy: The Real Reason that Brazil Ended Inflation?," *World Development*, 33(12), 2013–2028.

Armijo, Leslie Elliott. 2013. "Equality and Regional Finance in the Americas," *Latin American Politics and Society*, 55(3), Winter.

Armijo, Leslie Elliott. in press. "The Public Bank Trilemma: The BNDES and Brazil's New Developmentalism," in Peter Kingstone and Timothy Power (eds) *Democratic Brazil Ascendant*. Pittsburgh: University of Pittsburgh Press.

Armijo, Leslie Elliott, and Cynthia Roberts. 2014. "The Emerging Powers and Global Governance: Why the BRICS Matter," in Robert Looney (ed.) *Handbook of Emerging Economies*. New York: Routledge.

Bagchi, Indrain. 2012. "BRICS Summit: Member Nations Criticizes the West for Financial Mismanagement," *The Times of India*, March 31, 2012.

Beck, Asli Demirgüç-Kunt, and Ross Levine. 2000. "A New Database on Financial Development and Structure," *World Bank Economic Review*, 14, 597–605.

Bevins, Vincent. 2010. "BNDES: Climate for Casting a Wider Net," *Financial Times*, May 6, 2010.

Echeverri-Gent, John. 2004. "Financial Globalization and India's Equity Market Reform," *India Review*, 3(4) (October), 306–332.

Echeverri-Gent, John. 2007. "Politics of Market Micro Structure: Towards a New Political Economy of India's Equity Market Reform," in Rahul Mukherji (ed.) *India's Economic Reforms*. Delhi: Oxford University Press, pp. 328–358.

Echeverri-Gent, John. Under review. "India's Response to the Global Financial Crisis: From Quick Rebound to Endless Slowdown?," in Carol Wise, Leslie Armijo, and Saori Katada (eds) *Unexpected Outcomes: How Emerging Markets Survived the Global Financial Crisis*. Book manuscript.

Economist, 2008a. "Business: A New Economic Order," *Economist*, November 19, 2008.

Economist, 2008b. "Storm Clouds Gathering: What the World Recession will do to India's Economy," *Economist*, December 11, 2008.

Financial Express. 2011. "Era of Bank Secrecy is Over Manmohan Tells G20," *The Financial Express*, November 5, 2011.

Ganguly, Sumit, and Rahul Mukherji. 2011. *India Since 1980*. Cambridge: Cambridge University Press.

Government of India, Ministry of Finance. 2007. *Report of the High Powered Expert Committee on Making Mumbai an International Financial Centre*. Government of India, Ministry of Finance: New Delhi. Available at: http://finmin.nic.in/the_ministry/dept_eco_affairs/capital_market_div/mifc/fullreport/execsummary.pdf (accessed on September 21, 2007).

Government of India, Planning Commission. 2009. *A Hundred Small Steps: Report of the Committee on Financial Sector Reforms*. Delhi: Sage.

Hunter, Wendy. 2007. "The Normalization of An Anomaly: The Workers' Party in Brazil," *World Politics*, 59, 440–475.

Kingstone, Peter, and Adolfo F. Ponce. 2010. "From Cardoso to Lula: The Triumph of Pragmatism in Brazil," in Kurt Weyland, Raul Madrid, and Wendy Hunter (eds) *Leftist Governments in Latin America*. Cambridge: Cambridge University Press, pp. 98–123.

Kose, M. Ayha, Eswar Prasad, Kenneth Rogoff, and Shang-Jin Wei. 2007. "Financial Globalization: Beyond the Blame Game," *Finance and Development* 44(1), March 2007. Available from <http://www.imf.org/external/pubs/ft/fandd/2007/03/kose.htm>.

Lane, Philip R., and Gian Maria Milesi-Ferretti. 2007. "The External Wealth of Nations Mark II," *Journal of International Economics*, 73, November, 223–250.

Malamud, Andrés. 2011. "A Leader without Followers? The Growing Divergence Between the Regional and Global Performance of Brazilian Foreign Policy," *Latin American Politics and Society*, 53(3), 1–24.

Mukherji, Rahul, 2010. "India's Foreign Economic Policy," in Sumit Ganguly (ed.) *India's Foreign Policy: Retrospect and Prospect*. New Delhi: Oxford University Press, pp. 301–322.

Reserve Bank of India. 2010. *Report on Currency and Finance 2008–09*. Mumbai: Reserve Bank of India.

Stallings, Barbara, and Rogerio Studart. 2006. *Finance for Development: Latin America in Comparative Perspective*. Washington, DC: Brookings Institution Press and United Nations Economic Commission for Latin America and the Caribbean.

Tett, Gillian. 2009. "Brazil Catches Banks Adept at Capital Flight," *Financial Times*, November 252009.

Wheatley, Jonathan. 2009. "Brazil's Leader Blames White People for Crisis," *Financial Times*, March 27, 2009.

4
The End of Monetary Mercantilism in Southeast Asia?

Natasha Hamilton-Hart

Since the financial crisis at the end of the last century, Southeast Asian countries, along with the rest of the wider East Asian region, have amassed extraordinary levels of foreign currency reserves.[1] The region's accumulation of foreign reserves is unprecedented in scale and unmatched by that of countries in other world regions. Reserve accumulation has provided ammunition for foreign critics, who have touted the region's staggeringly large reserves as evidence of unfair manipulation of currency values in order to boost exports. There are also domestic critics. In some countries, there is now a level of debate and contestation over exchange rate policy that has not been seen in nearly half a century. What lies behind the renewed attention to international monetary policy in East Asia? Is a form of mercantilism pervasive across much of the region? If there is evidence of mercantilism, what are the implications of such a strategy?

This chapter argues that although there is evidence that some countries in Southeast Asia are pursuing strategies of what Aizenman and Lee (2008) have termed monetary mercantilism – the manipulation of currency values in order to boost export competitiveness – mercantilist strategies are subject to both domestic and international limits. In Southeast Asia's more democratic countries, it has become less acceptable in political terms to pursue export-surplus growth strategies. At the international level, the costs, risks, and vulnerabilities created by the accumulation of large financial stockpiles have become increasingly salient. In material terms, the tools of monetary statecraft represent costly and not very useful ammunition. Both export surplus and deficit countries in Southeast Asia are thus seeking alternative tools of economic statecraft in order to influence the international arena.

Viewed through the lens of financial statecraft (FS), the accumulation of foreign currency reserves has at least a dual quality. On the one hand, there is a strong precautionary, self-insurance motive for reserve accumulation and thus, as conceptualized by Armijo and Katada in Chapter 1, reserve accumulation can be seen as an element of defensive FS, with large reserves serving as a "shield" against future financial instability. After a certain point, however, reserve accumulation becomes excessive if pursued for defensive purposes, and in fact is implicated in macroeconomic imbalances that are cumulatively destabilizing at the global level. In this light, reserve accumulation can appear as a more offensive instrument of FS: a "sword" with the potential to be used as a strategic tool. However, this chapter argues that there is almost no evidence that regional countries currently view reserve accumulation and exchange rate management as instruments to achieve international strategic goals. In fact, their utility for achieving even defensive foreign policy objectives is sharply constrained, and these constraints have pushed regional countries to develop alternative means of exercising international influence.

This chapter first discusses the varieties of mercantilism that countries in the region have at times employed, and provides an explanation of the ways monetary tools may play a role in mercantilist strategies. Second, the chapter provides evidence that these strategies are not uniformly pursued across the region, and that there is increasing divergence between countries apparently wedded to export-surplus growth strategies and countries that have swung into the reverse pattern of deficits and increased domestic consumption. Those countries still accumulating large external surpluses have been forced to diversify their holdings of foreign assets and have developed different vehicles for managing large reserves, with the rise of sovereign wealth funds (SWFs) from the region being the most prominent example. As argued in the third section of this chapter, however, these external assets increasingly represent vulnerability rather than safety from future financial storms. They are also costly in standard economic terms. For these reasons, as shown in the fourth section, both external deficit and surplus countries have sought alternative tools of financial statecraft in the international arena.

Varieties of mercantilism and monetary statecraft

At its most basic, mercantilism is the pursuit of export surpluses. Classical mercantilism was associated with the pursuit of export surpluses in order to acquire specie – the gold and other precious metals that can be equated with the foreign currency assets that governments today acquire in the form of foreign exchange reserves. The overall macroeconomic futility of hoarding specie was apparent to the classical economists, including Adam Smith, at least in terms of the goal of maximizing growth. But specie could be used to pay for the buildup of war-making capacity, a political rather than an economic goal. Thus classical mercantilist strategies became associated with strategic competition and potentially destabilizing international rivalries (Viner 1948).

In contrast, East Asia since the end of World War II has pursued a different variety of mercantilism. Mercantilism here has been a domestically-driven strategy, a means of achieving economic growth in specific economic and political circumstances. East Asian states have not been motivated by a wish to accumulate foreign treasure (reserves) in order to further international strategic goals, but by the arithmetic of gross domestic product (GDP). GDP growth can occur through expansion in any one of its components: investment, consumption, government expenditure, and exports minus imports. One commonality that Southeast Asia shared with much of the rest of capitalist East Asia during the Cold War was a common reliance on increasing the investment and export surplus components of GDP as a more attractive, and apparently viable, growth strategy than increasing domestic consumption.

In the case of Japan, T. J. Pempel (1998) described the domestic political coalition and mechanisms for managing the trade-offs behind such an export-driven growth strategy as a system of "embedded mercantilism."[2] In the case of the Southeast Asian countries, where export-driven growth was powered in large part through foreign direct investment (FDI) in the manufacturing sector, Kanishka Jayasuryia (2003) identified a modified system of compensatory embedded mercantilism, resting on an implicit bargain between foreign investors in export-oriented manufacturing industries and privileged domestic groups in the non-tradables sector. Although in the Southeast Asian system of compensatory mercantilism manufacturing exporters were not politically powerful in their own right, politically dominant domestic interests recognized their importance and thus formed an implicit coalition that ensured export interests received at least intermittent policy support (Jesudason 1989; Ritchie 2005). Politically privileged domestic industries tended to be concentrated in inward-facing sectors such as property and finance, or in natural resource-based industries. The economic growth that ultimately sustained government-endowed privileges to these industries rested, however, on the performance of the export sector.

Various policy tools can serve the general mercantilist strategy of achieving export surpluses. The most obvious set of tools are trade policy restrictions on imports: tariffs, quotas, or other barriers to importing. A second set of tools can be conceived of as broadly financial: channeling financial resources (whether through the banking system or directly through fiscal means) to provide effective subsidies to the export sector, a strategy that Aizenman and Lee (2008) term financial mercantilism. Policy settings governing labor and social safety nets can also bolster investment and export-led growth over consumption, as labor-repressive industrial relations policies provide an implicit subsidy for exporters and limited public social safety nets incentivize savings. The fourth item on the menu of potential mercantilist tools is monetary instruments: engaging in exchange rate manipulation to make exported goods cheaper in foreign currency terms (and thus more competitive in world market terms) while simultaneously making imported goods more expensive in domestic currency terms, thus deterring imports.

Since the Asian financial crisis (AFC), monetary tools have become – almost by default – more significant in export-surplus growth strategies. After the crisis, under extreme economic and political pressure to restart growth, Southeast Asian governments turned to the export sector. Their means for doing so, however, were largely restricted to monetary tools. Trade policy interventions to limit imports and promote exports were increasingly constrained as a result of regional countries' commitments to trade liberalization (Sally and Sen 2011). A second change was that middle-income countries such as Malaysia and Thailand (and, in some industries, even low-income producers such as Indonesia and the Philippines) were increasingly squeezed by new entrants into global manufacturing value chains competing for FDI. The labor-repressive industrial relations regimes that had helped attract FDI in the past (Deyo 1989) were less viable post-AFC, as political elites in Southeast Asia were forced to reckon more seriously with electoral challenges and at least somewhat more influential labor or mass-based political movements. Finally, with the collapse of the banking sector and the financial vulnerability of most of the bank-based conglomerates in Southeast Asia, subsidies through the financial system also were not feasible (Hamilton-Hart 2008).

Together, these features of the post-AFC economic and political landscape in which much of Southeast Asia turned to export-driven growth to boost their economic recovery made these countries more sensitive than previously to considerations of exchange rate competitiveness. In the immediate aftermath of the crisis, currency values were of course well below most measures of fair value, providing an easy impetus for exports. But the currency revaluation that could be expected after the return to strong growth in the years after the crisis has been, with some exceptions, rather limited, as shown in the next section.

Evidence of deliberate management of exchange rates in order to make exports more competitive is necessarily speculative. In some cases, reserve accumulation is a desired policy end – to serve as self-insurance in the event of future financial instability. While this is a significant nonmercantilist objective, precautionary motives for reserve accumulation may sometimes be linked to mercantilism, albeit of a nonmonetary variety. Aizenman and Lee (2008) argue that a precautionary motive for reserve accumulation by Korea and Japan can in part be attributed to an earlier mercantilist strategy pursued by these countries: large-scale interventions in the financial system to direct resources to the export sector, a strategy they term financial mercantilism (see also Amsden 1989; Woo 1991). While it was integral to the export-led growth strategies of Japan and Korea in their high-growth periods, it came at the price of serious financial fragility in the banking system, which then created motives for precautionary reserve accumulation given a positive correlation between banking and currency crises. Reserve accumulation is thus consistent with precautionary motives, or financial statecraft as a shield, even if the necessity of holding such heavyweight shields stems at least in part from earlier strategies of financial mercantilism in some countries.

As shown in the next section, some Southeast Asian countries exhibit patterns of reserve accumulation, current account balances, and foreign exchange rate trends that are consistent with deliberate interventions to manage exchange rates. Although there is no transparency in the foreign exchange interventions carried out by regional central banks, several do report engaging in sterilization operations, through which large inflows of foreign capital have been absorbed through the issuance of domestic securities, the funds from which the authorities then convert into foreign currency assets. Several regional central banks have resorted to such operations in order to maintain domestic price stability at times of potentially destabilizing inflows of capital. On the current account side, the foreign currency earnings that accrue from running large trade surpluses, if not repatriated, necessarily result in the accumulation of foreign assets. It is certainly the case that, whether motivated by precautionary, defensive purposes or more outward-facing objectives (and whether brought about through strategic intervention in currency markets or not), the extent of foreign reserve accumulation that has occurred has meant that the region as a whole has acquired unprecedented financial resources, both in the form of official foreign currency reserves and other external assets managed more actively by SWFs.

Monetary statecraft: the rise and moderation of external surpluses

The new salience of monetary measures in Southeast Asia since the AFC is reflected in the region's accumulation of foreign exchange reserves, in exchange rate policies, and in current account balances. Although at a different order of magnitude for the global economy as compared to China's buildup of foreign currency reserves, the pace of reserve accumulation by other East Asian countries has been rapid since 2000. Table 4.1 shows that China is not alone in more than trebling its reserve holdings over a decade: Malaysia, Philippines, Thailand, and Indonesia have also increased their reserves at a comparable rate in percentage terms. Although reserve holdings of the region as a whole are particularly

Table 4.1 Southeast and Northeast Asia: foreign exchange reserves

	2000	2005	2008	2009	2010	2011	2012	2013 (May)
Southeast Asia								
Indonesia	29	35	52	66	96	110	113	105
Malaysia	29	70	91	97	106	134	140	141
Philippines	15	18	37	44	62	75	84	84
Singapore	80	116	174	188	226	238	259	258
Thailand	33	52	111	138	172	175	182	175
Vietnam	3.4	9	24	16.4	12.5	13.5	–	–
Northeast Asia								
China	172	822	2534	2418	2890	3255	3331	3500
Hong Kong	108	124	183	256	269	285	317	306
Taiwan	–	253	292	348	382	386	403	407
Korea	96	210	201	270	292	307	327	328
Japan	362	847	1031	1049	1096	1296	1268	1250

Note: All figures in billions of U.S. dollars.

Sources: IMF data on international reserves, available at http://elibrary-data.imf.org. World Bank data on total reserves (including gold), available at http://data.worldbank.org/indicator/FI.RES.TOTL.CD/countries, is used for years for which the IMF data is missing. The latest figure for Chinese reserves gives the reserve value as of June 2013, from the People's Bank of China's press release on "Financial Statistics, H1 2013," available from http://www.pbc.gov.cn/. Taiwanese data is from Central Bank of China (Taiwan), "Foreign Exchange Reserves," available from http://www.cbc.gov.tw.

high, there is significant intra-regional variation, both in the absolute size of reserves and when reserve holdings are scaled against the size of the national economy. On both measures, some countries hold much higher levels of reserves than others. However, the pace of reserve accumulation, even on the part of countries with very high reserves, has moderated significantly since 2008.

Although reserve accumulation does not necessarily signal a mercantilist motive at work, exchange rate policies in parts of the region are consistent with a concern for export price competitiveness. Officially, some countries declared a shift to more freely floating exchange rate policies post-AFC. Inflation targeting (IT) policies – which require exchange rate flexibility in order to maintain domestic price stability (Rose 2007) – have become increasingly popular. Some analyses have found that IT countries such as Korea have shown less commitment in recent years to managing the external value of their currency, in the sense of attempting to maintain it at a relatively low or "competitive" level, which would tend to promote exports (e.g., Kim and Lee 2008; Sanchez 2010). On the other hand, many countries appear to have a "fear of floating" and at least to some extent actively manage their exchange rates (Calvo and Reinhart 2002). Both China and Hong Kong have maintained openly-managed foreign exchange rate regimes, while Malaysia's currency peg, introduced in 1998, was maintained until 2005. The degree of actual flexibility exhibited by other East Asian countries is limited in practice (Cohen 2008; Fane 2005; Rajan 2009). Even formal IT countries employ mixed strategies and a degree of managed floating (Aizenman, Hutchison, and Noy 2011). Some accounts have gone as far as to detect a "Bretton Woods II" system in operation, under which export interests in East Asia are supported through de facto policies of exchange rate management, with the main reference currency being the U.S. dollar (Dooley, Folkerts-Landau, and Garber 2008).[3]

Depending on the country and time period selected, there are cases of both nominal and real appreciation against the U.S. dollar, but a number of analyses have suggested that regional policymakers have deliberately limited this appreciation. The Malaysian ringgit has returned to almost precisely the same nominal exchange rate against the U.S. dollar that it was at 40 years ago. As shown in Figure 4.1, the degree of real currency flexibility since 2000 shows that while some regional currencies have appreciated in real terms, others have shown very limited appreciation. Comparison with a broader set of countries shows that the variation within Southeast Asia puts some countries, such as Indonesia, closer to the high-appreciation countries such as New Zealand, while at the other end of the spectrum, countries such as Malaysia have experienced almost no real currency appreciation since 2000. However, no country in Southeast Asia has sustained the kind of long-term currency depreciation that Northeast Asian economies (despite large current account surpluses) such as Hong Kong have experienced since 2000.

These exchange rate trends gain added salience when viewed in conjunction with current account imbalances over the same time period. As shown in Table 4.2, all Southeast Asian countries in a sense exported their way out of the economic downturn associated with the AFC, but in some countries large export surpluses have been sustained well after this period. Table 4.2 provides prima facie support for the contention of many countries that their foreign reserves buildup is simply the consequence of running trade surpluses (rather than currency manipulation). As argued, for example, by the governor of Malaysia's central bank in response to calls for currency revaluation to reduce global trade imbalances:

> It needs to be recognised that Asia's comparative advantage is not derived from the exchange rate. Wages, prices and other costs are significantly lower in Asia. It is precisely for this reason that multinationals have relocated their operations to Asia. Furthermore, studies have in fact shown that Asian currencies would have to appreciate by 50 to 60% to have any discernible impact in reducing the global imbalances. (Zeti 2005: 192)

While it is not possible to determine definitively whether the surpluses would have been achieved had currencies been allowed to float freely, it is noticeable that the countries with the largest and most persistent current account surpluses are also the ones that have shown only modest exchange rate appreciation (see Figure 4.1 and Table 4.2). Malaysia and Singapore, in particular, have sustained large export surpluses but have not experienced the exchange rate appreciation that such surpluses might be expected to lead to under free float currency regimes.

As well as being channeled into official foreign exchange reserves, the foreign assets accumulated by these countries have also been managed via special-purpose vehicles that have come to be known as sovereign wealth funds (SWFs). Since definitions of SWFs vary (and some, e.g., exclude government pension funds) and many SWFs are not transparent, estimates of total numbers of SWFs and their assets vary considerably. Edwin Truman, who has done much to develop metrics for the management of SWFs, puts the total foreign assets of all SWFs (including

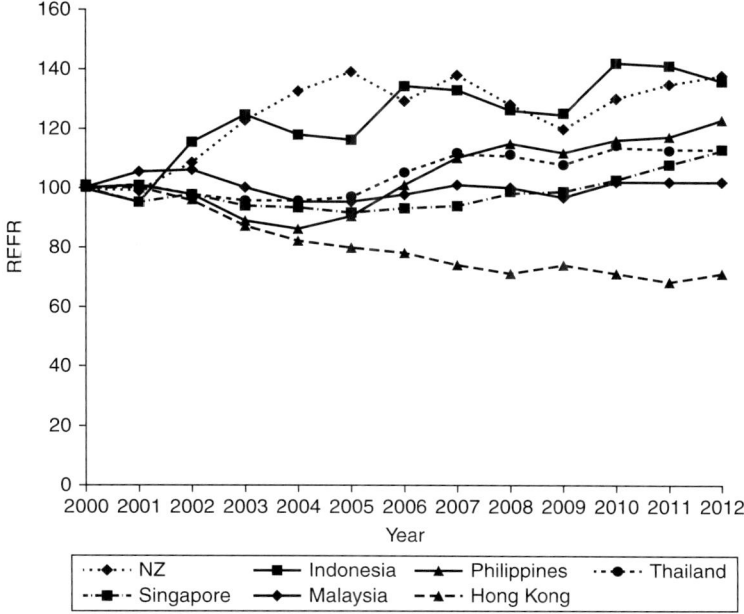

Figure 4.1 Southeast Asia: exchange rate trends

Notes: Trends in the real effective exchange rate (REER) are based on annualized exchange rate data, calculated on the basis of trade-weighted averages of bilateral exchange adjusted by relative consumer prices. The source data has been re-indexed to 2000 as the base year.
Source: Bank for International Settlements, www.bis.org/statistics/eer/index.htm.

Table 4.2 Southeast Asia: current account balances as percentage of GDP

	2003	2005	2007	2008	2009	2010	2011	2012	2013e
Surplus countries									
Malaysia	11.7	14.4	15.4	17.1	15.5	11.1	11.0	6.4	6.0
Philippines	0.3	1.9	4.8	2.1	5.6	4.5	3.2	2.9	2.4
Singapore	22.9	21.4	26.1	15.1	17.7	26.8	24.6	18.6	16.9
Deficit/in flux									
Indonesia	3.5	0.6	1.6	0.1	2.0	0.7	0.2	−2.8	−3.3
Thailand	3.4	−4.3	6.3	0.8	8.3	3.1	1.7	0.7	1.0
Vietnam	−4.9	−1.1	−9.8	−11.9	−6.6	−4.1	0.2	7.4	7.9

Notes: There are in some cases significant discrepancies across different WEO reports. This table uses the most recent figures available as of July 2013.

Source: IMF, *World Economic Outlook Database*, April 2013. Available from http://www.imf.org/external/pubs/ft/weo/2013/01/weodata/index.aspx.

government pension funds) at U.S.$3,740 billion, of which U.S.$1,154 are held by Asian funds (Truman 2011: 253). Among Southeast Asian countries, although SWFs have been established by Vietnam, Thailand, Timor-Leste, Brunei, and Malaysia, the SWFs operated by Singapore are by far the largest.

Singapore operates two SWFs, both established well before the vehicles proliferated globally in the 2000s. One, Temasek Holdings (Temasek), was established in 1974 as a holding company for government stakes in largely domestic firms and began expanding its foreign assets only in the 1990s. It now reports total assets of S$317 billion (U.S.$253 billion at end-2013 exchange rates) and a net portfolio of U.S.$215 billion, of which 70 percent is held in non-Singaporean assets.[4] Geographically, it reports a distribution of 58 percent of its assets in "mature economies" and 42 percent to "growth regions." It has a strong Asia-orientation in its portfolio, with 71 percent of its portfolio in Asia including Singapore. The second Singapore SWF was established in 1981 with an explicit mandate to invest part of the government's foreign exchange portfolio. It was until mid-2013 called the Government of Singapore Investment Corporation, but in July 2013 officially changed its name to GIC Private Limited (GIC). It is much less transparent than Temasek and only acknowledged holding assets of "well over U.S.$100 billion" in its first ever annual report issued in 2008 – a figure that has not changed since in official Singaporean disclosures. Outside estimates of its total assets suggest around U.S.$248 billion as of 2010 (Truman 2011: 251; Yeung 2011: 627). Geographically, it is oriented to developed country assets and reports holding 28 percent of assets in Asia, 44 percent in the Americas (36 percent in the United States), and 25 percent in Europe as of 2013 – a slight shift in its orientation compared to 2008, when it reported holding 23 percent of assets in Asia, 40 percent in the Americas (34 percent in the United States), and 35 percent in Europe.[5] Despite the uncertainty over the total size of Singapore's government-controlled foreign currency assets, at a minimum they amount to over U.S.$500 billion – approaching 200 percent of the country's GDP.[6] If financial resources are a measure of a country's ability to engage in financial statecraft, it would appear that Singapore at least among Southeast Asian countries has the potential to be a serious player on the world stage.

In contrast to the sustained surpluses and very modest currency appreciation experienced by Malaysia and Singapore, other Southeast Asian countries have diverged from this somewhat mercantilist pattern of growth based on export surpluses and a competitively valued currency. Indonesia in particular experienced significant real exchange rate appreciation between 2002 and 2010, while its current account surpluses narrowed and then swung into deficit from 2010. From 2012, the weakness of the Indonesian currency became a cause for concern, as the central bank embarked on a series of countermeasures to shore up the value of the rupiah, including mandating the repatriation of export earnings and drawing down on the country's foreign exchange reserves. The Indonesian case underlines the political foundations of Southeast Asia's version of embedded mercantilism.[7] As the Southeast Asian country undergoing the most significant post-crisis political change and democratization, it is here that the old compensatory bargain between foreign-owned export interests and a privileged domestic business elite came under the most serious challenge. Political demands for more domestic consumption in an economy fueled by strong commodities prices for much of this period have led to domestic rebalancing away from export surpluses and savings and toward more consumption-based growth – despite Indonesia being a much lower-income country than either Malaysia or Singapore.

Mixed motives and paradoxes

No single motive accounts for the significant buildup of foreign assets by Southeast Asian countries since 2000. In the terms of this volume, the accumulation of foreign assets controlled by governments creates the potential for financial statecraft (FS), defined as the "intentional use, by national governments, of a country's monetary or financial capabilities or conditions for the purposes of achieving on-going foreign policy goals" (Armijo and Katada, Chapter 1). As discussed in this section, there is most evidence of a defensive and inward-oriented motivation behind the accumulation of external surpluses by Southeast Asian countries. There is almost no evidence that countries in the region have sought to use external surpluses as a means of altering either the behavior of other states (bilateral) or the conditions of the international environment (systemic). To the extent they have pursued such externally oriented goals, they have primarily relied on nonfinancial policy tools. Paradoxically, however, the buildup of financial resources as a "shield" has produced unintended consequences both domestically and internationally. Although most countries in Southeast Asia are not systemically significant players, when combined with similar or even more pronounced export-surplus growth strategies on the part of larger players in Northeast Asia, their actions contribute to the development of destabilizing international conditions.

Rapid increases in reserve holdings came in the wake of the devastating financial and currency crises of 1997–1998. Not only did Southeast Asian countries experience the financial crisis of 1997–1998 and learn either first-hand or from their neighbors how costly such crises could be, they also learnt that reliance on outside sources of support via the IMF created particular economic and political problems. As highly internationalized economies with very open capital accounts, all countries in the region are potentially very vulnerable to financial turbulence. A strong precautionary self-insurance motive thus almost certainly accounts for much of the buildup in East Asian reserves after 1998 (Aizenman and Lee 2008). Reserve accumulation for these purposes fits this project's characterization of FS as a shield – a means of protecting the national economy from future financial instability.

It is hard to say with certainty how large precautionary reserve holdings need to be, and uncovering motives for accumulation of reserves is even more difficult given the lack of transparency surrounding exchange rate and reserve management policies. Because "the switch to large hoarding of reserves coincides frequently with the collapse of growth, it is difficult to disentangle monetary mercantilism from precautionary hoarding" (Aizenman and Lee 2008: 596). Status concerns may also lie behind the accumulation of large foreign reserves (Cheung and Qian 2009). Despite these uncertainties, a number of accounts suggest that the region as a whole has over-accumulated foreign reserves since around 2003. That is, since around that time, reserve levels have surpassed most measures of reserve adequacy for precautionary purposes (e.g., Park and Estrada 2009: 3–8). It is important to note, however, that many such analyses of reserve adequacy treat countries in Southeast Asia as part of a larger "developing Asia" grouping of countries, and this grouping is dominated by the massive buildup of reserves by China. Individually, as discussed in the previous section, not all countries in Southeast Asia hold particularly large reserves.

Despite this caveat, it is still the case that the perception of extremely large external surpluses is commonly held outside of the region and this perceived over-accumulation of reserves has fueled allegations by both popular and political actors that the broader East Asian region is succeeding at the expense of its principal trading partners, the United States and Europe. Academic analyses suggesting a "Bretton Woods II" system (Dooley, Folkerts-Landau, and Garber 2008) reinforce the popular view that export surplus countries have somehow won out – their success resting on the willingness of the United States to act as it did during the Cold War, as a provider of public goods that allowed trading partner allies to realize substantial relative gains. The export surplus countries (Japan then, emerging Asia now) are often depicted as free riders, refusing their role as consumer markets, acquiring manufacturing capacity shed from importing countries, and piling up ammunition in the form of financial resources. Much popular speculation has focused on the potential that such financial resources may serve to increase the influence of holders of foreign assets, providing them with bargaining leverage as creditors and through a comparatively greater capacity to fund bilateral and multilateral initiatives. If these concerns are justified, the region's mercantilist monetary policies look like "swords" pointed outwards, instruments of an increasingly proactive, if not offensive, financial statecraft.

In addition to official foreign exchange reserves, some regional countries have developed special-purpose vehicles for more active management of their foreign currency resources. The rising visibility of SWFs during the global financial crisis (GFC) triggered a great deal of speculation about their political implications (e.g., Helleiner 2009). The "reversal of fortunes" precipitated by the GFC of 2007–2008 has been described as a "reversal of neo-colonialism" (Lee 2009). In another account, the new activity of SWFs during the GFC is described as an element of "the new mercantilism", with the authors citing John Maynard Keynes to the effect that "international cash flows are always political" (Gilson and Milhaupt 2007–2008: 1345). Overseas investments by Singapore's SWFs have been analyzed as part of the nation's economic diplomacy (Yeung 2011), again creating the perception of outwardly oriented financial statecraft.

On closer inspection, however, what we do know about the operation of SWFs suggests strongly defensive and inward-oriented motivations. In the first place, the diversification out of traditional passive reserve management instruments (namely gold and sovereign debt issued in large developed money markets, primarily the market for U.S. government securities) has been explicitly motivated by the search for higher yields, as a means of offsetting the large opportunity costs associated with high reserve holdings (Devlin and Brummitt 2007; Park and Estrada 2009). This was openly articulated in the case of Singapore's early reorganization of its reserves management system in 1981, when the GIC was established to take over the management of part of the reserves held by the country's central bank. The underlying rationale was a search for internal legitimacy via economic performance, a strong and recurrent theme in the political rhetoric of Singapore's leaders (Shih 2009; Clark and Monk 2010; Yeung 2011). The lack of transparency associated with SWFs, a cause of much of the political concern about them in outside countries, is also justified in defensive terms. The Singapore government, for example, justifies its need for exceptionally high reserves and nondisclosure of its reserve holdings in this way:

> It is not in our national interest to publish the full size of our reserves. If we do so, it will make it easier for markets to mount speculative attacks on the Singapore dollar during periods of vulnerability. Further, our reserves are a strategic asset, and especially for a small country with no natural resources or other assets. They are a key defence for Singapore in times of crisis, and it will be unwise to reveal the full and exact resources at our disposal. (Ministry of Finance, n.d.)

As a number of accounts have argued, ulterior motives in the form of rent-seeking by domestic sectional interests are also a plausible reason for deliberate nontransparency (Eaton and Ming 2010). To the extent they exist, however, such motives are very far from the kind of offensive attempts to manipulate the countries hosting SWF investments that critics in some of these countries have alleged. Although most academic authors are quick to dismiss the more alarmist and protectionist responses to SWF investments as unfounded, the underlying shift in the distribution of wealth in the international system does constitute significant change in the international geopolitical balance of power (Kirshner 2009). There is, however, no straightforward metric for assessing the implications of such a shift. As the rest of this section argues, the new resources at the disposal of external surplus countries have so far yielded at least as many liabilities as gains.

In the first place, the perception that the buildup of financial resources in the form of official reserves and SWF assets represents politically useful ammunition has real consequences, regardless of the actual intent and actions of the states owning the SWFs. However unrealistic, this perception is real and is in itself is a factor shaping responses to SWFs, including instances where their investments have been blocked by political actors on either security or protectionist grounds (Truman 2011; Park and Estrada 2009). This puts significant constraints on the ability of surplus countries to manage foreign assets in ways that yield higher financial returns. Even in the case of Singapore's SWFs, which are much more experienced and – by most accounts – have much higher levels of institutional capacity than most of their newer counterparts from developing countries, its foreign excursions into nonportfolio investments have at times run into significant political pitfalls (Goldstein and Pananond 2008).

Second, although the imagery of FS as a "sword" is politically persuasive in conditions of persistent low growth, fiscal austerity, and high unemployment in Europe and North America, it falls short of capturing the nature of East Asia's changing and uneven mercantilism. The benefits (and costs) of economic growth in the export surplus countries of East Asia are real, but there are severe limits to their ability to translate their success as exporters into increased influence internationally. Financial statecraft requires more than financial resources. As Hung Ho-Fung (2009) has argued with respect to China's massive reserve stockpile, these assets represent a point of vulnerability more than useable ammunition at China's disposal. Hung points out that Chinese and other holders of U.S. dollar assets are hostage to their principal debtor, making any strategic sell-down of dollar holdings an exercise in self-harm. Efforts at currency diversification of international reserves (and implied threats to do so) have not produced any aggregate move away from U.S. dollar assets, which account for a similar percentage of world foreign exchange reserves as they did two decades ago. However, as also shown in Table 4.3, holdings by "emerging and developing economies" – which are dominated by China's official reserves – have shown a proportional shift away from the U.S. dollar. Such diversification notwithstanding, it

Table 4.3 World: currency composition of foreign exchange reserves

	1995	2000	2005	2010	2011	2012p
World						
Total foreign exchange holdings	1390	1936	4320	9262	10204	10952
Allocated Reserves	1034	1518	2844	5158	5648	6084
U.S. dollars (%)	59	71	67	62	62	61
Advanced economies						
Total foreign exchange holdings	932	1217	2078	3092	3399	3691
Allocated Reserves	767	1108	1822	2708	3012	3282
U.S. dollars (%)	54	70	69	65	67	62
Emerging and developing economies						
Total foreign exchange holdings	458	719	2242	6170	6806	7261
Allocated Reserves	267	410	1022	2450	2636	2802
U.S. dollars (%)	74	75	63	58	58	60

Notes: All figures are in billions of U.S. dollars, except percentage held in U.S. dollars.
Source: IMF, "Currency Composition of Official Foreign Exchange Reserves," April 2013.

remains that East Asia has a great deal invested in the continuing health of the U.S. dollar.

Beyond the financial vulnerability of reserve-holding countries, the underlying condition enabling the buildup of reserves in the first place sometimes represents a source of political vulnerability rather than leverage, particularly if most of the exporting country's surplus is earned vis-à-vis a single large foreign partner. As argued in 1945 by Albert Hirschman in his analysis of pre-war trading patterns between Germany and its neighbors, political leverage accrues to the deficit country, not the successful exporter (Hirschman 1980). With the exception of surplus countries that export mainly scarce and nonsubstitutable goods, the threat of closing market access by a deficit country that is a monopsony purchaser is more potent than any credible threat of trade retaliation by the surplus country. This asymmetry is probably less important in the current situation than the overall degree of mutual interdependence, which is unprecedented on a number of measures (Ravenhill 2009), but it does suggest additional reasons for doubting scenarios in which external surplus countries use their financial wealth as coercive bargaining resources.

Excess foreign exchange reserves are not very useful in political terms. In addition, the buildup of large foreign exchange reserves is costly economically, particularly for the countries engaged in reserve hoarding. For this reason, whether considered as a shield (precautionary motives) or a sword (export-promoting mercantilist objectives), the costs of reserve hoarding as a tool of financial statecraft are paid primarily by the hoarding country. The current account surpluses of the East Asian exporters are both destabilizing and inefficient. They represent an extraordinary and prolonged transfer of savings from East Asia to developed economies, principally the United States. The destabilization attendant on the recycling of these surpluses through the capital account aggravated the monetary policy choices that compounded regulatory failure prior to the U.S. financial crisis of 2008. For East Asia, the surpluses represent enormous consumption transfers from relatively low-income, developing countries to the United States – transfers that are suboptimal on standard calculations of welfare, which assume a declining marginal utility of consumption as income levels increase.

The steep rise in the foreign exchange reserves of East Asian countries has been costly in other ways. Because the rise in East Asian reserves is due in part to extensive sterilization operations by regional central banks, which have at a number of moments in the last decade been forced to confront large surges in capital inflows, these countries have been paying the considerable quasi-fiscal costs of extensive sterilization (e.g., Suryadarma and Sumarto 2011; Fane 2005; IMF 2011a). A direct cost is incurred as the intervention rate at which regional central banks have issued bonds or other instruments to mop up the excess liquidity due to large capital inflows has typically been much higher than the rate of return earned when the proceeds are invested in foreign currency assets. In addition, the exercise exposes these countries to further risks: sterilization of capital inflows (which have almost certainly been fed by the carry trade that has recycled funds from low-interest economies) creates further incentives for investors to make short-term bets on that country's currency. To the extent that domestic financial institutions respond to the interest rate differential by adding to their foreign currency liabilities, they add to the financial risks incurred by the country – risks that warrant offsetting taxes or other interventions by financial regulators, but which are politically difficult to sustain (Aizenman and Pinto 2011). The current recycling of liquidity back to emerging markets thus threatens to reproduce many of the macroeconomic pressures associated with short-term capital inflows that created incentives for perverse monetary policy choices and aggravated financial fragility in Asia in the lead-up to the AFC.

Finally, East Asia's current account surpluses and strategies of reserve accumulation help sustain what Barry Eichengreen (2011) has termed the "exorbitant privilege" of the United States – the ability to live for decades beyond its means by recourse to issuing currency that others are prepared to accept in payment for real goods and services. This privilege rests on the U.S. dollar's unique status as an international currency. Reduced reliance on the U.S. dollar by East Asian currencies would serve as a way of reducing the potential for the United States to abuse its position as the issuer of the world's most widely used currency (Kwan 2001). If the dollar's international role significantly declines, the United States would become a much more ordinary country, subject to the same risks (hence perhaps incentives for prudence) that other countries are, subject to the "original sin" of having to issue foreign currency-denominated debt (Eichengreen and Hausmann 2005). Although, as Eichengreen (2011) argues, the world will almost certainly move to a multipolar currency system in the future, the lack of an alternative, equally attractive currency has so far limited options for moving away from the dollar.

Financial statecraft and diplomacy

The significant costs and constraints facing regional countries in their use of financial resources to pursue even defensive aims put sharp limits on strategies of financial statecraft. It would be wrong to conclude that regional countries do not wish to engage in more proactive financial statecraft, or to see their increased financial resources translate into greater influence and voice in multilateral arenas. Several indicators suggest that many of the larger countries, including China and Indonesia, do wish to play a more assertive role internationally (Katada 2011). China, for example, has been prominent in calling for reform of the IMF in ways that would give countries such as itself voting rights more in line with their economic significance. Chinese officials have also occasionally made calls to diversify away from reliance on the U.S. dollar as the primary international currency.

The Southeast Asian countries have generally had low profiles in such debates, particularly after the retirement of Malaysia's outspoken former Prime Minister Mahathir in 2003, under whose leadership Malaysia had pushed strongly for much greater regulation and monitoring of international capital flows and reform of the IMF. Despite the lower profile in recent years, Southeast Asian countries have been supportive of initiatives for greater voice in multilateral arenas tasked with managing the international financial system. Malaysia, for example, has supported efforts to expand the resources of the IMF and simultaneously reform its governance structure in ways that would give emerging economies greater influence. Malaysia and the Philippines were both among the G20 emerging market economies to commit funds to the IMF's "second line of defense" facility announced in conjunction with the June 2012 G20 meeting in Mexico, and Indonesia shortly afterward announced it would also provide $1 billion in such contingent funding, on condition the funds were not used exclusively for lending to European countries (Xinhua 2012). As noted in official remarks by the IMF's Managing Director, the Fund "welcomed Malaysia's support for the IMF, including for our governance reforms, and for strengthening the IMF's resources, which will ensure that emerging Asia has a strong voice at the IMF and a stronger partner to help respond to future crises" (IMF 2012). As of October 2013, however, reforms of the IMF's governance structure remained blocked by the United States and European countries, underlining the limits of leverage provided by the new financial resources of emerging economies.

Southeast Asian countries have also taken up roles in new fora tasked with developing frameworks for international financial governance, particularly the G20 and the Financial Stability Board (FSB). The FSB developed out of a post-AFC initiative as a more representative institution than the IMF in terms of reflecting the financial and economic importance of members. It now includes 11 developing country members, including Singapore and Indonesia from Southeast Asia (Helleiner 2010). It has not, however, emerged as an influential, independent, agenda-setting organization, and its leadership remains dominated by developed country members – its current chair is the governor of the Bank of England, and its secretariat is hosted by the Bank for International Settlements (BIS) in Switzerland.

In the G20, Indonesia has taken its role seriously and repeatedly called for greater voice for emerging economies (Hermawan et al. 2011). Indonesia has had some success in influencing the G20, with its proposal for a global initiative on infrastructure financing gaining endorsement in 2012 (Wihardja 2012). The G20 has not, however, emerged as an arena for major restructuring in global institutions, even after the GFC of 2008, when Europe's need for external financing led to speculation that the financial resources of the emerging market members of the G20 would usher in major reform. As noted in a press account, "the excitement in the heady days of 2008 when the G20 finally gave leading emerging markets a place at the top table of global economic government" had changed by 2011, when at the G20 finance ministers' meeting in Paris "it was made clear that those newcomers continued to sit below the salt – and this by the ageing aristocracy whose sense of self-worth exceeds the cash they have on hand" (Beattie 2011). Much of the G20 agenda has in fact been taken up with defensive moves by China and other surplus economies to deflect pressure over their trade surpluses and currency policies, with conflicts between these countries and the United States over the measurement and understanding of trade imbalances threatening to derail talks (Rowley 2011). More recently, G20 attention has been drawn away from economic governance to security issues. Thus although Indonesia attended the 2013 G20 summit in St. Petersburg with the express intention of hearing – and being heard – on global economic conditions and policies (Saragih 2013), the summit was in fact dominated by disagreement over the question of military intervention in Syria, on which Indonesia joined the group of mostly emerging market countries (including China, India, Argentina, and Brazil, as well as Germany) rallied by Russia to oppose intervention (Murphy 2013).

Other attempts to exercise systemic and assertive FS include Singapore's proactive role in participating in the development of the Generally Accepted Principles and Practices, known as the Santiago Principles, adopted in October 2008. The Santiago Principles are a voluntary code of conduct for SWFs developed by the International Working Group of Sovereign Wealth Funds, consisting largely of developing countries with SWFs. The development of the Principles – which in themselves are unremarkable – was an explicit attempt to ward off protectionist responses to SWF purchases of distressed assets during the GFC (Truman 2011).

Finally, Southeast Asian countries have continued to pursue a regional financial agenda that would promote greater regional resilience and cooperation, as discussed by Katada and Sohn in this volume (Chapter 6). Regional institutions for financial and monetary coordination remain modest, but the groundwork for a significant regional infrastructure has been laid (Volz 2010; Katada 2011). The substantive implications of such regional cooperation capacities, even if they should develop as more authoritative organizations endowed with a degree of decision-making capacity, are not yet clear. Particularly on the issue of whether standards for regional financial surveillance and regulation would differ from those of the global organizations such as the IMF and BIS, there is no articulated regional vision that suggests an alternative set of priorities or approaches to financial governance. An examination of post-GFC statements from the two leading regional organizations, ASEAN (Association of Southeast Asian Nations) and its extended "plus three" variant that includes China, Japan, and South Korea, concluded that, "it is hard to read them as anything other than even more 'orthodox' than the prevailing mood in western capitals and multilateral organisations such as the IMF" (Hamilton-Hart 2012: 244). Individual Southeast Asian government officials do at times articulate critiques of the current international financial architecture, but there is as yet no unified and distinctive regional position setting out an alternative set of governance standards. For the time being, Southeast Asian countries seem more concerned with the procedural and structural issues around gaining more influential voices within multilateral arenas, rather than pursuing any particular substantive agenda.

The very fact that such countries have made use of such multilateral, diplomatic fora, both new and old, suggests that what may appear as structural sources of financial power – such as the accumulation of large international reserves – are not in themselves directly useful in foreign policy terms. The attempts to engineer shifts in decision-making procedures and organizational structure have also not been noticeably fruitful, as developed economies have exercised continued blocking power and have largely remained in control of the ideational and bureaucratic resources of both new groupings such as the FSB and old organizations such as the BIS and IMF. It is telling that, despite the country's initial enthusiasm for the G20, Indonesian observers see the country as having achieved relatively little as a result of G20 membership, one describing the G20 as "a sword of WTO. When they could not reach an agreement on some policies multilaterally in the WTO meetings, they will bring the issue on the G-20 agenda, where it has to be authoritatively implemented. If G-20 member-states implement those policies, then the other nations with low GDP cannot do anything" (quoted in Hermawan et al. 2011: 26).

Conclusion

Southeast Asia's domestic political economy was until recently fairly captured by the notion of "embedded mercantilism" (cf. Pempel 1998) – a sustained commitment to export-driven growth underpinned politically by a compensatory bargain between domestic elites and foreign-owned exporting interests, with labor largely marginalized in political terms (Jayasuryia 2003). An entrenched reliance on export-driven growth in Malaysia and Singapore, both countries marked by elite continuity and little democratization, has endured in the period since the AFC at the end of the last century. In this period, these countries pursued policies that approximate the notion of "monetary mercantilism" – the pursuit of external surpluses manifesting in the buildup of foreign currency reserves and at least plausibly supported by deliberate foreign exchange rate management. In contrast, the underlying political bargain sustaining export-driven growth and the accumulation of external surpluses has unraveled in the countries where political change has been greatest, most notably in Indonesia.

Although Southeast Asia does not conform to a single pattern of growth and external balance, the region as a whole is undoubtedly in a stronger position than it was a decade ago. Foreign exchange reserves are higher and few countries run large current account deficits. The purpose and usefulness of the accumulation of foreign assets remains contested. Most evidence points to defensive FS motivations for strategies of external accumulation, primarily to shield the domestic economy from the risks of economic openness. Although the comparative strength of regional economies in the face of the 2008

GFC centered on the United States and Europe attests to the relative resilience of Southeast Asia, the more open economies in the region were vulnerable to the downstream effects of the crisis, with the transmission being both through a trade shock and a reversal of financial flows – in contrast to the greater resilience shown by the larger, less-trade dependent economies of Indonesia and the Philippines (Isnawangsih et al. 2013).

This chapter has described pursuit of and limits to financial statecraft, both in terms of the structural power and protection that might be thought to accompany the accumulation of financial resources, and in terms of the diplomatic leverage that might be enjoyed by holders of such resources. Although the tangible gains from such FS have been modest, the economic growth and financial resources now at the disposal of Southeast Asian countries create a striking contrast with the condition of the region during and in the immediate aftermath of the AFC. Then, Thailand and Indonesia were forced into emergency lending and reform programs under the direction of the IMF, and the economic crises they experienced brought down ruling parties in both countries. The contrast was drawn explicitly by the Indonesian president (and the Indonesian press) when he hosted the Managing Director of the IMF in Jakarta in 2012:

'Now we can punch as powerfully as the IMF. We dissolved the CGI. We stand upright. We don't have to ask, ask, ask.'[8]

Notes

1. Parts of this chapter are based on Hamilton-Hart (2014).
2. Pempel (1998: 48–62) describes the policy complex of embedded mercantilism as consisting of, inter alia, a protectionist economic nationalism aimed at nurturing domestic industries to enable them to compete with those of more developed countries.
3. Eichengreen (2004) critiques the idea of such a system, arguing that countries currently benefitting from currency management do not show signs of any unified commitment to supporting the system.
4. Unless otherwise stated, figures for Temasek's assets are from two websites operated by Temasek Holdings, http://www.temasek.com.sg and http://www.temasekreview.com.sg. The reporting date for portfolio size and distribution is March 31, 2013.
5. Figures as of 31 March, as reported in GIC 2008 and GIC 2013.
6. This is a conservative estimate as of 2013, based on Temasek's foreign assets at $120 billion, official reserves managed by the Monetary Authority of Singapore at $250 billion, and GIC assets of $130 billion.
7. These diverging domestic political economies are discussed in Hamilton-Hart (2014).

8. Quoted in Liauw (2012). The CGI was the Consultative Group for Indonesia, a consortium of foreign donors wound up by Indonesia after it repaid its loans to the IMF in 2007.

References

Aizenman, Joshua, and Jaewoo Lee. 2008. "Financial versus Monetary Mercantilism: Long-run View of Large International Reserves," *The World Economy*, 31(5), 593–611.

Aizenman, Joshua, Michael Hutchison, and Ilan Noy. 2011. "Inflation Targeting and Real Exchange Rates in Emerging Markets," *World Development*, 39(5), 712–724.

Aizenman Joshua, and Brian Pinto. 2011. "Managing Financial Integration and Capital Mobility – Policy lessons from the past two decades," University of California Santa Cruz Economics department working paper, July.

Amsden, Alice. 1989. *Asia's Next Giant: South Korea and Late Industrialization.* Oxford: Oxford University Press.

Beattie, Alan. 2011. "G20's Ageing Aristocracy Stands in Way of New Ideas," *Financial Times*, October 16, 2011.

Calvo, Guillermo, and Carmen Reinhart. 2002. "Fear of Floating," *Quarterly Journal of Economics*, 117(2), 379–408.

Cheung, Yin-Wong, and Xianwang Qian. 2009. "Hoarding of International Reserves: Mrs Machlup's Wardrobe and the Joneses," *Review of International Economics*, 17(4), 824–843.

Clark, Gordon, and Ashby Monk. 2010. "Government of Singapore Investment Corporation (GIC): Insurer of Last Resort and Bulwark of Nation-State Legitimacy," *The Pacific Review*, 23, 429–451.

Cohen, Benjamin. 2008. "After the Fall: East Asian Exchange Rates since the Crisis," in Andrew MacIntyre, T. J. Pempel, and John Ravenhill (eds) *Crisis as Catalyst: Asia's Dynamic Political Economy.* Ithaca: Cornell University Press, pp. 25–44.

Devlin, Will, and Bill Brummitt. 2007. "A Few Sovereigns More: The Rise of Sovereign Wealth Funds." In *Economic Roundup: Spring 2007.* Canberra: Commonwealth of Australia, pp. 119–132.

Deyo, Frederic. 1989. *Beneath the Miracle: Labor Subordination in the New Asian Industrialism.* Berkeley: University of California Press.

Dooley, Michael, David Folkerts-Landau, and Peter Garber. 2008. "Life on the Tri-Polar Sphere: How Should Interest and Exchange Rates Realign Next?" in Takatoshi Ito and Andrew Rose (eds) *International Financial Issues in the Pacific Rim: Global Imbalances, Financial Liberalization, and Exchange Rate Policy.* Chicago: University of Chicago Press, pp. 13–37.

Eaton, Sarah, and Zhang Ming. 2010. "A principal–agent analysis of China's sovereign wealth system: Byzantine by design," *Review of International Political Economy*, 17(3), 481–506.

Eichengreen, Barry. 2004. "Global Imbalances and the Lessons of Bretton Woods." NBER Working Paper 10497.

Eichengreen, Barry. 2011. *Exorbitant Privilege: The Rise and Fall of the Dollar and the Future of the International Monetary System.* Oxford: Oxford University Press.

Fane, George. 2005. "Post-Crisis Monetary and Exchange Rate Policies in Indonesia, Malaysia and Thailand," *Bulletin of Indonesian Economic Studies*, 41(2), 175–195.

GIC (Singapore). 2008. "Report on the Management of the Government's Portfolio for the Year 2007/08."

GIC (Singapore). 2013. "Report on the Management of the Government's Portfolio for the Year 2012/13."

Gilson, Ronald, and Curtis Milhaupt. 2007–2008. "Sovereign Wealth Funds and Corporate Governance: A Minimalist Response to the New Mercantilism," *Stanford Law Review*, 60, 1345–1369.

Goldstein, Andrea, and Pavida Pananond. 2008. "Singapore Inc. Goes Shopping Abroad: Profits and Pitfalls," *Journal of Contemporary Asia*, 38, 417–438.

Hamilton-Hart, Natasha. 2008. "Banking Systems a Decade After the Crisis," in A. MacIntyre, T. J. Pempel, and J. Ravenhill (eds) *Crisis as Catalyst: Asia's Dynamic Political Economy*. Ithaca, NY: Cornell University Press.

Hamilton-Hart, Natasha. 2012. "Regional and Multi-level Governance: East Asian Leadership after the Global Financial Crisis," *Asia-Europe Journal*, 9, 237–254.

Hamilton-Hart, Natasha. 2014. "Monetary Politics in Southeast Asia: External Imbalances in Regional Context," *New Political Economy*.

Helleiner, Eric. 2009. "The Geopolitics of Sovereign Wealth Funds: An Introduction," *Geopolitics*, 14, 300–304.

Helleiner, Eric. 2010. "What Role for the New Financial Stability Board? The Politics of International Standards after the Crisis," *Global Policy*, 1(3): 282–290.

Hermawan, Yulius, Wulani Sriyuliani, Getruida Hardjowijono, and Sylvie Tanaga. 2011. *The Role of Indonesia in the G-20: Background, Role and Objectives of Indonesia's Membership*. Jakarta: Friedrich Ebert Stiftung.

Hung, Ho Fung. 2009. "America's Head Servant? The PRC's dilemma in the global crisis," *New Left Review*, 60, November–December, 5–25.

IMF (International Monetary Fund). 2012. "IMF Managing Director Christine Lagarde Visits Malaysia, Meets Prime Minister Najib." Press Release No. 12/433, 14 November. Available at http://www.imf.org/external/np/sec/pr/2012/pr12433.htm.

Isnawangsih, Agnes, Vladimir Klyuev and Longmei Zhang. 2013. "The Big Split: Why Did Output Trajectories in the ASEAN-4 Diverge after the Global Financial Crisis?" IMF Working Paper WP/13/222. Available at www.imf.org/external/pubs/ft/wp/2013/wp13222.pdf.

Jayasuriya, Kanishka. 2003. "Embedded Mercantilism and Open Regionalism: The Crisis of a Regional Project," *Third World Quarterly*, 24(2), 339–355.

Jesudason, James. 1989. *Ethnicity and the Economy: The State, Chinese Business and Multinationals in Malaysia*. Singapore: Oxford University Press.

Katada, Saori. 2011. "Seeking a Place for East Asian Regionalism: Challenges and Opportunities under the Global Financial Crisis," *The Pacific Review*, 24(3), 273–290.

Kirshner, Jonathan. 2009. 'Sovereign Wealth Funds and National Security: The Dog that will Refuse to Bark,' *Geopolitics*, 14(2), 305–316.

Kwan, C.H. 2001. *Yen Bloc: Toward Economic Integration in Asia*. Washington, D.C.: Brookings Institution.

Lee, Yvonne. 2009. "A Reversal of Neo-Colonialism: The Pitfalls and Prospects of Sovereign Wealth Funds," *Georgetown Journal of International Law*, 40, 1103–1149.

Liauw, Hindra. 2012. "Presiden: Sekarang Indonesia Gagah Bertemu IMF," *Kompas*, July 10, 2012.

Ministry of Finance (Singapore). n.d. 'Section I: What comprises the reserves and who manages them?' Available at http://app.mof.gov.sg/reserves_sectionone.aspx.

Murphy, Joe. 2013. "Divided they Stand: G20 Ends with East and West Still Split over Syria Action," *The Independent*, September 7, 2013.

Park, Donghyun, and Gemma Estrada. 2009. "Developing Asia's Sovereign Wealth Funds and Outward Foreign Direct Investment," ADB Economics Working Paper Series No. 169, Asian Development Bank.

Pempel, T. J. 1998. *Regime Shift: Comparative Dynamics of the Japanese Political Economy*. Ithaca: Cornell University Press.

Rajan, Ramkishen. 2009. *Exchange Rates, Currency Crisis and Monetary Cooperation in Asia*. New York: Palgrave Macmillan.

Ravenhill, John. 2009. "The economics-security nexus in the Asia-Pacific region," in William Tow (ed.) *Security Politics in the Asia-Pacific: A Regional-Global Nexus?* Cambridge: Cambridge University Press, pp. 188–207.

Ritchie, Bryan. 2005. "Coalitional Politics, Economic Reform, and Technological Upgrading in Malaysia," *World Development*, 33(5), 745–762.

Rose, Andrew. 2007. "A stable International Monetary System Emerges: Inflation Targeting is Bretton Woods, Reversed," *Journal of International Money and Finance*, 26, 663–681.

Rowley, Emma. 2011. "G20 Paris: last-ditch China deal saves summit," *The Telegraph*, February 19, 2011.

Sally, Razeen, and Rahul Sen. 2011. "Trade Policies in Southeast Asia in the Wider Asian Perspective," *The World Economy*, 34(4), 568–601.

Sanchez, Marcelo. 2010. "What does South Korean inflation targeting target?," *Journal of Asian Economics*, 21, 526–539.

Saragih, Bagus B. T. 2013. "SBY Heads East and Eyes Greater Role for RI in G20," *Jakarta Post*, September 2, 2013.

Shih, Victor. 2009. "Tools of Survival: Sovereign Wealth Funds in Singapore and China," *Geopolitics*, 14, 328–344.

Suryadarma, Daniel, and Sudarno Sumarto. 2011. "Survey of Recent Developments," *Bulletin of Indonesian Economic Studies*, 47(2), 155–181.

Truman, Edwin. 2011. "Are Asian Sovereign Wealth Funds Different?," *Asian Economic Policy Review*, 6, 249–268.

Viner, Jacob. 1948. "Power versus Plenty as Objectives of Foreign Policy in the Seventeenth and Eighteenth Centuries," *World Politics*, 1(1), 1–29.

Volz, Ulrich. 2010. *Prospects for Monetary Cooperation and Integration in East Asia*. Cambridge, MA: MIT Press.

Wihardja, Maria Monica. 2012. "Indonesia and the G20: A Door Left Half Open," *East Asia Forum* June 29, 2012. Available from www.eastasiaforum.org.

Woo, Jung-En. 1991. *Race to the Swift: State and Finance in Korean Industrialization*. New York: Columbia University Press.

Xinhua. 2012. "Indonesia confirms 1 bln USD loan for IMF as 'second-line defense'," July 11, 2012. Available from ASEAN-China Free Trade Area, http://www.asean-cn.org/Item/5548.aspx.

Yeung, Henry W.C. 2011. "From national development to economic diplomacy? Governing Singapore's sovereign wealth funds." *The Pacific Review*, 24(5) 625–652.

Zeti, Akhtar Aziz. 2005. "Intervention by Tan Sri Dato," Dr. Zeti Akhtar Aziz, Governor, Bank Negara Malaysia at the Frankfurt European Banking Congress, November 18, 2005, Frankfurt. *Quarterly Bulletin* (Bank Negara Malaysia), 2005, Quarter 4.

5
All Politics Is Local: The Renminbi's Prospects as a Future Global Currency

Ulrich Volz

Recent years have seen a heated discussion over Chinese capital account liberalization and internationalization of China's currency, the renminbi (RMB). Against the backdrop of a weak U.S. economy and China's growing international economic clout, there has been speculation about the RMB replacing the U.S. dollar as the world's leading currency. Subramanian (2011: 1), for instance, maintains that "the renminbi could become the premier reserve currency by the end of this decade, or early next decade." Much of the current discourse recalls past discussions when other currencies, especially the Japanese yen (Burstein 1988; Kwan 1994; Taguchi 1994) and the Euro (Chinn and Frankel 2007), were seen as candidates to "dethrone" the dollar.

China is often portrayed as aggressively trying to achieve global leadership, and RMB internationalization is seen by many as the epitome of China's quest for global dominance. However, it is important to understand the complex motivations behind RMB internationalization in order to allow for a more balanced and nuanced debate on China's changing role in the international economy. Understanding the reasons for which China might pursue RMB internationalization also is key to predicting the speed at which it might proceed.

I argue that what may appear to be a rather assertive, offensive, and systemic use of financial statecraft (FS), through which China would actively be redefining the global currency structure by promoting an increased global use of the RMB and displacing the U.S. dollar, has additional and more complex layers of meaning within China's domestic political economy. As discussed below, the drive for RMB internationalization has been triggered mostly by China's domestic need for financial reform along with the country's defensive reaction to its excessive dependence on the U.S. dollar. Hence at present, the Chinese "challenge" to the existing global currency hierarchy through RMB internationalization comes largely from the Chinese reformers' desire to restructure the country's rigid and inefficient financial sector and improve the effectiveness of domestic monetary policy.

This chapter reviews the current state of RMB internationalization and highlights the links between capital account opening and RMB convertibility, on the one hand, and the controversies within the Chinese Communist Party (CCP) leadership over the speed of economic and financial liberalization, on the other. I argue that the Chinese discussion about RMB internationalization is mainly motivated by domestic debates about financial sector reform. In particular, the widely popular notion of establishing the RMB as a global currency has been promoted by those seeking domestic financial reform as a way to overcome the reform resistance coming from various factions within the Chinese government and economy. International currency policy is therefore primarily used for the purpose of achieving domestic policy goals, rather than for changing the global financial order or supporting larger foreign policy goals. My argument thus relates to earlier literature on China's economic opening and reform, much of which highlighted "domestic politics [as] the primary source of policy changes in China's reform and opening" (Moore 2002: 35).

The chapter is structured as follows. After briefly reviewing the literature on international currencies in the first section, the second section summarizes the incremental steps toward currency internationalization that the Chinese authorities have taken thus far. A third section analyzes the political economy of China's domestic financial market and capital account reforms and establishes the link to the discussion on RMB internationalization. It suggests that neither a foreign policy lens nor a purely economic efficiency one captures key elements in the decision-making process of today's Chinese leadership; instead, domestic political economy considerations appear to play a major role. While there are domestic interests that support RMB internationalization, they are opposed by powerful party factions, state banks, and state-owned enterprise constituencies that perceive themselves as likely to lose from such policies. The fourth section addresses China's broader ambitions to augment its stature in the regional and global economy, and discusses the ways in which FS – the active use of monetary and financial instruments, including promotion of the RMB as an international reserve currency – has been employed to pursue this foreign policy goal.

My conclusion argues that a rapid and comprehensive liberalization of China's capital account is improbable. It is therefore unlikely that the RMB will take on the U.S. dollar's role as the premier investment and reserve currency anytime soon, even as the RMB is established as a leading currency for trade. The likeliest scenario in the next two decades is the emergence of a multipolar international monetary system, with the U.S. dollar, the Euro, and the RMB in the leading roles, and smaller regional lead currencies in Africa, Latin America, the Middle East, and Central Asia in the second tier.

International reserve and investment currencies

The international monetary system is characterized by currency competition and a hierarchy of currencies. Cohen (1998: 114) compares currency competition to a "vast, three-dimensional pyramid: narrow at the top, where a few popular currencies dominate; increasingly broad below, reflecting varying degrees of competitive inferiority." Several factors establish a currency's rank in this international currency hierarchy, and whether a currency will be able to become a major international or "global" currency, which will be used not only as invoicing currency for trade, but that will also be a major investment currency in the portfolios of international investors and reserve currency held by central banks.[1]

As Minsky (1986: 228) observed, "everyone can create money; the problem is to get it accepted." The easiest way to have one's IOUs (promises to pay) accepted is to generate liabilities for others that can only be extinguished through possession of these IOUs (Kregel 2006). A government can enforce the acceptance of its currency domestically through the fiscal system (and up to a certain degree through the legal system) by creating a tax liability on its citizens that can only be redeemed in the form of money issued by the government. But this does not work internationally, as a government can tax its own citizens, who are subject to government regulations, but cannot force nonresidents to hold claims on the government as financial assets. The only way to make the currency internationally accepted is by building an expectation that these liabilities will act as perfect substitutes for the liabilities of other countries' monetary authorities.

A number of conditions can be identified that contribute to building such expectations. First, confidence in a currency's future value is dependent on the political stability of the country of origin (Cohen 2000). This is the quintessential precondition for establishing a track record of relatively low inflation and low inflation variability. Second, countries need sound and credible fiscal institutions. In conjunction with noninflationary wage and price policies, a sound fiscal framework lays the groundwork for a noninflationary monetary environment with low nominal as well as real interest rates. Third, countries need to establish credible monetary regimes. Unpredictable monetary policy makes market participants unsure about the future real value of their assets issued in domestic currency and may lead them to denominate them in international currency (Jeanne 2005). Establishing a strong, (de facto) independent central bank with strong inflation aversion and a clear monetary policy objective is an important way to pin down inflationary expectations and to reduce this uncertainty.

Fourth, avoiding international debt, and instead striving for a surplus in the trade and current account, helps to create expectations of an appreciation of the national currency. From a long-term development perspective, it is not the short-term stabilization of the exchange rate that is of central importance but rather the currency's long-term value. The quality of a nation's currency is undermined when a currency regime is chosen that achieves price and exchange rate stabilization at the cost of an increase in the country's foreign debt. Instead, countries need to develop the ability to generate foreign reserves by generating export surpluses.[2] Such a strategy is helped by a tendency toward an undervaluation of the currency, as illustrated by the successful adopters of this development strategy such as West Germany in the 1950s and Japan in the 1960s and 1970s. The East Asian tiger economies – and then China – have very successfully followed this strategy more recently.

But developing sound fiscal and monetary institutions and generating export surpluses will not suffice to achieve key currency status. The literature on the determinants of key currency status points to another factor, namely the size of the economy. Matsuyama, Kiyotaki, and Matsui (1993) explain the international use of currencies and, succinctly, the determinants of key currency status as a function of relative country size and the degree of international economic integration. Because of network externalities and transaction costs, the global portfolio is concentrated in only a handful of currencies. In some ways, money is comparable to language, whose usefulness is also dependent on the number of people with whom one can communicate; similarly a currency's utility rises with the number of other market participants using the same currency (Dowd and Greenaway 1993). A currency's attractiveness also increases with its transactional liquidity, which in turn is dependent on the existence of well-developed and broad domestic financial markets that offer a wide range of short- and long-term investment opportunities in that currency, as well as fully operating secondary markets (Cohen 2000). Eichengreen, Hausmann, and Panizza (2005) point out that larger countries offer significant diversification possibilities, while smaller countries add fewer diversification benefits relative to the additional costs they imply.

As a result of these factors, the global portfolio is concentrated in a small number of currencies (those at the top of the international currency pyramid) for reasons partly beyond the control of even those countries that follow sound domestic policies. Developing key currency status is hence a very difficult and perhaps even impossible endeavor for small economies. Eichengreen, Hausmann, and Panizza (2005) show larger economies to have less of a problem borrowing in their own currency than do smaller economies. Using different measures of size, their estimates suggest that economic size is robustly and negatively correlated to "original sin," that is, a situation where it is impossible for a country to borrow abroad in its domestic currency.

Taking into account these conditions, China certainly has the economic potential to elevate the RMB to key currency status. Assuming continuous economic and political stability in China (admittedly a significant assumption), China can be expected to replace the United States as the world's largest economy in the foreseeable future, even if the country's growth rate slows significantly compared to the 10 percent annual average recorded over the past three decades. Although the People's Bank of China (PBOC, sometimes abbreviated as PBC), China's central bank, is not institutionally independent, China's leadership is generally inflation-averse and likely to continue to grant the PBOC sufficient operational independence to prevent high inflation, given that the latter could cause social unrest.[3] Last but not least, China has been running significant current account surpluses, which have been driving appreciation expectations.

However, as many studies have highlighted, there are also conditions that China does not fulfill at the moment: in particular, China is currently lacking deep and liquid capital markets; the RMB is not fully convertible (i.e., it is not freely tradable in global currency markets); and the capital account is still tightly regulated (e.g., Prasad and Ye 2011; Volz 2013). Without a further opening of the capital account and convertibility of the RMB, the latter cannot assume a major international role besides being an invoicing country in (mostly regional) trade. Nonetheless, China's government could, in theory, implement the necessary policies fairly quickly, and with foreign portfolio capital inflows domestic Chinese capital markets would probably then see considerable growth. Moreover, taking into account the historical experience of the U.S. dollar, which went from having no international role to being the leading international currency in less than a decade (Eichengreen 2011), we could indeed see the RMB rise to key currency status very quickly.

In practice, however, reform of the capital account and convertibility of the RMB are hotly contested issues in China. Moreover, these reforms necessarily are linked with reform of the domestic financial sector, since the capital account cannot be fully liberalized before the overhaul of the interest rate setting system, among others, is completed. The speed of reform is hence not yet decided. Before analyzing the preferences of different interests within China with respect to these issues, and what they imply for the reform process and hence RMB internationalization, the next section will briefly review the steps already taken toward capital account opening and RMB internationalization.

China's evolving roadmap for RMB internationalization

Since a number of recent studies, including Cohen (2012a), Prasad and Ye (2012), and Volz (2013), have reviewed the steps taken to liberalize China's capital account and promote the internationalization of the RMB, the following overview is kept very short. A summary of China's framework for capital controls is provided in Table 5.1. Major steps taken by the Chinese authorities toward RMB internationalization are listed in Table 5.2. Table 5.3 provides information on the 24 bilateral currency swap agreements that the PBOC had entered into with other central banks as of December 2013.

Various initiatives have been announced and implemented over recent years to promote RMB internationalization, including a subnational pilot program on RMB cross-border trade settlement (later extended to the country as a whole); the issuance of sovereign RMB-denominated bonds and permission for the issuance of corporate bonds in Hong Kong and elsewhere; pilot programs for RMB-denominated outward foreign direct investment (FDI) for residents of 20 cities and provinces; and, most recently, the establishment of a special zone to experiment with direct currency convertibility in Shenzhen, the city that designated as China's first special economic zone and test-case for economic reforms in 1980. However, as Table 5.1 demonstrates, China's capital account is still tightly regulated, with the exception of inward FDI. Direct investment inflows still need approval, but face less severe restrictions than portfolio inflows. Since 2002, licensed foreign investors, the so-called

Table 5.1 China: framework of capital controls

Major items		Inflows	Outflows
Direct investment		Free; three-tier classification of foreign exchange activities: encouraged, restricted, prohibited	
Stock market	NR	Local purchase of B shares and QFIIs subject to a set of limitations	Sale of A and B shares locally with no restrictions and QFIIs
	R	Sale of B, H, N, and S shares abroad and QDIIs locally	QDIIs, insurance companies, qualified banks purchase abroad
Bonds and other debt securities	NR	QFIIs purchase locally Purchase RMB bonds offshore in HK, Singapore	Financial and nonfinancial firms, international agencies issue RMB-denominated bonds in HK, Singapore, and locally
	R	Commercial and policy banks, selected firms are permitted to sell RMB bonds in HK	QDIIs, insurance companies, qualified banks purchase abroad
Money market	NR	QFIIs purchase money market fund locally but no permission to participate in interbank foreign exchange market Overseas monetary authorities, the designated RMB clearing banks, and participating banks to invest in interbank bond market with their legally acquired RMB assets	No permission
	R	Bonds with less than one-year duration	QDIIs and qualified banks
Collective investment securities	NR	QFIIs purchase open-end and closed-end funds locally	No permission
	R	Prior approval by SAFE	QDIIs, insurance companies, qualified banks subject to quota
Derivatives and other instruments	NR	No permission	No permission
	R	Regulated financial institutions with the approval of CBRC may sell for the purposes of hedging, gaining profit, and providing transaction services for clients with limit on open foreign exchange position	Regulations on sale apply

Notes: R stands for residents; N stands for nonresidents; QFII stands for Qualified Foreign Institutional Investors; QDIIs stands for Qualified Domestic Institutional Investors; SAFE is the State Administration of Foreign Exchange; CBRC is the China Banking Regulatory Commission.

Source: Adapted from Gao (2012).

Table 5.2 China: major steps toward RMB internationalization

November 2002. Qualified Foreign Institutional Investors (QFII) can buy and sell RMB-denominated shares in China's mainland stock exchanges, licensed by China Securities Regulatory Commission (CSRC). QFII investors need to obtain investment quotas from China's foreign currency regulator (SAFE) before they can start buying Chinese securities.

February 2004. Retail RMB business starts in Hong Kong and Macau (following permission given in November 2003). The PBOC provides clearing arrangement for relevant banks in Hong Kong and Macau via Bank of China, Hong Kong and Macau.

October 2005. First two RMB-denominated bond from a non-Chinese issuer ("Panda bonds") are sold in mainland China by the International Finance Corporation and the Asian Development Bank.

May 2006. A PBOC Study Group publishes a report "Timing, Path, and Strategies of RMB Internationalization."

January 2007. RMB bonds (also known as "dim sum bonds") can be issued in Hong Kong.

July 2007. First dim sum bond issued by China Development Bank.

December 2008. Currency swap with South Korea.

December 2008. Premier Wen announces a pilot scheme of RMB cross-border trade settlement with Hong Kong, Macau, and ASEAN countries.

April 2009. State Council announces pilot program on RMB cross-border settlement in five cities.

April 2009. First cross-border trade settlement between Shanghai Silk group (China exporter) and Zhong Ye Trading (Hong Kong importer).

June 2009. PBOC and HKMA sign memorandum of cooperation for RMB cross-border trade settlement pilot scheme.

July 2009. PBOC and other five authorities issued administrative rules for RMB settlement pilot scheme with HK, Macau, and ASEAN countries.

July 2009. Launch of the pilot scheme for RMB cross-border trade settlement between Mainland Designated Enterprises (MDEs) in five cities (Shanghai, Guangzhou, Shenzhen, Dongguan, and Zhuhai) and corporations in Hong Kong, Macau, and ASEAN countries.

September 2009. Ministry of Finance issues the first sovereign RMB-denominated bond in Hong Kong.

November 2009. Interbank Market Clearing House is founded in Shanghai.

March 2010. PBOC and the National Bank of Belarus sign local-currency settlement agreement, the first of its kind with a non-neighboring country.

May 2010. Rules for issuance of Panda bonds are liberalized and more issuers are allowed. Bank of Tokyo-Mitsubishi UFJ (China) Ltd. is the first foreign bank to sell bonds in China.

June 2010. RMB trade settlement program is extended to 20 provinces and to trading partners worldwide.

June 2010. RMB bonds extended to allow banks to develop all types of RMB products and services and open type of participation to all types of financial intermediaries.
July 2010. Bank of China (Hong Kong) authorized to clear RMB bank notes in Taiwan.
July 2010. Hong Kong financial institutions allowed to open RMB accounts.
July 2010. Hopewell Highway issues the first corporate RMB-denominated bond in Hong Kong.
August 2010. First offshore RMB mutual fund is started.
August 2010. Qualified financial institutions (overseas central banks, cross-border settlement banks, and RMB clearing banks) can invest in China's interbank bond market.
September 2010. First foreign-issued dim sum bond by a nonfinancial company (McDonald's) in Hong Kong.
October 2010. Overseas institutions allowed to apply for RMB accounts for trade settlement.
October 2010. Pilot project for deposits of export proceeds abroad launched in four areas.
October 2010. Asian Development Bank issues first supranational dim sum bond.
December 2010. Trade settlement scheme expanded; number of Chinese exporters eligible for cross-border settlement (MDEs) rises from 365 to 67,359.
January 2011. PBOC announces a pilot scheme under which residents of 20 provinces and cities are allowed to use RMB for outward FDI.
January 2011. Bank of China allowed to offer RMB deposit accounts in New York City.
April 2011. First RMB IPO by Hui Xian listed on the Hong Kong Exchange.
August 2011. Cross-border trade settlement in RMB is extended to the whole nation.
August 2011. Initial RMB 20 billion Mini-QFII Program launched.
September 2011. At the UK-China Economic and Financial Dialogue, Vice Premier Wang Qishan and British Chancellor of the Exchequer George Osborne agree on a cooperation project on the development of RMB-denominated products and services in London and welcome a private sector-led development of the offshore RMB market in London.
October 2011. Banks are allowed to provide settlement services to overseas entities that made RMB-denominated investments.
November 2011. JP Morgan Asset Management is allowed to create a $1 billion RMB-denominated fund under the Qualified Limited Partners Program, making it the largest foreign manager of an RMB-denominated fund so far.
December 2011. China and Japan sign currency pact to promote use of their currencies for bilateral trade and investment flows.
January 2012. Shanghai city government and NDRC outline a plan for developing the size of the city's capital markets and open them more widely to foreign investors by 2015.

Continued

Table 5.2 Continued

April 2012. China Securities Regulatory Commission announces an expansion of the QFII scheme from the previous limit of $30 billion to $80 billion and increases the total amount of RMB that foreign investors can raise in Hong Kong for investment on the mainland from RMB20 billion to RMB70 billion.

April 2012. HSBC issues a three-year RMB-denominated bond in London, the first dim sum bond to be issued outside China and Hong Kong.

June 2012. Announcement of plans to create a special zone to experiment with currency convertibility in Shenzhen.

November 2012. First Chinese bank (China Construction Bank) issues RMB-denominated bond in London.

January 2013. Qianhai, a special zone located in the western part of Shenzhen, is allowed to launch China's first cross-border RMB lending program (with Hong Kong). Fifteen banks in Hong Kong – nine branches of mainland lenders and six foreign banks – sign $320m RMB loans to Chinese mainland firms relating to 26 projects registered in Qianhai.

May 2013. The State Council announces that by the end of the year the government would outline a plan for full convertibility of the RMB.

July 2013. The State Council announces the intention to establish a pilot zone in Shanghai as a test ground for financial reforms, including interest rate liberalisation and full convertibility of the RMB.

October 2013. Singapore-based investors are allowed to buy RMB-denominated securities.

November 2013. China's biggest bank (Industrial and Commercial Bank of China) issues its first dim sum bond in London.

Source: Based on Volz (2013) and Prasad and Ye (2012) and amended and updated by the author.

Table 5.3 China: bilateral swap agreements with other central banks (as of December 2013)

Country/area	Amount (in billion RMB)	Date of agreement	Expiration date
Albania	2	September 2013	September 2016
Argentina	70	March 2009	March 2012
Australia	200	March 2012	March 2015
Belarus	20	March 2009	March 2012
Brazil	190	March 2013	March 2016
Eurozone (ECB)	350	October 2013	October 2013
Hong Kong	200	January 2009	January 2012
	400	November 2011	November 2014
Hungary	10	September 2013	September 2016
Iceland	3.5	June 2010	June 2013
Indonesia	100	March 2009	March 2012
Kazakhstan	7	June 2011	June 2014
Korea	180	December 2008	December 2011
	360	October 2011	October 2014
	360	June 2013	October 2017
Malaysia	80	February 2009	February 2012
	180	February 2012	February 2015
Mongolia	5	May 2011	May 2014
	10	March 2012	May 2014
New Zealand	25	April 2011	April 2014
Pakistan	10	December 2011	December 2014
Russia	Local-currency settlement agreement, no limitation	June 2011	
Singapore	150	July 2010	July 2013
	300	March 2013	March 2016
Turkey	10	February 2012	February 2015
Thailand	70	December 2011	December 2014
United Arab Emirates	35	January 2012	January 2015
United Kingdom	200	June 2013	June 2016
Ukraine	15	June 2012	June 2015
Uzbekistan	0.7	April 2011	April 2014

Source: Compiled by author with enhanced and updated data from Garcia-Herrero and Xia (2013).

"Qualified Foreign Institutional Investors" (QFII), have been granted permission to invest in China's capital markets, but they still face quota restrictions and are constrained to invest only in certain asset classes. Capital outflows, except for direct investments, are also tightly regulated or banned altogether. Although the goal of capital account liberalization was put forward in the 12th Five-Year Plan outlining the policy for the years 2011–2015, the authorities had not as of late 2013 provided details on how quick liberalization should proceed and how far it should go, even as the goal of capital account liberalization was reiterated at the CCP's Third Plenum in November 2013.

The discussion within China on capital account liberalization recently intensified, with the unveiling of a PBOC blueprint for an accelerated opening of China's financial sector. In a February 2012 interview to the "China Securities Journal," one of the country's most influential newspapers, a senior PBOC official outlined a three-step plan for liberalizing the capital account over the next ten years (Sheng 2012).[4] According to this plan, the next three years would see a loosening of direct investment controls and a liberalization of capital flows out of China to take advantage of lower valuations for Western companies. Over the next three to five years, the plan also foresees deregulation of commercial credit controls and an increase in foreign RMB-denominated lending by Chinese banks to raise the RMB's global status. In the third step, within five to ten years, China would "gradually open up trading of real estate, stocks and bonds to foreign investors". By the end of the plan's third phase, China would have achieved a great (yet not clearly specified) degree of RMB convertibility.

Even though the PBOC's plan does not reflect the government's official position, it represented the first time any Chinese government body had proposed a concrete timeline for RMB internationalization. The draft plan thus boosted discussion about the costs and benefits of capital account liberalization and RMB internationalization, as well as the time horizon over which both should be achieved. The costs and benefits of RMB internationalization will be outlined in the following section, and complemented by an analysis of which domestic interests are set to benefit, and which would lose, from capital account and domestic financial market liberalization, both of which are essential preconditions for turning the RMB into a truly global currency.

The intertwined political economies of RMB internationalization, capital account liberalization, and domestic financial market reforms

This section details the benefits and costs of RMB internationalization for the Chinese economy, then discusses the implications of related reforms of capital account opening and domestic financial deregulation, and the overall political economy of Chinese financial reforms across these various arenas. It concludes with a brief recap of the current reform policies.

Benefits and costs of RMB internationalization

From a Chinese perspective, there are several potential benefits of RMB internationalization.[5] Besides the political prestige of issuing a global key currency, benefits for Chinese firms arise if they can use the domestic currency for international transactions, which means that they can shift exchange rate risk to their trading partners and hence need not hedge.[6] Wider RMB use also would improve Chinese financial firms' international competitiveness. As the international use of the RMB expanded, international loans and investments increasingly would be executed through Chinese financial institutions, which would also help to boost Shanghai as a financial center (Gao and Yu 2011). Furthermore, China would earn additional seigniorage through the international use of the RMB.[7]

Moreover, reforms related to RMB internationalization addressing these problems would yield benefits in terms of macroeconomic rebalancing and improved financial stability. Keeping nominal interest rates low has led to negative real interest rates for deposits. The average annual real return on one-year deposits in Chinese banks has been negative since 2003, in contrast to an average annual real return of 3 percent over the period 1997–2003 (Lardy 2012a). These negative real deposit rates are an implicit "financial repression tax imposed on Chinese households" (Pettis 2012: 9), because they reduce households' income from their financial investments. Besides depressing household income, low interest rates have arguably contributed to the buildup of the country's property bubble, by causing a much larger allocation of investment into realstate, where real returns on property investment have been much higher than those on bank deposits. The prevailing exchange rate system has thus contributed to serious distortions in capital allocation and exacerbated macroeconomic imbalances of the Chinese economy (Lardy 2012a; Ito and Volz 2013).

There are, however, also costs of currency internationalization. First, greater international use of a currency implies that international demand for that currency will increase beyond what is needed for domestic uses, which will tend to drive up the currency's value, reducing export competitiveness. For precisely this reason, the German Bundesbank and the Bank of Japan both opposed larger international roles for the deutschmark and the yen, respectively. Given the constant stream of capital inflows into U.S. financial markets over the past decades, which have generated pressure for dollar appreciation and eroded the competitiveness of

U.S. exports, Pettis (2011) referred to the dollar's special status as an "exorbitant burden," a refutation of Valéry Giscard d'Estaing's famous characterization of the dollar's special role as a "privilège exorbitant." For China, full RMB internationalization also eventually would imply an end to the dollar link, which likely (although not necessarily) would result in significant appreciation against the U.S. dollar. Chinese export industries, supported by the powerful National Development and Reform Commission (NDRC), the macroeconomic management agency under the State Council, and the Ministry of Commerce, have long been trying to prevent this from happening.[8]

Second, a currency's greater international use to some degree compromises monetary policy independence, as it makes more difficult for the central bank to control the domestic money supply. The German and Japanese monetary authorities, for instance, tried to increase their influence over the money supply by imposing controls on capital flows in the 1970s and into the 1980s (Tavlas 1991: 36–37; Schobert and Yu forthcoming). In the United States, former Federal Reserve Chairman Alan Greenspan repeatedly complained that the steady inflow of capital into U.S. financial markets made it impossible for the Fed to raise long-term bond yields.

However, in the case of China, the situation looks a bit different, since China's monetary policy autonomy *already* has been compromised by the current link to the U.S. dollar (Reade and Volz 2012). While employing capital controls and relying on instruments other than the interest rate have granted the PBOC leeway to exert relatively autonomous monetary policy, the current arrangement has serious costs. In particular, the PBOC has been constrained in its ability to use interest rate policy effectively. It must keep interest rates low to avoid attracting capital inflows, which would put upward pressure on the country's exchange rate and require the PBOC to intervene in the foreign exchange market and sterilize these interventions through open market operations. It is hence understandable that the PBOC has been seeking to push reform of the exchange rate regime with a view to strengthening of the monetary policy transmission mechanism and overcoming the need to continuously accumulate dollar reserves – which comes at great cost for the Chinese economy. On a more general level, RMB internationalization thus can be seen as a means to overcome the dependency on the U,S. dollar.

Winners and losers from capital account opening and domestic financial liberalization

Since exchange rate and capital account reform have ramifications for domestic interest rate liberalization and hence for reform of China's financial sector at large, the discussion on RMB internationalization has to be seen in the context of the interests of the different stakeholders that will be affected by such reforms. As is often the case with reforms, financial market reform in China will produce both winners and losers. Many interests benefit from the status quo and thus tend to oppose either RMB internationalization per se, or other policy shifts such as domestic financial liberalization that are logically linked to RMB internationalization. These typically antireform constituencies include large state banks, state-owned industrial enterprises, the NDRC, and the Ministry of Finance (MOF).

For Chinese banks – which are primarily state-owned and enjoy oligopolistic rents – the negative real deposit rates have been like subsidies. With a ceiling on deposit rates and a floor on lending rates, banks have gotten used to living with a "comfortable margin of around 3 percent" (Borst 2012a). According to Borst (2012a), "Xiao Gang, the chairman of the Bank of China, estimated in 2010 that the non-liberalized interest rate regime in China gave banks a net interest spread twice as large as that for foreign currency loans in the international market." With interest income accounting for 80 percent of bank income in 2011, Borst (2012b) points out that "a narrowing of the interest rate spread has serious implications for bank profitability." It is hence not surprising that the major banks have been strongly opposing interest rate reform – which would be unavoidable if the capital account were to be opened. In April 2012, then Premier Wen Jiabao, generally considered a champion of the pro-reform faction in government, openly criticized the "monopoly" profits of state-owned banks and called for a shake-up of the current system. The four biggest state-owned banks, which dominate the banking system, had an average return on equity of about 26 percent in 2011 (*WSJ* 2012: C24). They would be clear losers from financial market reform. Not only would the banking sector have to forego the negative real deposit rate subsidy it currently enjoys. Capital account opening would also open the Chinese financial sector to outside competition and erode the profits banks were able to extract in a hitherto oligopolistic (state-owned) system.

Low interest rates have also benefited state-owned enterprises (SOEs), which have enjoyed monopoly privileges in many sectors, and which also have received cheap funding from the state-owned banking system. According to Unirule (2011), a Chinese think tank, "easy access to bank loans at a third of the market rate" has been one of the reasons behind the relatively high profitability of SOEs (cf. Breslin 2012a: 37–38).[9] Like the banks, the SOEs strongly oppose financial market reform as they would have to cede to rely on cheap (and essentially subsidized) finance and face increasing competition from the private sector. While competition would benefit overall welfare, the SOEs would be hurt. It should be noted that in the Communist Party hierarchy, top executives of large SOEs routinely wield as much power as the government ministers who formally supervise them. Their strong opposition to domestic financial liberalization has therefore been a significant blockage to reform. Interest rate liberalization and a lifting of the restrictions on capital outflows would also hurt the real estate and construction industries, which have profited from the negative real deposit rates and a lack of alternative investment opportunities that have made residential property a preferred asset class (so much that this has led to a property bubble). Moreover, moving toward a more market-based financial system would also require the government (and the CCP) to give up much of their influence over the domestic banking system, which thus far has been one of the state's most powerful tools in steering the economy. State banks also increasingly have been used to enlarge Chinese influence abroad, as discussed below. As Breslin (2012a: 36) points out, the state's control over the financial sector has been central to remaining at the "commanding heights" of the economy.

Finally, financial market reform would also have far-reaching and in the short run adverse implications for public finances. As pointed out by Shih (2012), the central government is directly or indirectly the largest debtor of the financial system. Interest rate liberalization, which would drive up deposit and lending rates, would significantly raise the government's borrowing costs. Shih estimates that every basis point increase of the interest rate imposes an additional RMB6.9 billion of interest payments on state-owned debtors. Moreover, market-based interest rates may also threaten the survival of numerous SOEs, which would create additional costs for the government.

On the winning side of financial liberalization would be households, who would be freed of the current financial repression tax. Lardy (2012a) estimates that interest rate liberalization would boost household income by 2 percent.[10] In addition, abolishing the cap on deposit rates and increasing bank competition would improve small and medium enterprises' access to credit. While the current lending rates are low, these benefit SOEs, while small and medium private enterprises are typically excluded from credit, and have been forced to either rely on internal earnings or seek credit in the shadow banking sector. Market-based interest rates would help alleviate this problem and reduce the power of SOEs over the economy. The majority of the Chinese private sector therefore supports market-oriented financial reform since they can expect improved access to credit. Indeed, small and medium private enterprises have called for speeding up reforms, but generally speaking lack political clout. Finally, there have been also calls from private Chinese investors, frustrated with the limited range of investable assets in China, to allow capital outflows.

Vested interests and the political economy of financial reforms

The pro-reform constituencies have had a strong ally in the central bank, the PBOC, whose officials believe that financial liberalization is necessary to rebalance the economy and improve the functioning of the economy at large. Moreover, it is clear that interest rate reform – as well as exchange rate reform – would further increase the PBOC's authority and control over banking and macroeconomic policy. The PBOC has, over a long period, made great efforts to reform the conduct of monetary policy and push interest rate liberalization, moving in the direction of more market-determined interest rates, designed to improve the allocation of credit and improve the transmission mechanism of monetary policy. Yet the shift toward the use of more price-based mechanisms has been impeded by the PBOC's lack of independence. Indeed, much of the influence over Chinese monetary policy rests with the National Development and Reform Commission (NDRC), which dominates decisions over macroeconomic policy, and the Central Leading Group on Finance and Economic Affairs (CLGFEA), the "advisory and co-ordinating agency of the CCP's Politburo in managing economic affairs, and a core leading and decision-making body for the Chinese economy" (Bell and Feng 2013: 50). The NDRC, which is responsible for SOEs as the "quasi-central planning" agency under the State Council and assumed to care more about economic growth than inflation, has been very reluctant to move forward with domestic financial market reform. A "major power contender against the PB[O]C in the finance sector [already] in the reform era," the NDRC has "fought hard to maintain its formidable but narrow power in the financial sector" (Bell and Feng 2013: 51). The NDRC strongly has favored quantitative measures aimed at steering the amount, rather than the price, of credit, thus effectively preventing the PBOC from using its entire monetary toolkit.

Another direct challenger to the PBOC's pro-financial liberalization position has been the Ministry of Finance (MOF), with which the PBOC has fought a "turf war" over authority over financial reform since 2003 (Bell and Feng 2013). Until the present, the MOF has retained control of the "Big Four" state-owned commercial banks (Bank of China, China

Construction Bank, Industrial and Commercial Bank of China, and Agricultural Bank of China) through its control over Central Huijin Investment Ltd., a state-owned investment company established in 2003. Even though most economists (including those within China) would agree that financial market reform is needed and that it would benefit the overall economy, expert opinion differs as to the urgency and ideal sequencing of reforms. Moreover, reforms are hampered by the vested interests of the beneficiaries of the current system. As Huang (2012) observes, "policymaking is not as unified as it seems to the amateur observer," and "[r]esponsibilities are compartmentalised under different senior leaders and 'leading groups' and therefore they are vulnerable to capture by vested interests."

The NDRC and other branches of government that are hesitant to move ahead with financial market reform and capital account opening regularly point to the dangers that capital account opening can bring for financial stability. Indeed, a fast liberalization of the capital account entails the risk of financial crisis, as seen by the crises experienced in countries like South Korea and Mexico shortly after financial opening. It is particularly risky to open too fast without having a sound domestic financial sector and a well-developed capital market – as is the case in present China. Since financial and economic crisis could cause social unrest and political instability, and threaten the survival of the current political system, it is unlikely that the reformers will be able to go forth with a swift liberalization and economic reform.

Against this backdrop, coming forward with the abovementioned three-step plan for liberalizing the capital account over the next decade can be seen as an affirmation by the PBOC of the irreversible goal of RMB internationalization in response to recent increasing domestic doubts and debates (Gao and Volz 2012). It also transmits the message that the strategic time for China to open up its capital account is now, and that the risks of opening are controllable. The PBOC downplays the risks of opening the capital account and argues that the need to establish preconditions such as domestic interest rate marketization, the introduction of greater exchange rate flexibility, and similar policies *before* capital account opening should not be overemphasized. Specifically, the PBOC has highlighted four reasons why the potential risks of financial opening are small (cf. Gao 2012): (1) the risk of currency mismatches is limited since both the assets and the liabilities of Chinese commercial banks are mainly denominated in domestic currency; (2) Chinese foreign reserves are mainly invested in bond markets, so that market fluctuations have minimal impact on revenues; (3) short-term foreign liabilities account for a small portion of China's overall foreign debt; and (4) domestic property and asset price developments are under control. There is no doubt that PBOC is aware of the risks of current account opening. Hence, one can safely assume that it does not actually expect the proposed reforms to proceed within its suggested time frame, in the context of determined resistance from the antireform camp. Given the public's benign view on RMB internationalization as a reflection of China's growing statue in the world, the current debate on RMB internationalization may be understood as an attempt of the PBOC to push for domestic financial market reform – which is the precondition for current account opening – and also for a reform of monetary and exchange rate policy (Gao and Volz 2012).[11] Some would even argue that PBOC Governor Zhou Xiaochuan "conned" CCP leaders when he convinced them "in 2009 to try to make the yuan an international standard" by using "the language of economic nationalism to push an agenda that ultimately would loosen state control of the economy by making the yuan...more dependent on market forces than government orders" (Davis 2011). Davis (2011) referred to this approach as "a Trojan horse strategy: Make the policy arguments so attractive that decision makers will approve the ideas without realizing the implications – like the Trojans accepting that beautiful horse from the Greeks without realizing what was inside."

The PBOC's announced tentative three-stage liberalization plan thus may have been in the nature of a trial balloon to test for public sentiment on this matter – with the Chinese public's responses including both applause and anger. As noted by Gao (2012: 10–11), immediately after the PBOC publicized its three-stage plan, "an instant critique appeared in both Chinese and overseas media," with some pundits comparing the proposed current account liberalization to an "opening of the floodgate" and inviting foreign "wolves" into the Chinese "sheep's house." Reformers utilize the RMB internationalization discussion as a means of fostering financial sector reform, similar to the way that the earlier goal of China's entry into the World Trade Organization (WTO) was used to push through far-reaching economic reforms in the late 1990s.[12] This discourse is still ongoing, and the speed at which the reforms will move ahead is not yet determined. To overcome opposition to reforms, the new Chinese leadership will have to show "political courage to deal with vested interests" and the willingness "to cushion the cost of change for those who will lose out in the reform process" (Huang 2012).

However, sooner or later, policymakers will need to enact some type of financial reform. The problems associated with the current financial repression are building up, and the case for financial market reforms, especially interest rate reform, is becoming ever stronger. The negative real interest rates offered on deposits have led investors to consider alternative financial investments.[13] Increasingly, banks have to compete for funds by offering the so-called "wealth management products," which are short-term savings instruments with yields higher than the regulated deposit rates. While wealth management products offer choices for more affluent investors and reduce the profit margins of banks – which in the view of some "amounts to a de-facto liberalisation of interest rates" (*Economist* 2012) – the proliferation of such structured and largely unregulated investment vehicles also leads to a buildup of risk in the (shadow) financial system.

Furthermore, financial repression and the constrained access to formal credit for small and medium enterprises have caused the informal financial sector to mushroom. By some accounts, at least one-quarter of all financial transactions are now carried out in the informal financial sector (Ayyagari, Demirgüç-Kunt, and Maksimovic 2010). A 2013 report by the Chinese Academy of Social Sciences put the size of the shadow banking sector (comprising all shadow-lending activities including wealth management products, trusts to interbank business, finance leasing, and private lending) at RMB20.5 trillion ($3.35 trillion) at the end of 2012, the equivalent of 40 percent of GDP, although foreign banks and rating agencies have come up with much larger estimates (Zhu 2013). According to Allen, Qian, and Qian (2005), credit created outside formal bank lending through alternative financing channels – including through informal financial intermediaries, internal financing, trade credit, and alliances of various forms between firms, investors and local governments – has been crucial for supporting the growth of the Chinese economy. However, the growth of shadow finance, which also includes loans arranged by banks but not recorded in their books, has created considerable risks for financial stability. To reign in these risks and prevent a further uncontrolled development of the informal and shadow financial sector, financial reform is crucial.

Recent advancements with reforms

Despite the difficult political economy of reform just detailed, progressives have continued to push for reforms, and modest progress has been recently made in some areas. For instance, in June 2012, the PBOC granted banks more flexibility in setting deposit and lending rates, while banks hitherto had no room at all to deviate from the official benchmark deposit rate and lending rates were only allowed to be 10 percent below the benchmark lending rate at most, the new rules for setting interest rates allowed banks to offer interest rates to depositors that are 10 percent higher than the benchmark deposit rate and make loans at 80 percent of the benchmark lending rate. A month later, the limit on lending rates was further reduced to 70 percent of the benchmark rate set by the PBOC. But even if this liberalization was a move in the right direction, it introduced only little flexibility to the interest rate setting system.

In July 2013, the PBOC made further advancements in reforms when it announced to remove the floor on lending rates and allow financial institutions to price loans by themselves, which is a significant step toward interest rate liberalization. China's domestically traded banking shares fell sharply the first trading day after the PBOC made this announcement, reflecting the expectation that interest rate reform will hurt the bank's profitability (*WSJ* 2013).[14] However, the PBOC did not remove the ceiling on deposit rates, which arguably is the most binding interest rate control (Feyzioğlu, Porter, and Takáts 2009). Relaxing controls on deposit rates will have much more significant effects on the profitability of banks and the wider economy. How long it takes for interest rate liberalization to be completed remains to be seen.

An experiment that has generated huge interest and fueled the hopes of reformers is the financial liberalization pilot program in the city of Wenzhou, which was approved by the State Council in March 2012.[15] Under this program, private lenders – which had been operating informally before – are allowed to operate loan companies and provide credit to small and medium-sized enterprises. Moreover, the State Council is considering to allow residents of Wenzhou to invest up to $200 million abroad, with a maximum of $3 million per resident. If these reforms get implemented, Wenzhou could indeed become a test ground for financial reforms for all of China.

But whether and at what speed market-oriented interest rate reform and particularly capital account opening will proceed remains an open question. The Chinese government is risk-averse, and there is no domestic political pressure to liberalize the capital account soon – especially not at times of a volatile world economy and excessive global liquidity seeking returns in emerging economies (Volz 2012). Since RMB internationalization without a clear sequencing strategy could cause trouble for China's banking system, capital account liberalization can be expected to proceed very gradually – probably at a pace that is much slower than the PBOC plan would suggest. This is particularly true in the face of fierce opposition to reforms from the beneficiaries of the current system, which have "acquired disproportionate influence over economic policy" and which to date "have been able to block much-needed policy reforms" (Lardy 2012b).

Given that financial repression and regulated interest rates are "at the heart of the Chinese financial machine" (Sender 2012: 22) and a key element to the CCP's influence over the Chinese economy, financial reform is hardly a minor technical change to the current system, but rather a very far-reaching structural policy shift and a major regime change. But as Pettis (2013: 3) points out, it is not clear yet whether the Party leadership has developed the "political will to face down opposition to any change in a growth model that has been extremely profitable for some very powerful sectors within the economy." Many of the largest beneficiaries of China's past growth model oppose reform. Even Premier Li Keqiang acknowledged the problem of vested interests blocking reforms at his inaugural press conference, where he reportedly said that "[s]ometimes, stirring vested interests may be more difficult than stirring the soul" (Economist 2013).

After completion of the "Third Plenary Session of the 18th CCP Central Committee" in November 2013, the new administration of President Xi Jinping published a blueprint for economic and social reforms, comprising 60 points which are to be implemented by the year 2020. The plan emphasizes that "[e]conomic structural reform is the focus of deepening reform" and that the Chinese leadership will "ensur[e] that the market has a decisive function in resource allocation" (CCP 2013, (3)). In the document, the Party also vows to "vigorously and reliably move marketization reform forward in breadth and depth, substantially reduce direct government allocation of resources, promote that resource allocation is based on market principles, market prices and market competition, to realize productivity maximization and efficiency optimization" (CCP 2013, (3)). Relating to financial market reforms, the leadership reiterated its commitment to "[e]xpand domestic and international financial openness, under the precondition of strengthening supervision and management," create "[p]erfect mechanisms for the formation of Renminbi exchange marketization," "accelerate with moving interest rate marketization forward," "[p]romote bidirectional openness for capital markets, raise the extent of convertibility of cross-border capital and financial trading, establish and complete foreign debt and capital flow management systems under prudential macro-level management frameworks, [and] accelerate the realization of the convertibility of Renminbi capital accounts" (CCP 2013, (12)). The state media (unsurprisingly) lauded the outcome of the Third Plenary, with the People's Daily (2013) remarking that "with the reform blueprint in place, the key now is to put that blueprint into reality step-by-step."

Thus, it appears that, at least rhetorically, President Xi's administration is committed to sweeping economic reform, including financial liberalization. However, this was also true for President Hu's administration, whose reform record is widely seen as disappointing. Possibly the most significant decision taken at the Third Plenum was to set up a "Leading Small Group on Comprehensively Deepening Economic Reform" to manage the economic transformation and coordinate the work of powerful ministries and commissions (Anderlini 2013). This new body, which will concentrate power over the economy directly under President Xi's control, may indeed increase the chance that reforms will progress in the direction indicated at the Plenum and that they will be completed as planned by 2020. Yet success will not be automatic. As Moses (2013) observes, "China's reformers are still plodding along a very tough track. The path they've laid out is laudable, but it's still far from certain that they will be able to navigate it to the end."

China's international ambitions and the diversity of its FS

This chapter primarily has focused on the *domestic* political economy of Chinese financial policymaking. Does this imply, then, that decisions on international financial choices such as currency internationalization and capital account liberalization are really not *foreign* economic policies at all? No. As discussed, the notion of developing the RMB into a major – and in the longer run perhaps *the* major – international currency resonates well with the Chinese public and the political leadership. Elevating the RMB to a prominent status in the world economy that can rival the dollar is part and parcel of an ambitious vision to reposition China as the leading economic power, not only in Asia, but in the world economy. Although this vision is not framed as an official foreign policy goal, it is backed by the belief, widely held by policy elites as well as the general public, that China is now leaving behind a century of humiliation and regaining its deserved role in the world. Policymakers harken back to China's golden era of wealth and power before it fell prey to imperial subjugation from the late 19th century onward. A leading international role for the RMB resonates well with "the Chinese Dream of the great rejuvenation of the Chinese Nation" (CCP 2013).

Given the growing strength of China's economy and the swelling of China's foreign exchange reserves over the past decade, FS has been a powerful way for China to extend its stature in the regional and global economy. Besides the steps taken toward RMB internationalization, Chinese leaders have verbally criticized "reckless" fiscal and monetary policy on the part of the United States, which China accuses of destabilizing the global monetary system. China's international FS also includes contributions to regional financial and monetary cooperation (see this volume's Chapter 6), granting of credit and aid to foreign entities through the state-owned financial system, and the country's engagement with international fora such as the G20 and BRICS.

But despite its potential, it appears that China thus far has lacked a coherent strategy of international FS, as it often responds to outside developments rather than attempting to actively shape the international agenda. In other words, China's FS often appears defensive and reactive, rather than offensive and creative. Its role in regional financial and monetary cooperation in East Asia is a case in point. Although China, now the largest Asian economy, aims to be a regional leader, it has been hesitant to fill this leadership position. Most of its moves toward greater regional financial and monetary cooperation have come as a response to initiatives from other East Asian countries, especially Japan, whose government has sought to position Japan as the leading economic power in the region. Both countries appear to be involved in a strategic game for regional leadership that has developed into a "competition for regional cooperation" (Volz and Fujimura 2009; Volz 2010).

Examples of Japan–China competition spurring the Chinese government to greater initiative in the international financial sphere are not difficult to discover. For instance, the Chinese government at first responded negatively to the Japanese proposal in 1997 to create an Asian Monetary Fund. Yet only two years later, it was the Chinese foreign minister who called on the ASEAN+3 Finance Ministers to establish a framework for regional financial cooperation, which then resulted in the launch of the Chiang Mai Initiative (CMI) in 2000. But even after its establishment, China has been hesitant to support bold moves to develop the CMI into a full-fledged regional monetary fund and was seen as responding to proposals by the other ASEAN+3 nations rather than actively setting the agenda. In particular, China has been reluctant to increase its financial contributions and also to de-link disbursement under the CMI (or CMIM, as it has been called since it was "multilateralized" in 2010) from the International Monetary Fund (IMF). Apparently Chinese leaders have been worried about the risk of moral hazard, whereby countries would be encouraged to be less prudent than they otherwise would be, knowing that the regional fund was available to bail them out.[16] China has thereby missed an opportunity to show leadership in strengthening the regional financial architecture.[17]

A similarly careful and defensive pattern of financial policymaking has been apparent on the global, multilateral stage, where China has been very cautious about committing itself to binding agreements or new financial contributions. China's response to the global financial crisis of 2008–2009 provides an illustration. While China was quick to announce a huge, RMB 4 trillion fiscal stimulus package in November 2008 to boost domestic demand and counter a slump in global demand for its exports – a policy that won the Chinese government international praise – the Chinese leadership was slower than many other G20 members to follow up on the agreement reached at their London G20 Summit in April 2009 to contribute to a tripling of the IMF's lending capacity to $750 billion. In contrast to Japan, the first country to heed the chance to sign a $100 billion lending agreement with the Fund in February 2009 (almost two months prior to the G20 Summit) and thereby show its readiness to assume international responsibility, the Chinese leadership waited until June to signal its intention to invest up to $50 billion in notes issued by the IMF (the final agreement was signed in September 2009).[18] Although this was the third largest contribution by an individual country (after the $100 billion each pledged by Japan and the Unites States), it came too late to be perceived as leadership. Of course, Chinese policymakers rightly point out that China still has a relatively low per capita income, but given that the country has by far the world's largest foreign exchange holdings (which are largely invested at very low or even negative returns in U.S. treasuries), and that lending money to the IMF is virtually risk-free, the opportunity cost of stepping up to the plate and announcing a big contribution to IMF finances early on in the crisis would have been zero, whereas the political gains would have been large. Of course one may argue that China's hesitation to engage in or contribute to the multilateral system is due to its underrepresentation in the governance structure of international financial institutions like the IMF and the World Bank. But if anything, increasing its contributions would strengthen China's demand for a greater say in these institutions.

One international forum in which China has acted with relative ease is the BRICS, where China has joined Brazil, Russia, India, and more recently South Africa, in criticizing both the fiscal and monetary policies of the United States since 2010, and in exerting collective pressure on its fellow members of the IMF and World Bank to expand the voting rights allocated to the BRICS as well as other large developing countries (e.g.,

Armijo and Roberts forthcoming). Within the BRICS, China has agreed to commit $41 billion of its foreign exchange reserves to a Contingent Reserve Arrangement (CRA), a $100 billion currency reserve pool to which Brazil, India, and Russia have pledged $18 billion each and South Africa $5 billion. However, as with the CMIM, China seems to insist on linking the CRA to IMF conditionality – another hint that China, which is set to become the third largest member country in the IMF, does not seek a complete remake of the existing international financial system (and supplant institutions like the IMF where it has increasing sway).

China's reluctance to engage more in the multilateral financial system may be due at least in part to a widely held view among Chinese scholars and policy makers that "Western attempts to enlist greater Chinese involvement in global management and governance is a dangerous trap aimed at tying China down, burning up its resources, and retarding its growth" (Shambaugh 2011: 13). But as Katada and Sohn (2012: 19) point out, despite apparent suspicion and skepticism regarding global governance in Chinese policy circles, policy makers believe that China must involve itself in regional and multilateral cooperation at least to a certain extent, since they do not wish to tarnish China's international image "by behaving like a free-rider on the international system." There seems to be an uneasy relationship between the desire to be seen as a great power and the responsibilities that being a great power might carry with it. As Breslin (2012b: 1) remarks, "[i]t seems rather clear that China wants to change its role in global politics, and also to change some of the ways in which the global order is governed," but it is "less clear...how this should come about and with what conclusions.

In general, China has been much more at ease when acting unilaterally, and here it has made the greatest efforts to use its economic and financial power abroad. In particular, besides entering bilateral central bank swap agreements, as mentioned above, China has been actively using its state-owned financial system not only to grant credit to domestic (mostly state-owned) firms investing abroad, but also to fund foreign activities, using its financial leverage as a means of foreign diplomacy and a way to secure the country's strategic interest in gaining access to natural resources or strengthening its commercial ties with other countries. In many cases, Chinese firms and banks have been able to offer comprehensive and financially very competitive packages to foreign governments, for instance in the area of infrastructure financing.[19] Such financing, often in the form of foreign aid, has repeatedly been provided to develop infrastructure in resource-rich countries, helping to expand China's access to energy and other natural resources (Weston, Campbell, and Koleski 2011).[20] In the framework of this volume, such use of financial and monetary levers to win friends, prestige, and influence abroad clearly is a form of offensive and bilateral FS.

Summing up, China has been actively trying to employ its financial power overseas, but this has mostly happened unilaterally. It typically has been reluctant to engage in regional or global initiatives. Given that a comprehensive reform of the international financial and monetary system – negotiated in a new Bretton Woods-type conference – is very unlikely, the unilateral approach that has dominated Chinese policies thus far may not appear to be the worst strategy, since benefits may accrue more directly. But although investments in strengthening the regional and global financial architecture may be more costly and not yield the same immediate returns as unilateral (or bilateral) initiatives, in the long run a solid multilateral financial architecture would be in China's best interest, given that China has a lot to gain from a stable global economy – and conversely a lot to lose from international financial and monetary instability. Moreover, a stronger commitment to multilateral cooperation would also help to build trust in the Chinese leadership – and trust is certainly needed to develop the RMB into a truly international currency.

Conclusions and outlook

Eichengreen (2011) recently observed that the U.S. dollar went from having no international role to being the leading international currency in less than a decade. Similarly, the RMB could be very quickly accepted as a major currency for invoicing and settling trade, as a currency for undertaking financial transactions and investments, and as a major reserve currency for central banks. Whether and when the RMB will become a global lead currency depends to a large extent on economic and political stability in China and on the ability of China's leadership to reform the domestic financial system so that it can stand international competition after financial opening. As argued above, in the face of strong opposition from various special interests and rivaling party lines as well as the risks to overall economic stability from (badly managed) financial opening, rapid liberalization of China's capital account and the domestic financial system is unlikely. However, a strategy of gradual opening is quite likely so that the RMB can be expected to further gain in international importance not only as an invoicing currency for trade, but also for financial transactions. Government-led initiatives, such as arrangements with other central banks, will support this process, but will not be the deciding factor.

What have we learned about FS? One lesson from this chapter's case study of RMB internationalization is that what may appear to the outside world as a rather assertive, offensive, and systemic use of a country's financial capabilities – such as the not infrequent announcements on the part of some Chinese financial officials that their plan is to promote the increased global use of the RMB, displacing the U.S. dollar – may have additional layers of meaning within a country's domestic political economy. Thus one may understand many Chinese domestic political battles around the goal of currency internationalization to be disguised disagreements over the pace of other domestic economic reforms – rather than struggles over Chinese foreign policy. Hence at present, the Chinese "challenge" to the existing global currency hierarchy through the RMB internationalization comes largely from the Chinese reformers' desire to restructure the country's rigid and inefficient financial sector.

In the short to medium run, then, we may expect Chinese FS to continue to focus on bilateral and offensive initiatives – such as foreign aid tied to natural resource contracts, or bilateral currency swap arrangements – or on systemic FS, ranging from participation in regional currency arrangements to joining with other large emerging economies in fora such as the BRICS to lobby for greater clout in the international financial institutions. In the medium to long run, however, China's options for employing its national financial capabilities for a wide variety of foreign policy goals, political as well as economic, are much wider than those of any other emerging power. Among the BRICS countries, for example, *only* China has a realistic possibility of providing a major global reserve and investment currency sometime in the future. Yet this chapter has shown why that future will not arrive any time soon.

Nevertheless, RMB internationalization is progressing, and there are already signs that the RMB is becoming a regional lead currency in East Asia (Fratzscher and Mehl forthcoming; Subramanian and Kessler 2012). Given the great importance of the Chinese economy and its central role in the East Asian trade production network, other countries in the region are now cautiously managing their exchange rates vis-à-vis the RMB, and one can safely assume that it will continue to play a central role in the evolving regional monetary cooperation of East Asian countries (Volz 2010, forthcoming). Interestingly, it should be noted that the RMB can play this regional role *without* complete opening of China's capital account. For the RMB to become a serious alternative to the dollar on the global stage, in contrast, a full liberalization of China's capital account will be required. But this would imply that the Chinese government would have to relinquish control over much of its financial system and economy, something the government is not at present prepared to do.

Finally, whether or not the RMB can displace the U.S. dollar as the world's major currency also will depend in no small part on U.S. policies for maintaining the internal and external value of the dollar and keeping U.S. financial markets attractive for international investors. In this respect, the incapacity of the U.S. political system to put the country's fiscal system on a sustainable path and the resulting recurrent threat of debt default certainly do not help to increase the dollar's attractiveness. The future role of the euro and European financial markets, in turn, will depend on European countries' willingness to further integrate their economies and financial systems. The most likely scenario over the next two decades is the emergence of a multipolar international monetary system, with the U.S. dollar, the euro, and the RMB in the lead roles and smaller regional lead currencies in Africa, Latin America, the Middle East, and Central Asia in the second tier.

Notes

1. The chapter was largely written while I was a Visiting Professor at Peking University in 2012. The research is based on informal interviews conducted with Chinese officials and scholars at the time. Given the sensitiveness of the topic, the interviewees were promised anonymity. I would like to thank Peking University's School of Economics for its hospitality and Joshua Aizenman, Leslie Elliott Armijo, Shaun Breslin, Benjamin Jerry Cohen, Hiro Ito, Saori Katada, Arthur Kroeber, Michael Pettis, as well as participants of the two workshops on "Financial Statecraft and Ascendant Powers,", held at the University of Southern California on April 5, 2012, and July 28, 2012, for very helpful discussions and comments on previous versions of this study. The usual disclaimer applies.Thimann (2010) distinguishes between global and international currencies, where the former are currencies that play a major role in the global economy, while the latter are currencies that are used outside the constituency where they are issued.
2. For example, the fact that the United States has been running a current account deficit since 1982 (except for a small surplus 1991) has contributed to the worry about the long-term stability of the dollar and questions about its status as the world currency.
3. As shown by Bell and Feng (2013), the PBOC has been able to gradually but steadily increase its authority in the area of monetary and financial policy.
4. The plan is based on an unpublished research project conducted by the PBOC's Statistics Department.
5. For an overview of the costs and benefits of international currencies, see, for instance, Cohen (1971; 2000; 2012b).
6. Chinese firms engaging in international trade did not face any exchange rate risk between 1994 and July 2005, when the RMB was pegged to the dollar at

an exchange rate of 8.28 RMB to the dollar, or between July 2008 and June 2010, when China reinstalled a tight peg against the dollar in the face of the global financial crisis, at a rate of 6.8 RMB to the dollar. However, a freely floating RMB would expose Chinese firms to currency risk if transactions are denominated in foreign currency.
7. According to estimates by Jefferson (1998), total seignorage earnings in the United States may amount to as much as 3 percent of total annual tax revenue or 0.5 percent of GDP. Since the 1990s, more than 50 percent of U.S. dollars have circulated outside the United States.
8. On the politics shaping China's exchange rate policy, see Kaplan (2006) and Liew and Wu (2007).
9. Other factors are subsidized rent on land, lower tax rates than for private corporations, and tax breaks on energy.
10. This would also help boost the household consumption rate, which in turn is an important condition for rebalancing the economy and reducing its export dependency (cf. Ito and Volz 2013). As Lardy (2012b) explains: "Negative real deposit rates have had a double-barrelled adverse effect on private consumption expenditures. First, negative rates have depressed the growth of household income, leading to lower consumption. Second, in response to sustained negative real deposit rates, households have sharply increased the share of their after-tax income that goes to savings, further depressing the share of private consumption expenditure in China's GDP."
11. On the sequencing of reforms, see Yu (2012).
12. According to Chow (2003), "[t]he main motivation of Premier Zhu Rongji in promoting China's entry into WTO was to use foreign competition to speed up economic reform in both the industrial and service sectors," where reforms had slowed down in the late 1990s "because of the inertia coming from vested interests of a group of formerly appointed managers holding on their positions." On reforms in the agricultural and financial sector ahead of China's WTO entry, see Lin (2000).
13. As a recent article in the *Financial Times* put it, "[p]ublic anger is mounting at the banks' huge profits and their monopolistic power. It is not quite Occupy Jinrongjie (Financial Street) in Beijing, but regulators are finding themselves on the back foot as they try to defend banks.... Industrial and Commercial Bank of China, the country's largest bank, has recorded average profit growth of 35 per cent over the past five years.... China has been spared the expense of a direct bailout, but the rules that cap deposit rates and limit bank competition add up to a large hidden tax on savers.... More worrying for China's mollycoddled banks is that popular frustration is beginning to turn into action that could hurt them: not complaints or protests, but withdrawal of money. Savers are depositing cash outside traditional bank accounts in a growing array of 'wealth management products'. These offer savers higher deposit rates, forcing banks to compete on interest rates, eroding margins and denting profits. While far from a crisis yet, it is an alarming trend for banks. Public anger, not pure economics, might be the undoing of the Chinese banking model." (Rabinovitch 2012: 20).
14. It also raised expectations that banks may need to raise new capital (Wei 2013).
15. See Borst (2012a) for details on the Wenzhou experiment.

16. The fear of moral hazard is shared by Japan, the other big contributor to the CMIM.
17. The development of regional financing arrangements has also been a means for emerging economies to demand a greater say in the governance of the IMF. See McKay, Volz, and Wölfinger (2011).
18. See IMF (2012).
19. Through public backing, China has emerged as a major financer of infrastructure projects in Asia, Latin America, and Africa (e.g., World Bank 2008).
20. By pursuing its interest largely outside the multilateral framework, China has repeatedly received criticism for undermining international standards, such as those set by the members of the OECD Development Assistance Committee for the conduct of their development cooperation programs.

References

Allen, Franklin, Jun Qian, and Meijun Qian. 2005. "Law, Finance, and Economic Growth in China," *Journal of Financial Economics*, 77(1), 57–116.

Allen, Franklin, Jun Qian, Chenying Zhang, and Mengxin Zhao. 2012. "China's Financial System: Opportunities and Challenges," in Joseph Fan and Randall Morck (eds) *Capitalizing China*. Chicago, IL: University of Chicago Press, http://www.nber.org/chapters/c12071.pdf

Anderlini, Jamil. 2013. "China: The Road to Reform," *Financial Times*, November 13, 2013.

Armijo, Leslie Elliott, and Cynthia A. Roberts. forthcoming. "The Emerging Powers and Global Governance: Why the BRICS Matter," in Robert Looney (ed.) *Handbook of Emerging Economies*. New York: Routledge.

Ayyagari, Meghana, Asli Demirgüç-Kunt, and Vojislav Maksimovic. 2010. "Formal Versus Informal Finance: Evidence from China," *The Review of Financial Studies*, 23(8), 3048–3097.

Bell, Stephen and Hui Feng. 2013. *The Rise of the People's Bank of China*. Cambridge, MA: Harvard University Press.

Borst, Nicholas. 2012a. "Are Chinese Banks Too Profitable?" China Economic Watch, Peterson Institute of International Economics, March 29,2012, http://www.piie.com/blogs/china/?p=1191

Borst, Nicholas. 2012b. "Wen Jiabao Has the Wrong Solution for China's Banks," China Economic Watch, Peterson Institute of International Economics, April 4, 2012, http://www.piie.com/blogs/china/?p=1237

Breslin, Shaun. 2012a. "Government-Industry Relations in China: A Review of the Art of the State," in: Andrew Walter and Xiaoke Zhang (eds) *East Asian Capitalism. Diversity, Continuity, and Change*. Oxford: Oxford University Press, pp. 29–45.

Breslin, Shaun. 2012b. "China as Rising Power," forthcoming in *International Affairs*.

Burstein, Daniel. 1988. *Yen! Japan's New Financial Empire and its Threat to America*. New York: Simon and Schuster.

CCP. 2013. "CCP Central Committee Resolution concerning Some Major Issues in Comprehensively Deepening Reform," Passed at the 3rd Plenum of the 18th Central Committee of the Chinese Communist Party on 12 November

2013, http://chinacopyrightandmedia.wordpress.com/2013/11/15/ccp-central-committee-resolution-concerning-some-major-issues-in-comprehensively-deepening-reform/

Chinn, Menzie D., and Jeffrey A. Frankel. 2007. "Will the Euro Eventually Surpass the Dollar as Leading International Reserve Currency?," in Richard Clarida (ed.) *G7 Current Account Imbalances: Sustainability and Adjustment.* Chicago and London: University of Chicago Press, pp. 283–322.

Chow, Gregory C. 2003. "The Impact of Joining WTO on China's Economic, Legal and Political Institutions," *Pacific Economic Review*, 9(2), 105–115.

Cohen, Benjamin. 1971. *The Future of Sterling as an International Currency.* London: Macmillan.

Cohen, Benjamin J. 1998. *The Geography of Money.* Ithaka and London: Cornell University Press.

Cohen, Benjamin J. 2000. "Life at the Top: International Currencies in the Twenty-First Century," Essays in International Economics No. 221, Princeton University, Princeton, NJ.

Cohen, Benjamin J. 2012a. "The Yuan Tomorrow? Evaluating China's Currency Internationalisation Strategy," *New Political Economy*, 17(3), 361–371.

Cohen, Benjamin J. 2012b. "The Benefits and Costs of an International Currency: Getting the Calculus Right," *Open Economies Review*, 23(2), 13–31.

Davis, Bob. 2011. "Were China's Leaders Conned?," *Wall Street Journal*, June 2, 2011, http://online.wsj.com/news/articles/SB10001424052748703730804576313000018581230.

Dowd, Kevin, and David Greenaway. 1993. "Currency Competition, Network Externalities and Switching Costs: Towards an Alternative View of Optimum Currency Areas," *The Economic Journal*, 103(420), 1180–1189.

Economist. 2012. "Finance: Bending not Breaking," *The Economist*, May 26, 2012, http://www.economist.com/node/21555766

Economist. 2013. "The New Prime Minister. A Talker or a Walker?", *The Economist*, March 21, 2013, http://www.economist.com/news/china/21574023-despite-sounding-ebullient-li-keqiang-manages-expectations-downwards-talker-or-walker?fsrc=nlw|wwp|3-21-2013|5342771|77780131|EU

Eichengreen, Barry J. 2011. *Exorbitant Privilege: The Rise and Fall of the Dollar and the Future of the International Monetary System.* Oxford: Oxford University Press.

Eichengreen, Barry J., Ricardo Hausmann, and Ugo Panizza. 2005. "The Mystery of Original Sin," in Barry J. Eichengreen and Ricardo Hausmann (eds) *Other People's Money: Debt Denomination and Financial Instability in Emerging Market Economies.* Chicago and London: University of Chicago Press, pp. 233–265.

Feyzioğlu, Tarhan, Nathan Porter, and Előd Takáts. 2009. "Interest Rate Liberalization in China," IMF Working Paper No. 09/171, International Monetary Fund, Washington, DC.

Fratzscher, Marcel, and Arnaud Mehl. forthcoming. "China's Dominance Hypothesis and the Emergence of a Tri-polar Global Currency System," *The Economic Journal.*

Gao, Haihong. 2012. "Convertibility as a Step for RMB Internationalization," mimeo, CASS, Beijing.

Gao, Haihong and Yongding Yu. 2011. "Internationalisation of the Renminbi," in: BIS and Bank of Korea (eds) *Currency Internationalisation: Lessons from the Global*

Financial Crisis and Prospects for the Future in Asia and the Pacific, Proceedings of a joint conference organised by the BIS and the Bank of Korea in Seoul on 19–20 March 2009, BIS Paper No.61, Bank for International Settlements, Basel, pp. 105–124.
Gao, Haihong and Ulrich Volz. 2012. "中国是否准备好开放资本账户?" [Is China Ready to Open its Capital Account?], 新产经 [*New Industrial Economy*], June, p. 728.
Garcia-Herrero, Alicia, and Le Xia. 2013. "China's RMB Bilateral Swap Agreements: What Explains the Choice of Countries," BOFIT Discussion Paper No. 12-2013, Bank of Finland, Helsinki.
Huang, Yukon. 2012. "Grading China's Leadership: A for Intentions; F for Actions," *Financial Times*, April 3, 2012, http://carnegieendowment.org/2012/04/03/grading-china-s-leadership-for-intentions-f-for-actions/a698
IMF. 2012. "Bolstering the IMF's Lending Capacity," International Monetary Fund, Washington, DC, June 18, 2012, http://www.imf.org/external/np/exr/faq/contribution.htm
Ito, Hiro, and Ulrich Volz. 2013. "China and Global Imbalances from a View of Sectorial Reforms," *Review of International Economics*, 21(1), 57–71.
Jeanne, Olivier. 2005. "Why Do Emerging Economies Borrow in Foreign Currency?," in Barry J. Eichengreen and Ricardo Hausmann (eds) *Other People's Money: Debt Denomination and Financial Instability in Emerging Market Economies*. Chicago and London: University of Chicago Press, pp. 190–217.
Jefferson, Philip N. 1998. "Seigniorage Payments for Use of the Dollar: 1977–1995," *Economics Letters*, 58(2), 225–230.
Kaplan, Stephen B. 2006. "The Political Obstacles to Greater Exchange Rate Flexibility in China," *World Development*, 34(7), 1182–1200.
Katada, Saori N. and Injoo Sohn. 2012. "Regionalism as Financial Statecraft: Pursuit of Counterweight Strategies by China and Japan," Paper prepared for the "Pacific Rim Emerging Economies in the Post Global Financial Crisis" writers' workshop on July 27 and 28, 2012 at University of Southern California.
Kregel, Jan. 2006. "Chances and Limits of South-South Monetary Coordination," in Barbara Fritz and Martina Metzger (eds) *New Issues in Regional Monetary Coordination: Understanding North-South and South-South Arrangements*. Houndmills, Basingstoke: Palgrave, pp. 42–53.
Kwan, Chi Hung. 1994. *Economic Interdependence in the Asia-Pacific Region: Towards a Yen Bloc*. London and New York: Routledge.
Lardy, Nicholas. 2012a. *Sustaining China's Economic Growth after the Global Financial Crisis*, Peterson Institute for International Economics, Washington, DC.
Lardy, Nicholas. 2012b. "Sustaining Economic Growth in China," East Asia Forum, February 5, 2012, http://www.eastasiaforum.org/2012/02/05/sustaining-economic-growth-in-china/
Liew, Leong H., and Harry X. Wu. 2007. *The Making of China's Exchange Rate Policy. From Plan to WTO Entry*. Cheltenham: Edward Elgar.
Lin, Justin Yifu. 2000. "China's Accession to WTO: Impacts on Agriculture and Financial Sector," CCER Working Paper No. 2000–11, China Center for Economic Research, Peking University, Beijing.
Matsuyama, Kiminori, Nobuhiro Kiyotaki, and Akihiko Matsui. 1993. "Toward a Theory of International Currency," *Review of Economic Studies*, 60(2), 283–307.

McKay, Julie, Ulrich Volz, and Regine Wölfinger. 2011. "Regional Financing Arrangements and the Stability of the International Monetary System," *Journal of Globalization and Development*, 2(1), Article 5.
Minsky, Hyman P. 1986. *Stabilizing an Unstable Economy*. New Haven: Yale University Press.
Moore, Thomas G. 2002. *China in the World Markets: Chinese Industry and International Sources of Reform in the Post-Mao Era*. Cambridge: Cambridge University Press.
Moses, Russell Leigh. 2013. "A Significant Warning on Reform Roadblocks in China," Real Time Economics, Wall Street Journal Online, December 8, 2013, http://blogs.wsj.com/economics/2013/12/08/a-significant-warning-on-reform-roadblocks-in-china/?mod=WSJBlog
People's Daily. 2013. "人民日报评论员：一分部署，九分落实——三论贯彻落实十八届三中全会精神 本报评论员" [Issuing one strategic plan is 10% whereas the Actual Implementation of the Plan is 90%], December 6, 2013, http://opinion.people.com.cn/n/2013/1206/c1003-23760285.html
Pettis, Michael. 2011. "An Exorbitant Burden," *Foreign Policy*, September 7, 2011, http://carnegieendowment.org/2011/09/07/exorbitant-burden/51um
Pettis, Michael. 2012. "China Needs a New Growth Model, Not a Stimulus," *Financial Times*, March 14, 2012, p. 9.
Pettis, Michael. 2013. "What I will Watch in 2013," China Financial Markets, January 14, 2013.
Prasad, Eswar, and Lei Ye. 2012. "The Renminbi's Role in the Global Monetary System," IZA Discussion Paper No. 6335, Institute for the Study of Labor, Bonn.
Rabinovitch, Simon. 2012. "China's Banks are Still Not a Model for the World to Copy," *Financial Times*, March 21, 2012, p. 20.
Reade, J. James, and Ulrich Volz. 2012. "Chinese Monetary Policy and the Dollar Peg," in Yin-Wong Cheung and Jakob de Haan (eds) *The Evolving Role of China in the Global Economy*. Cambridge, MA: MIT Press, pp. 265–299.
Schobert, Franziska, and Lijun Yu. forthcoming. "The Role of Reserve Requirements – The Case of Contemporary China Compared to Postwar Germany," in Frank Rövekamp and Hanns Günther Hilpert (eds) *Currency Cooperation in East Asia*. Berlin and Heidelberg: Springer.
Sender, Henny. 2012. "China Should Give its People Greater Freedom on Investment," *Financial Times*, March 30, 2012, p. 22.
Shambaugh, David. 2011. "Coping with a Conflicted China," *The Washington Quarterly*, 34(1), 7–27.
Sheng, Songcheng. 2012. "The Basic Conditions are Mature for Accelerating China's Capital Account Opening," *China Securities Journal*, February 23, 2012.
Shih, Victor. 2012. "Awash in Debt: State Liabilities and Monetary and Welfare Implications for China," mimeo, Northwestern University, Evanston, IL.
Subramanian, Arvind. 2011. "Renminbi Rules: The Conditional Imminence of the Reserve Currency Transition," PIIE Working Paper No. 11–14, Peterson Institute for International Economics, Washington, DC.
Subramanian, Arvind, and Martin Kessler. 2012. "The Renminbi Bloc is Here: Asia Down, Rest of the World to Go?," PIIE Working Paper No. 12–19, Peterson Institute for International Economics, Washington, DC.

Taguchi, Hiroo. 1994. "On the Internationalization of the Japanese Yen," in Takatoshi Ito and Anne Krueger (eds) *Macroeconomic Linkage: Savings, Exchange Rates, and Capital Flows*. Chicago, IL: University of Chicago Press, pp. 335–357.

Tavlas, George. 1991. "On the International Use of Currencies: The Case of the Deutsche Mark," Essays in International Finance No. 181, Princeton University, Princeton, NJ.

Thimann, Christian. 2010. "Global Roles of Currencies," in Wensheng Peng and Chang Shu (eds) *Currency Internationalization: Global Experiences and the Implications for the Renminbi*. Houndsmills and New York, NY: Palgrave Macmillan, pp. 3–41.

Unirule. 2011. "Guoyou Qingye de Xingxhi, Baoxian yu Gaige" (The Nature, Performance, and Reform of State-owned Enterprises), Tianze (Unirule) Economic Research Institute Discussion Group, 12 April, 2011, http://unirule.org.cn/xiazai/2011/20110412.pdf

Volz, Ulrich, and Manabu Fujimura. 2009. "The Political Economy of Japanese Monetary and Exchange Rate Policy: With Special Reference to Regional Monetary Cooperation in East Asia," *Economic Review*, 1(1), 3–46.

Volz, Ulrich. 2010. *Prospects for Monetary Cooperation and Integration in East Asia*. Cambridge, MA: MIT Press.

Volz, Ulrich (ed.). 2012. *Financial Stability in Emerging Markets: Dealing with Global Liquidity*. Bonn: German Development Institute.

Volz, Ulrich. forthcoming. "RMB Internationalisation and Currency Co-operation in East Asia," in Frank Rövekamp and Hanns Günther Hilpert (eds) *Currency Cooperation in East Asia*. Berlin and Heidelberg: Springer.

Weston, Jonathan, Caitlin Campbell, and Katherine Koleski. 2011. "China's Foreign Assistance in Review: Implications for the United States," Staff Research Backgrounder, U.S.-China Economic and Security Review Commission, Washington, DC.

World Bank. 2008. *Building Bridges: China's Growing Role as Infrastructure Financier for Sub-Saharan Africa*, Washington, DC: World Bank.

Wall Street Journal (WSJ). 2012. "China Takes on its Dinosaur Banks," *Wall Street Journal*, April 5, 2012, p. C24.

Wall Street Journal (WSJ). 2013. "China Bank Shares Fall as Beijing Loosens Grip on Interest Rates," China Real Time Report, Wall Street Journal Online, July 22, 2013, http://blogs.wsj.com/chinarealtime/2013/07/22/china-bank-shares-fall-as-beijing-loosens-grip-on-interest-rates/?mod=djemChinaRTR_h

Yu, Yongding. 2012. "Revisiting the Internationalization of the Yuan," ADBI Working Paper No. 366, Asian Development Bank Institute, Tokyo.

Zhu, Grace. 2013. "Chinese Think Tank Puts Shadow Banking at 40% of GDP," *Wall Street Journal China Real Time*, October 9, 2013. http://blogs.wsj.com/chinarealtime/2013/10/09/chinese-think-tank-puts-shadow-banking-at-40-of-gdp/

6
Regionalism as Financial Statecraft: China and Japan's Pursuit of Counterweight Strategies

Saori N. Katada and Injoo Sohn

East Asia's regional financial cooperation emerged from the Asian Financial Crisis (AFC) in the late 1990s, as East Asian governments realized their vulnerability in the face of global financial forces. For them, crisis resolution led by the International Monetary Fund (IMF) had been insufficient and politically problematic. More than ten years later, East Asia has obtained tangible results from cooperation among the ten members of the Association of Southeast Asian Nations, plus China, South Korea, and Japan (ASEAN+3). The Chiang Mai Initiative (CMI) emergency funding mechanism, in particular, has developed into a concrete regional institutional arrangement with legally binding agreements that are considered rare in East Asia (ADB 2010; Kahler 2000). Skeptics of East Asian regionalism claim that the CMI is insignificant and untested: because it has never been activated since its formal inception in 2002, its effectiveness cannot be evaluated (Eichengreen 2009). Nonetheless, member governments, particularly the major regional powers of Japan and China, have invested significant policy effort and committed billions of dollars to fostering this regional financial cooperation. Why? The question is even more curious when one considers that these major creditor governments have on their own built massive walls of foreign exchange reserves to fend off any financial attack against the respective national economies.

In this chapter, we argue that East Asia's financial regionalism[1] illustrates the use of financial statecraft as a counterweight strategy (Katada 2004; Sohn 2007). A counterweight strategy involves a mixture of balancing and institutional building efforts to avoid overdependence on one-level institutional arrangements, namely global financial institutions. In terms of the analytical framework introduced in the first chapter of this collective project, East Asia's balanced behavior features both defensive (shield) and offensive (sword) purposes targeted at the systemic level. The strategy can be utilized to create supplementary or alternative regional institutions designed to protect East Asia's domestic economies against imported financial turmoil and maintain regional policy autonomy (shield). At the same time, the major regional powers of Japan and China may use a counterweight strategy to introduce a potential threat of defection from the international financial governance regime and, with such pressure, to thereby increase their influence in global financial governance (sword). In other words, regional options would enhance these major powers' ability to balance against the "Western monopoly" of the IMF policymaking paradigm and its neoliberal perspective.

In what follows, we first summarize the development of regional financial cooperation since the AFC to highlight the characteristics of East Asia's financial regionalism. In the next two sections, we analyze the strategies of Japan and China, respectively. Our fourth major section seeks to explain both differences and similarities between the international financial statecraft of Japan around the AFC and that of China during the global financial crisis (GFC) a decade later, emphasizing the delicate balancing act in which both countries are engaged. On the one hand each wants to use its regional clout to back up its hopes for changes in international financial governance, while on the other hand the two large East Asian powers also recognize that their budding regional financial architecture needs the IMF as a backup. We end with brief conclusions.

Financial regionalism in East Asia

In the aftermath of the AFC, East Asian governments launched various efforts to enhance regional financial cooperation so that the region would be able to avoid or better respond to future financial crises. Since its official announcement in May 2000, the CMI framework, a series of bilateral swap arrangements, has become the core of such efforts among the ASEAN+3. The CMI has two basic objectives: to provide emergency liquidity at the time of financial crises such as the AFC and, in the long term, to enhance regional cooperation in terms of both currency stabilization and financial monitoring and surveillance. The CMI and its multilateralized form, the Chiang Mai Initiative Multilateralized (CMIM), which pools the various bilateral swaps into a single reserve pool, embody East Asia's regional cooperation efforts at least in three ways.

First, the CMI/CMIM, although it evolved in the usual "Asian way" of regional cooperation that tends to be informal and is often criticized as being only a "talking shop," is today relatively institutionalized (Pekkanen 2012). The CMI began with the typical "institutionally light" characteristics of "few delegated powers, a lack of a permanent secretariat, and limited formal rules and legal structure" (ADB 2010: xviii), but later developed a visibly formal structure and increasingly explicit legal agreements among the well-defined membership of ASEAN+3, with each member's central bank agreeing on its activation conditions.[2] The CMI also expanded its scope from a total swap amount of $25.5 billion in 2002 to a potential maximum of $90 billion in 2009. Following multilateralization in March 2010, the overall amount of accessible emergency funding available was raised to $120 billion and a single contractual agreement was reached on governance and swap activation (Ciorciari 2011).[3] The CMI/CMIM also strengthened its capacity in balance of payments and macroeconomic surveillance and monitoring by establishing the ASEAN Macroeconomic Research Office (AMRO), an independent regional surveillance unit, in May 2011. In this manner, the CMI/CMIM has come a long way in the last ten years. Although this mechanism has never been activated, regional monetary authorities have vested significant efforts and resources into its creation.[4]

Second, the CMI/CMIM is clearly an East Asian intra-regional institution among the ASEAN+3 that excludes the United States (Lee 2006). Nonetheless, the mechanism is closely nested within the larger global financial governance led by the IMF (Grimes 2006). When the CMI was set up, member countries agreed to make 90 percent of the CMI bilateral swap agreements contingent on IMF involvement, with only the remaining 10 percent capable of activation without the crisis country being under an IMF loan agreement. By 2005, however, with solid backing from China, CMI members decided to increase the portion from 10 percent to 20 percent. Then, with the successful establishment and further expansion of ASEAN+3 Macroeconomic Research Office (AMRO) in 2009, member countries have agreed to increase the IMF de-linked portion of CMIM from 20 to 30 percent, which is to be further increased to 40 percent by 2014. The IMF–CMI/CMIM linkage is related to some East Asian countries' reluctance to activate the CMI/CMIM during the recent global crisis. For example, when South Korea faced an attack on its currency in the fall of 2008, it did not utilize the CMI swap line or the IMF lending facility. Instead, the Korean monetary authority signed a $30 billion swap arrangement with the U.S. Federal Reserve Board and expanded swap arrangements in yen and renminbi, respectively with its Japanese and Chinese counterparts. Such unwillingness to use the CMI is related to the Korean government's grave concern about the IMF–CMI linkage, which required at that time that CMI member countries drawing more than 20 percent of their respective swap lines engage in an agreement with the IMF. Because of the lingering bad memory of the "IMF crisis" in the Korean public's mind, the Korean government was reluctant to invite the IMF in again.

Finally, the CMI/CMIM is consistently supported by the two major powers in the region, China and Japan, whose rivalry and disagreements often are allegedly the fundamental causes of East Asian regionalism's underinstitutionalization (Rozman 2004; Kwack 2004). Despite frequent bilateral tensions over territorial issues and other subjects, the two governments have demonstrated consistent support and high level of collaboration on the issue of regional financial governance. Not only did they agree to set the exact same level of contribution to the CMI/CMIM,[5] the first two Directors of the newly established AMRO would rotate between a Chinese national and the Japanese appointed and inaugurated at the same time.

There is an historical backdrop as to why the two governments are both keenly interested in establishing a regional lender of last resort. When East Asian countries experienced the AFC, it was quite problematic for these governments to go to the IMF, whose loan conditionality imposed the hardship of austerity on crisis countries. East Asian governments also feared that the amount of IMF loans they would be able to access might be insufficient because of their low IMF quotas. Moreover, they were shocked by the lack of the U.S. contribution to the Thai rescue package, assembled under IMF leadership in August 1997.[6] There was, however, at that time no regional institution that could adequately address the balance of payments crisis of these countries: ASEAN was not strong enough, APEC was too diverse to generate solutions to the crisis (Webber 2001), and the Asian Development Bank (ADB) was too timid and inconsistent to serve as the regional lender of last resort (Wesley 1999). It is fully understandable for Malaysia or Thailand to want to put in place a regional emergency funding arrangement such as the CMI/CMIM (preferably without IMF strings attached) that would provide them with an alternative source of financial assistance to the IMF at a time of crisis. For the major creditor countries in the region, namely China and Japan, the CMI/CMIM could potentially be an expensive undertaking, and one might expect that they would be quite wary of making a commitment to fund such a mechanism. Nonetheless, it has become quite clear that the two large creditor governments of Japan and China also would greatly benefit from the CMI/CMIM and AMRO, not least because of AMRO's enhanced monitoring and surveillance mechanisms that would help to avoid a future regional financial crisis.

Despite Tokyo and Beijing's apparent interest in using regionalism to stake out a principled stand in contrast to the dominant economic paradigm, both countries remain ambivalent about using financial regionalism as a more explicit sword. Not only do these two large powers fear being ineffective in any direct challenge to the existing global financial architecture, they also recognize their need to retain good relations with global institutions in order to further shape regional arrangements and enhance their power in East Asia.

Japan's strategy

Establishment of a regional emergency funding mechanism was an important way for Japan to increase its financial shield for East Asia. The AFC had reaffirmed the magnitude of regional economic interdependence as East Asia's economic downturn severely impacted the Japanese economy. By the mid-1990s, East Asia was already quite financially vulnerable. Emerging countries such as Thailand had begun to liberalize their financial markets without proper sequencing, regulatory frameworks, or measures against massive inflows and outflows of capital due partly to pressure from the IMF and WTO, and partly to their competition to attract external funds. Many of these countries also pegged their currencies to the dollar to facilitate their exports, making them easy targets for currency speculation. Despite increasing informal economic integration through regional production networks and business activities (Hatch and Yamamura 1996; Peng 2002), East Asia had no regional financial cooperation mechanism that would allow the region to shield itself from global financial waves. Hence, many crisis-ravaged Asian countries had to turn to the IMF in 1997–1998 for financial help, despite their immense reluctance to do so amid fears of political backlash from potentially destabilizing economic conditionality imposed from abroad.

The region's largest financial power, Japan, was reluctant to shoulder the potential financial burden through *bilateral* rescues.[7] Japan at the time was undergoing its own financial woes, triggered by the bursting of its economic bubble in the early 1990s. Coincidentally, in the fall of 1997, major Japanese financial institutions collapsed and paralyzed the Japanese economy. The AFC hit Japan through contraction of Japanese exports to the region, disruption in regional production networks and operations of Japanese firms, and by Japanese banks' exit from lending in the region (Nordhaug 2005).

Despite its domestic financial troubles, Tokyo needed a regional strategy to address the hemorrhaging of foreign capital from East Asia and to counter normative pressures from those recommending that East Asian countries implement neoliberal economic policies consistent with the Washington Consensus. In response, Tokyo in 1997 proposed the Asian Monetary Fund (AMF), a regional emergency funding mechanism, which at the time was dubbed the Asian version of the IMF. The AMF idea began as a regional arrangement among the so-called "Friends of Thailand," a group of East Asian governments that participated in the Thai rescue in August 1997. The AMF expected to raise a $100 billion contribution, at least half of which was to come from the Japanese government. The proposal demonstrated Japan's willingness to take independent regional leadership as it advocated the importance of pursuing mutual interests among the members of the region by providing a financial and social safety net against the overwhelming forces of mobile cross-border capital. Some Asian leaders also hoped that establishment of a regional funding mechanism would enable them to avoid IMF involvement. The exclusion of the United States from the AMF was, in fact, key to increasing regional policy autonomy in the context of ongoing debate on the cause and the appropriate solution to the AFC taking place at that time. In the debate, the "Treasury-Wall Street-IMF Complex" (Wade 1998) insisted that "crony capitalism" was at fault in Asia, and demanded fundamental domestic economic reforms *a la* neoliberalism. In contrast, East Asian policymakers emphasized the dangers of premature liberalization and the responsibility of financial players' herd mentality (Hall 2003).

The AMF proposal was killed as early as November 1997 due to opposition from the United States, the IMF, and China (Amyx 2004; Grimes 2009). Meanwhile, criticisms of IMF policies mounted. Asian leaders, including those from Japan, became critical of the way in which the IMF dealt with the crisis, allocating limited funds, and imposing the strict conditionality of budget austerity and structural adjustments that reflected neither the nature of the crisis nor the macroeconomic conditions of the crisis-hit countries (Higgott 1998; Beeson 2003). The fact that these Asian countries, despite their increased economic clout in the global economy by the mid-1990s, did not have large enough quotas or voting power in the IMF was considered a problem of double-standards (Sohn 2005). The Japanese government advocated less stringent and more appropriate conditions to be attached to IMF loans, as well as increased quotas for member countries from the region.

To promote such a position vis-à-vis the IMF, Tokyo utilized the implicit but collective Asian clout that it had managed to assemble through its failed AMF attempt. In the place of the "radical" Asia-only AMF, the governments concerned in November 1997 set up, under the auspices of the IMF, a mechanism called the Manila Framework. Its four goals were to: (a) establish a regional surveillance mechanism; (b) foster technical assistance to strengthen Asia's financial sector; (c) enhance the IMF funding access limit; and (d) create a cooperative financing arrangement to complement IMF loans in times of need.[8] Following this regional initiative, Tokyo pushed forward its IMF reform proposals based on a more "accurate" understanding of the capital account crisis as perceived by the Asian leaders, a crisis which Tokyo attributed to short-term capital movements and premature financial liberalization. Japan recommended establishing preventive lending facilities, and cautioned against the cookie-cutter stabilization and structural adjustment that had been imposed on the crisis countries (Ito 2009).[9]

During this period, Tokyo also tried to utilize East Asian regional backing as a sword to launch a campaign at the G7/G8 summits. Japan advocated reform of the global financial architecture to guard against excessive short-term capital flows, regulate hedge funds, and legitimize establish capital controls under certain adverse global conditions. Japanese government officials and academics published their analyses of the AFC, asserting that the crisis was a capital account crisis involving a liquidity shortage due to sudden currency depreciation (after de-pegging) and the resulting large-scale exodus of foreign capital (Yoshitomi and Ohno 1999).[10] At the 1999 Köln Summit of the G7/G8M, in particular, Japan's Ministry of Foreign Affairs emphasized Japan's position as Asia's representative. On that occasion, Japan successfully modified the G8 communique to include a cautionary note on globalization and hedge funds, and insisted on the need for the IMF in future to consider country-specific economic conditions at the time of program implementation (Kondo 1999).

To underwrite these propositions on behalf of Asia's economic recovery and to counter the criticism that Japan had not done enough to help Asia, the Japanese government launched the New Miyazawa Initiative (formally known as "'The New Initiative to Overcome the

Asian Currency Crisis") in October 1998 with a total of $30 billion for Asia's economic recovery. Half this amount was in the form of medium- and long-term funding, while the other half was for short-term lending. Despite the country's own economic downturn, by the close of 2000 the Japanese government had provided $80 billion in total to support the Asian countries in crisis via various funding facilities. Furthermore, the Japanese government used a part ($3 billion) of the fund set aside for the New Miyazawa Initiative to set up the Asian Currency Crisis Support Facility (ACCSF) in the ADB, an initial step toward establishing the CMI.

Ten years later, when the subprime mortgage crisis in the United States and parts of Western Europe became a full-blown GFC after the collapse of Lehman Brothers in September 2008, the Japanese economy was on the verge of emerging from a decade-long financial overhaul. With abundant foreign exchange reserves (*gaitame tokkai*) in the Ministry of Finance (MOF) coffers, then Prime Minister Taro Aso lost no time in announcing Japan's $100 billion contribution to the IMF at the time of the first G20 summit in Washington DC in November 2008. During his speech there, Aso also provided advice from Japan's own experience of the lost decade(s) on how to quench the domestic financial crisis, and advocated reviews of both the IMF's governance structure and the global regulatory and supervisory structure.[11] He followed this proposal with further suggestions for IMF reforms, including higher quotas and voting shares for Asia's emerging market countries, a change in the traditional practice of selecting the IMF managing director from Europe, and review of the conditionality attached to IMF lending (Takei 2009). As for desirable reforms of global financial governance, the prime minister's statement did not, however, give any specifics on prudential regulations or accounting standards, except for a comment in favor of proper credit rating agency (CRA) regulations and the need for regionally based CRAs for locally issued bonds.[12]

Of course, at a moment when concerns over the reliability of many currencies were mounting, Aso also made certain to emphasize his government's unequivocal support for the U.S. dollar as the world's key currency well into the future. Overall, Japan's economy was impacted quite extensively by the GFC, particularly through export contraction and the deleveraging of American and European financial institutions that began to take money out from Japan to compensate for their losses elsewhere. Nonetheless, the Japanese government did not take any initiatives beyond those mentioned to shape the G20 agenda. Rather, its financial authority welcomed the efforts among members of the G20 and the Financial Stabilization Board (FSB) to better regulate derivatives, offshore markets, and CRAs in the future (Katada 2009).

On the regional front, the new crisis motivated Japan's Finance Ministry to make swift progress on CMI multilateralization, the basic framework for which already had been decided on in May 2007, by seeking quick agreement on specific quota allocations with China and other ASEAN+3 members. The $120 billion CMIM agreement came into effect in March 2010. Tokyo and Beijing's collaboration in the ASEAN+3 also resulted in the establishment of the office of regional surveillance mechanism called AMRO in May 2011. AMRO's first three-year directorship was jointly awarded to representatives from China and Japan, Benhua Wei, and Yoichi Nemoto. The European sovereign debt crisis began to emerge in full force during this period, and it became increasingly evident to Japanese monetary authorities that East Asia would require a regional financial shield against the financial crisis *in addition to* the IMF. Tokyo firmly encouraged and supported the European efforts to find a regional solution through the European Financial Stability Facility (EFSF) and the European Stability Mechanism (ESM). Meanwhile, Asia has to make sure that the CMIM is ready when needed.[13]

China's strategy

In the aftermath of the AFC, Beijing's growing concern about financial security led it to support regional options that would offer insurance against future financial crises. Even though China, like Japan, had not been directly hit by the AFC, Chinese leaders became intensely aware of the need to stabilize the East Asian region, an increasingly important source of investment into China and market for Chinese exports. Hence, the CMI, as an additional shield to protect China's neighboring countries from financial contagion, could serve China's national interest, even though China itself might be relatively immune to financial crises due to its comprehensive capital controls and huge foreign reserves.

Furthermore, the Chinese leadership had also begun to recognize the links between financial security and political security. Most notably, the political transition in Indonesia following the AFC had stunned the Chinese Communist Party (CCP). During Indonesia's financial crisis, economic hardship and dislocation triggered protests and violence there. Consequently, in May 1998, Suharto, Indonesia's autocratic leader, was forced to step down. Chinese leaders, cautious about maintaining political stability and committed to CCP regime survival, realized that financial and economic security would be crucial for these political goals. The

Chinese leadership also recognized the limitations of a purely unilateral defense against future international financial turmoil. Given the interdependent nature of financial globalization, a unilateral strategy of holding huge foreign exchange reserves in order to manage large yet infrequent threats of capital flight is extremely expensive.[14] With a new awareness of the importance of financial security, Beijing expected its involvement in regional financial cooperation to help protect China by providing financial information, expertise, and early-warning mechanisms in the post-AFC era.

Beijing's embrace of a regional financial defense mechanism was reinforced by its discontent with the IMF-prescribed solutions to the AFC. In East Asia, including in China, there was a strong sense that the United States had used the AFC to pursue a particular economic agenda aimed at serving its own interests. This led China to share with its Asian neighbors a common sense of (potential) victimhood vis-à-vis the West, and also to appreciate the need to secure policy autonomy for the region. Accordingly, in April 2002, People's Bank of China Governor Dai Xianglong said that the "Asian financial crisis has taught us the lesson that if Asian economies cannot work more vigorously to set up a mechanism for regional monetary cooperation, it will be difficult to avoid speculative attacks" (Dai 2002). Doubts about the existing international monetary system persisted even after the recent global crisis has led China to continue its defensive counterweight strategy in support of increased regional autonomy from the IMF. For instance, in July 2009, Li Ruogu, president of the Export–Import Bank of China and former vice governor of the People's Bank of China, stated that the GFC, "Let us clearly see how unreasonable the current international monetary system is" (Rabinovich 2009). Similarly, at the meeting of the IMF's International Monetary and Financial Committee in October 2009, People's Bank of China Deputy Governor Yi Gang observed that "the persistently misaligned quota shares and underrepresentation of emerging market and developing countries hamper [IMF] governance and even-handed surveillance. It undermines [IMF] legitimacy and effectiveness" (Yi 2009). Given China's ongoing skepticism about the current U.S.-centered global financial architecture, Chinese policy elites have consistently argued for the further development of regional mechanisms as additional shield to prevent a crisis.[15]

Beijing has also attempted to utilize financial regionalism as a systemic sword in order to increase its influence in regional economic governance and generate a more favorable environment for China's economic development and political rise. China took the lead in shaping regional initiatives such as the CMIM and fostering of regional bond market through Asian Bond Market Initiative (ABMI) in order to consolidate its image of "responsible great power" (*Lingdao Canyue* 2008). Beijing hoped that its more cooperative stance would help to diffuse the "China threat" perception among its neighbors and thereby establish a more favorable geostrategic landscape in the region.

But despite Chinese official rhetoric on reform of global financial architecture in the aftermath of the GFC, revising global financial governance has not been a primary focus of Chinese foreign financial policy. In fact, Beijing's actual policy behavior has been somewhat ambiguous or even inconsistent with its stated goal. Instead, Beijing has sought to use financial regionalism to enhance its political leverage in East Asia. For example, with the political support of other East Asian countries, Beijing has called for reform of international financial architecture. In November 2000, China highlighted its policy preference for becoming a rule-maker (as a member of the East Asia grouping) in global financial governance through the new regional financial arrangements such as the CMI (Sohn 2005; 2008). More recently, Chinese president Hu Jintao also declared at the G20 Summit in June 2012 that "all countries should work together to push for reform of international financial governance and increase the representation and powers of emerging economies and developing countries" (*Xinhua News* 2012). However, while continuing to call for more fundamental reforms of the existing global financial architecture, China has been neither a leading policy innovator nor a key opponent vetoing major policy initiatives in the post-GFC governance discussions. Although Beijing has played a constructive role in the institutionalization of the G20 summits and the upgrading of the Financial Stabilization Forum to the FSB, it did not assume a leading role in either of those global initiatives. Moreover, although China embraced the idea, initiated by Russia, of revamping the dollar-based reserve system, it has not pushed hard to implement such a system. In March 2009, People's Bank of China Governor Zhou Xiaochuan proposed the creation of a "supersovereign reserve currency" patterned after the Special Drawing Rights (SDR), as a way to wean international reserve currencies away from U.S. dollar dominance (Zhou 2009). Encountering strong U.S. government opposition to the idea, Chinese officials had ceased to raise the issue in their private contacts with American counterparts, as in President Hu Jintao's April 2009 meeting with President Obama. While Beijing intends to work with key developing countries (including countries in East Asia) on the modification of the dollar-based reserve system, it seeks neither to challenge the United States directly by creating a super-sovereign reserve currency, nor to actively promote the idea of the Asian Currency Unit (ACU), a basket of ASEAN+3 currencies, to complement an unstable dollar-based currency system (see also Chapter 5 in this volume).

Chinese behavior in global financial regulatory regimes has been equally cautious. Since 2008, China has joined key global standard-setting institutions including the Basel Committee on Banking Supervision (BCBS), the Technical Committee of the International Organization of Securities Commission (IOSCO), the Committee on Payment and Settlement Systems (CPSS), and the FSB. While joining these major global regulatory regimes, it has refrained from confronting major financial powers or articulating any Chinese or East Asian model of regulatory standards. In fact, as the GFC revealed weaknesses in the Anglo-Saxon neoliberal model underlying the Basel standard of prudential banking regulations, China began to openly express its concerns and criticism about the Basel standard. However, China's criticisms of the Basel norm of market self-regulation have largely echoed those of the United States and other G7 countries. As the global crisis deepened, G7 regulators accepted the criticism that Basel II's support for market price-based assessments encouraged banks to engage in excessive risk-taking during economic booms.

Explaining the limits to the exercise of systemic financial statecraft

How can we explain the attitudes and policies of Japan and China in relation to regional and global financial governance? As noted, Tokyo was quite active in shaping a regional financial option at the time of the AFC in the late 1990s, and at least attempted to use regional backing to promote IMF reform and reshape global financial architecture at that time as well. But in the aftermath of the GFC of 2008–2009, and despite progress in financial regionalism particularly in the form of CMIM, Tokyo seems to have lost its voice in using such measures as a foreign policy tool to influence the global debate. Meanwhile, Beijing, which emerged as an important global actor at the time of the GFC, nonetheless has been lukewarm about shaping global financial governance by using financial regionalism as a sword in the late 2000s and early 2010s. Three factors seem relevant.

Differing expectations of global financial governance

First, Japan's assertive use of systemic financial statecraft around the time of the AFC may have reflected that country's longer experience of participation in high-level global financial governance through membership in the G7 since the 1970s. By the late 1990s, Japanese leaders were already somewhat disillusioned with what they experienced as continuing U.S. hegemony and disinterest in hearing alternative viewpoints on international regulation and thus they resolved to speak up. For China, a neophyte in global financial governance, and unlike Japan still a developing country with a shallow and repressed domestic financial sector, mere inclusion in the senior multilateral financial and monetary bodies as a consequence of the GFC was a significant achievement. In the years of and immediately following the GFC, China lacked the experience and expertise to offer a full-blown critique of the international financial status quo. Moreover, Chinese leaders observed that Japan's participation in the G7 had led it to make significant sacrifices on several occasions in the 1990s, as for example by accepting currency revaluation via the Plaza Accord of 1985 for the sake of prolonging the U.S.-led system. China's policymakers did not want to find themselves similarly compromised.

In the 1980s and 1990s, Tokyo was repeatedly called upon to pay for the upkeep of U.S.-led global financial architecture without much power-sharing. Since the 1970s, in fact, Japan had pushed for increases in its IMF quota allocation (and thus its voting shares and influence), so that its governing role would be proportionate to the country's rapidly growing economic size (Ogata 1989). In the late 1980s, given the strong growth of the Japanese economy and East Asia's impressive economic miracles, the Japanese government launched a campaign to promote an alternative approach to the neoliberal dominance of the "Washington Consensus" (Wade 1996; Lee 2006). Yet Japan's voice continued to be underrepresented in both the international financial institutions and the G7, as were the voices and interests of most East Asian countries (Rapkin and Strand 2003; Dobson 2004; Bergsten and Henning 1996). During each global economic downturn, Japan was pressured to stimulate domestic demand (Putnam and Henning 1989) or appreciate its currency (Funabashi 1988). From the viewpoint of Japanese policymakers, ostensibly "global" rules, including the initial Basle Accord (Kapstein 1989), often were actually rules directed at curbing Japan's successful competitive edge. Given these experiences, Japan's leaders eagerly seized on the disarray generated by the AFC to promote its already well-developed alternative plans and interpretations of events.

China's low-key and modest behavior during the GFC, which stand in contrast to Japan's more assertive participation during and after the AFC a decade previously, may have arisen from a newly influential foreign policy doctrine, which Chinese scholars refer to as a strategy of "realpolitik multilateralism." This term is used to refer to a current that has emerged within the Chinese foreign policy community since the late 1990s. Moderate and comparatively liberal thinkers have emphasized the opportunities for win–win international cooperation – as opposed to the earlier dominant Chinese view that most international interactions would be competitive and zero-sum.[16] Advocates of "realpolitik multilateralism" therefore propose that a more developed China should shoulder responsibility for addressing a wide range of global governance issues commensurate with its position and power.[17] Their position echoes the views of liberal institutionalists in the West.

At the same time, however, hardline Chinese "realists" remain highly skeptical of the concept of global governance. As Shambaugh (2011: 13) notes, Chinese realists claim that the "Western attempt to enlist greater Chinese involvement in global management and governance is a dangerous trap aimed at tying China down, burning up its resources, and retarding its growth." Despite their suspicion of global governance, Chinese realists also feel that China should not undermine its own image and status by behaving like a free-rider on the international system. Attentive to both of these liberal and realist views, China's foreign policy establishment appears to support a middle-of-the-road policy: Beijing should increase its global involvement in a gradual and selective manner. This variant of realpolitik multilateralism maintains that China should continue to "maintain a low profile but do some things" (*taoguang yanghui, yousuo zuowei*) as Deng Xiaoping instructed.

Beijing's cautious strategic attitude also reflects its sober assessment of China's limited power in today's international monetary system. Despite China's rapidly growing economic and financial muscle, China has not achieved what Susan Strange (1994) termed the "structural power" that hegemonic states can exercise. China still lacks the capacity to set new global standards and revise existing institutions on its own. Hence, a significant segment of Chinese opinion denies that China is a global or hegemonic power, arguing instead that it is merely a regional power. In the minds of Chinese realists, it is reasonable for China to avoid confrontation, tensions, and clashes with major established powers given China's nonhegemonic, albeit growing, position in the international system.

Balancing against whom and in what arena?

Our second point of comparison highlights the ideational and normative aspects of global financial governance. Evolving beliefs about how best to regulate global finance have shaped the policy behavior of both Japan and China in the 2000s. At the time of the AFC in the late 1990s, it was easy to observe a dividing line between the "Washington Consensus" and the Asian perspective. As East Asian debtors were forced to stabilize and adjust under pressure from the creditor community and the IMF, it was clear who the "others" to be challenged were (Terada 2003). The "triumph of liberalism" in the early 1990s (Biersteker 1995) enabled a free market, deregulatory, open economy model to prevail over alternative perspectives on economic development and governance. In this context, Japan's challenge to the ongoing global governance debate at G7 summits was unambiguous, and East Asia was able to rally around Japan's position. Japan was the champion of the "developmental state" model and a promoter of a stronger government role in economic management, as seen in its efforts to encourage the World Bank to publish the "East Asian Miracle" book (World Bank 1993).

Normative fragmentation (or the absence of new global consensus) in the area of international finance in the first decade of the 21st century (Sohn 2011) has made it much more difficult to know whom and what to balance against and also what ideas to offer instead. On the one hand, the Japanese government, as well as many Japanese financial institutions that recently emerged from their decade-long restructuring, have welcomed American and European initiatives for greater prudential regulations and modification of the neoliberal commitment to deregulation. This more nuanced ideological environment should spare Japan for a while from being pressed to engage in further financial liberalization or deregulation. On the other hand, the developmental state model has become a thing of the past for Japan. Tokyo recently has become worried about domestic stimulus packages and protectionist tendencies appearing in many Asian countries, particularly in China, which gives Japanese leaders a disincentive to criticize premarket policies. Japan's political position between China and the West has also become increasingly ambiguous, making Tokyo more reluctant to take strong and ideologically unambiguous positions.

Devaluation of what became known as the free market "Washington Consensus," an old hegemonic idea, significantly undermined the "soft power" of the United States and other G7 countries in the wake of the GFC, and thereby potentially provides China with greater bargaining power over the redesign of global financial governance. The changing normative structure may have opened up an opportunity for China to become a rule-maker, as opposed to a rule-follower. Nonetheless, although some Western observers have played up China's apparent economic development model by coining the term "Beijing Consensus," Chinese policy elites remain skeptical about one-size-fits-all regulatory standards, stressing local context and variation.[18] In short, the normative vacuum invites not only opportunities but also challenges for China. Chinese leaders still feel incapable of leading global financial institutional reform as principal innovators. As compared to trade negotiations, global financial matters are relatively new to China, and Chinese elites still lack the sophisticated knowledge and experience necessary to address the technically complex nature of international financial policy.[19] As a result, while China has vocally called for global financial reforms, Chinese policy elites' statements have not given any specifics on the country's preferences for new prudential regulations or accounting standards. The Chinese leadership believes that China should selectively adopt certain elements of international norms and standards in accordance with specific local conditions in order to achieve its domestic financial reform (Walter 2010). Normative fragmentation, combined with China's weak soft power, thus far has constrained China's global activism in the arena of international finance.

Employing connections with global institutions to influence the region

Although their international financial assertiveness in the wake of the GFC has been cautious, the governments of both China and Japan have utilized both financial regionalism and their respective relations with global institutions to increase their political influence *within* the region. Both Tokyo and Beijing frequently allude to the advancement of regional financial cooperation as evidence of East Asia's solidarity and as a basis for pushing for a greater Asian voice in global financial governance. Political rhetoric aside, however, it is also the case that Tokyo and Beijing's efforts in building regional financial institutions such as the CMIM have been used to increase their influence within East Asia. Japan and China have achieved this feat by borrowing capacity from the international financial establishment rather than the other way around. Despite their desire for regional solidarity, potential creditors such as China and Japan would be hard pressed to agree to lend funds to countries whose operations were not under regular surveillance. The IMF has better institutionalized surveillance mechanisms than any country or international institution in Asia. Thus, linking the CMI to the IMF can ensure that funds lent have a better chance of being repaid, even if China and Japan remain critical of IMF conditionality per se.

Even the "independent" regional surveillance institution headed by Japanese and Chinese experts, AMRO, collaborates closely with the IMF staff in implementing its surveillance duties.[20] With AMRO's development, the Japanese government has come to support the gradual increase of the de-linked portion of the CMIM from 20 to 30 percent, and then to 40 percent, as the size of the CMIM resources was doubled from $120 billion to $240 billion in May 2012. Nonetheless, the Japan's finance ministry has insisted on the stringent screening of eligibility and conditionality as the CMIM funds are activated.[21]

Advocating regional causes on the global stage has given Japan and China increased powers and instruments to influence their smaller and weaker neighbors. Japanese experts have been heavily involved in technical assistance to the ABMI to ensure that Asia's bond markets have in place rules, technical expertise, and investor protections that meet global standards. In the context of the 2009 East Asia Summit, a report on "An Assessment of Financial Sector Capacity Building Needs of East Asian Summit Countries" was produced with collaboration of the Tokyo-initiated think tank Economic Research Institute for ASEAN and East Asia (ERIA), which consists of 16 Asia-Pacific members (i.e., ASEAN+6). The report assessed the member nations' progress in financial liberalization and implementation of their appropriate prudential regulation.

Similarly, Beijing has proactively used financial regionalism to increase its political influence over regional policymaking and to burnish its credentials as a benign regional hegemon. For example, China has attempted to increase its voice and influence in regional financial governance by chairing meetings of new regional bodies and track-two (semi-official) dialogues. In 2008, the People's Bank of China assumed the first chairmanship of the Monetary and Financial Stability Committee, which was established in 2007 to enhance regional collaboration in the area of macro-monitoring and crisis management. China also sought to play an active role in track-two dialogues to exert indirect influence over official track-one policy making. A notable example is the Network of East Asian Think Tanks (NEAT). The NEAT's working group addresses a variety of issues concerning East Asian community building, including East Asian Financial Cooperation (steered by China). As co-chairman of the 2007 ASEAN+3 Finance Minister's Meeting, China also conducted a joint study on the idea of reserve pooling with collective decision-making for the CMI. With a positive result from the joint study, Beijing made efforts to get other Asian countries to agree on the CMI's multilateralization.

Moreover, Beijing has promoted the development of the bond market through ABMI, which has given China another opportunity to show Beijing's sense of responsible leadership. Beijing's rationale for its promotion of the ABMI, as summarized by leading Chinese policy elites in their internal government report, is worth quoting at length:

> even if substantial progress happens to be made in the ABMI in the near future, our country's economic benefit would be very limited... China's active participation and leadership in the development of the ABMI would not merely improve China's international environment and peaceful development, but also help to reinforce China's image of a responsible great power and thereby facilitate China's integration with Asia and the world, and further comprehensive regional cooperation. (*Lingdao Canyue* 2004)

This internal policy discourse lays bare the political as well as the strictly economic reasons why China pushes for multilateral financial regionalism. This is related to China's proactive regional multilateral diplomacy in order to improve inter-state relations around its periphery.

In short, instead of using regional arrangements as a tool of systemic and offensive financial statecraft to influence global financial governance, both Japan and China recently have tended to deploy their international financial statecraft in the opposite direction, utilizing their presence in *multilateral* frameworks to shape *regional* arrangements and enhance their powers vis-à-vis their neighbors.

Conclusion: financial regionalism as financial statecraft

Since its inception in the late 1990s, both Japan and China have viewed regional financial cooperation in East Asia as an important element in their international financial statecraft. For Japan, whose commitment to financial regionalism started immediately after the AFC, its regional leadership has constituted an essential tool for its counterweight strategy to shield the region from global financial forces and advocate reforms in the IMF and global financial architecture. China was also keenly interested in fostering a regional shield after its leaders observed the massive economic and political disruption of the AFC.

Despite the arguably quite successful development of East Asia's regional emergency funding mechanism, the CMI/CMIM, in the last ten years, the political and economic environment has become much more complex since the GFC. With the American economy facing ongoing repercussions from the 2008–2009 crisis and the neoliberal paradigm under scrutiny, normative fragmentation has made it difficult for Japan and China to know whom to challenge and how. While welcoming global regulatory moves in the aftermath of the GFC, Tokyo has remained mostly silent in the contemporary debates over global financial governance. At the same time, with the world holding high expectations for China's rising power, policymakers in Beijing have been reluctant to engage in active restructuring of the global financial architecture, either unilaterally or using regionalism. In this uncertain environment, both Tokyo and Beijing have been much more interested in shaping the regional financial governance structure than the global one, which they might not have much leverage to reform. Regional financial cooperation has been one of the few subjects on which Tokyo and Beijing have managed to collaborate in recent years, due to their high levels of mutual interest. If the recent security and economic tensions between the two countries do not derail the entire regionalism project, East Asia might in due course have an entity that may clearly influence both financial preferences and policies at the global level.

Notes

1. This chapter distinguishes between the intentional process of financial regionalism and the relatively apolitical integration of regional financial markets (or regional financial interdependence). We are here concerned with financial regionalism, defined as the policy-led process of creating cohesive financial arrangements or institutions in the region.
2. A well-defined membership appears more significant as it is contrasted with East Asia's regional trade arrangements where bilateral free trade arrangements prevail with highly contentious (until recently) and competing proposals for regional trade areas of ASEAN+3 (China's proposal), ASEAN+6 (Japan's proposal), and FTAAP (the U.S. proposal).
3. As the European Sovereign debt crisis raged, the ASEAN+3 Finance Ministers and Central Bank Governors doubled the total size of the CMIM reserve pool from $120 billion to $240 billion at their meeting in Manila in May 2012.
4. Besides these cases, East Asian governments since the AFC have been extremely vigilant against currency and financial crises and have accumulated substantial foreign exchange reserves that would allow them to fend off currency attacks. East Asia has accumulated $6 trillion in foreign exchange reserves (World Bank 2011), three quarters of which is in China ($3.3 trillion) and Japan ($1.3 trillion).

5. China and Japan agreed to split their top subscriber status to the CMIM with each contributing 32 percent. In the case of China, its 32 percent comes with the PRC contributing 28.5 percent and Hong Kong the remaining 3.5 percent.
6. It was particularly strongly felt due to the contrast with the U.S. assembly of a $50 billion rescue package for Mexico two years earlier, to which the U.S. government had pledged $20 billion ("The Generosity of the United States, Our Great Friend, Is Even More Scarce in Time of Crisis" Bangkok Matichon, FBIS January 15, 1998).
7. For the story of how the Thai government first approached the Japanese government prior to going to the IMF, see Lee (2006).
8. Kunihiko Kuroda, Saikin no Kokusai Kinyuu josei ni tuite [最近の国際金融情勢について], Kokusai Kinyu, #1006. June 1, 1998. This was the speech by Mr. Kuroda, International Finance Bureau Chief of MOF, on March 23, 1998.
9. Finance Minister Miyazawa's (1998) speech at the IMF/World Bank Annual Meeting in 1998 included these points. The IMF introduced Contingent Credit Lines (CLL) in 1999 for preventive purposes.
10. The report on the Japanese position from the IMF Interim Committee Meeting on October 4, 1998 noted in Miyazaki (1998: 35–36).
11. The Prime Minister Aso's speech on November 15, 2008, "Overcoming the Current Crisis: Taro Aso's proposal to the short, mid- and long terms," in English available at http://www.kantei.go.jp/foreign/asospeech/2008/11/081115tarosproposal.pdf.
12. See Aso's speech.
13. The Japanese government demonstrated further willingness to support a global solution to the crisis with additional $60 billion contribution to the IMF in April 2012 despite facing its own difficult fiscal consolidation challenge in the aftermath of the triple disasters (earthquake, tsunami, and nuclear fallout) of March 11, 2011.
14. A similar view of the limitation of unilateral response was articulated by Hu Jintao in his recent speech entitled "携手合作　同舟共济" [Let Us Join Hands and Tide over Difficulties] at the second Group of 20 (G20) financial summit in London in April 2009 (China News 2009).
15. For instance, see Lujiazui Forum (2008, p. 10).
16. For detailed discussion of the emerging positive-sum view among Chinese foreign economic policy experts, see Injoo Sohn (2008).
17. For instance, see the remarks of Foreign Minister Yang Jiechi (2010), "Our own interests and those of others are best served when we work together to expand common interests, share responsibilities, and seek win-win outcomes. This is why, while focusing on its own development, China is undertaking more and more international responsibilities commensurate with its strength and status."
18. As for Beijing's rationale for delegitimizing the universal model, for instance, see Wen Jiabao (2009). Chinese premier Wen Jiabao stated that "Many people are trying to offer prescriptions for Africa's development, such as the 'Washington Consensus' or the 'Beijing Model.' Yet it seems to me that Africa's development should be based on its own conditions and should follow its own path, that is, the African Model. All countries have to learn from other countries' experience in development. At the same time, they

have to follow a path suited to their own national conditions and based on the reality of their own countries."
19. Author's interviews in Beijing, June 2012.
20. Statement by Jun Azumi, Minister of Finance, Japan, at 25th Meeting of International Monetary and Financial Committee, April 21, 2012. Available online at http://www.imf.org/External/spring/2012/imfc/statement/eng/jpn.pdf.
21. The CMIM also mimics IMF in developing funding facilities. The CMIM members put in place the CMIM Precautionary Line following the installment of preventive funding mechanisms such as the Flexible Credit Line (FCL) and Precautionary and Liquidity Line (PLL) at the IMF.

References

Amyx, J. 2004. "Japan and the Evolution of Regional Financial Cooperation in East Asia," in Ellis S. Krauss, and T. J. Pempel (eds) *Beyond Bilateralism: U.S.–Japan Relations in the New Asia-Pacific*. Stanford, CA: Stanford University Press, 198–219.

Asian Development Bank (ADB). 2010. *Institutions for Regional Integration: Toward an Asian Economic Community*. Manila: Asian Development Bank.

Beeson, M. 2003. "East Asia, the International Financial Institutions and Regional Regulatory Reform: A Review of the Issues," *Journal of the Asia Pacific Economy*, 8(3), 305–326.

Bergsten, C. F., and C. R. Henning. 1996. *Global Economic Leadership and the Group of Seven*. Washington, DC: Institute for International Economics.

Biersteker, T. 1995. "The 'Triumph' of Liberal Economic Ideas in the Developing World," in Barbara Stallings (eds) *Global Change and Regional Response: The New International Context of Development*. Cambridge: Cambridge University Press.

China News. 2009. Hujintao G20 fenghui fabiao jianghua (胡锦涛G20峰会发表啕话) [Hujintao's speech at G20 submit]. April 3. http://www.chinanews.com/gn/news/2009/04-03/1630685.shtml (accessed on January 9, 2011).

Ciorciari, J. D. 2011. "Chiang Mai Initiative Multilateralisation International Politics and Institution-Building in Asia," *Asian Survey*, 51(5), 926–952.

Corsetti, G., P. Pesenti, and N. Roubini, 1999. "What Caused the Asian Currency and Financial Crisis?" *Japan and the World Economy*, 11, 305–375.

Dai, X. 2002. China's Financial Opening-Up and Financial Cooperation in Asia. *The People's Bank of China-Speeches*, April 15. http://www.pbc.gov.cn/english//detail.asp?col=6500&ID=6 (accessed on June 5, 2006).

Dobson, H. 2004. *Japan and the G7/8: 1975–2002*. London: Routledge.

Eichengreen, B. 2009. "Bad Credit History," *Current History*, January, 14–19.

Funabashi, Y. 1988. *Managing the Dollar: From the Plaza to the Louvre*. Washington, DC: Institute for International Economics.

Grimes, W. W. 2009. *Currency and Contest in East Asia: The Great Power Politics of Financial Regionalism*. Cornell Studies in Money. Ithaca, NY: Cornell University Press.

Grimes, W. W. 2006. "East Asian Financial Regionalism in Support of the Global Financial Architecture? The Political Economy of Regional Nesting," *Journal of East Asian Studies*, 6(3), 353–380.

Hall, R. B. 2003. "The Discursive Demolition of the Asian Development Model," *International Studies Quarterly*, 47, 71–99.
Hatch, W., and K. Yamamura. 1996. *Asia in Japan's Embrace: Building a Regional Production Alliance*. Cambridge: Cambridge University Press.
Higgott, R. 1998. "The Asian Economic Crisis: A Study in the Politics of Resentment," *New Political Economy*, 3(3), 333–356.
Ito, T. 2009. Sekai kinyu kiki to kokusai tsuka taisei: kinyu aakitekuchya ha kawattaka? [世界金融危機と国際通貨体制：金融アーキテクチャーは変わったか？] (The Global Financial Crisis and the International Currency System: Has the Financial Architecture Transformed?) *Kokusai mondai*. No. 582. June 5–18.
Kahler, M. 2000. "Legalization as Strategy: The Asia-Pacific Case," *International Organization*, 54(3), 549–571.
Kapstein, E. 1989. "Resolving the Regulator's Dilemma: International Cooperation among Financial Regulators," *International Organization*, 43(2).
Katada, S. N. 2004. "Japan's Counterweight Strategy: U.S. – Japan Cooperation and Competition in International Finance," in Ellis S. Krauss, and T. J. Pempel (eds) *Beyond Bilateralism: U.S. –Japan Relations in the New Asia-Pacific*. Stanford, CA: Stanford University Press, 176–197.
Katada, S. N. 2009. "Mission Accomplished, or a Sisyphean Task? Japan's Regulatory Response to the Global Financial Crisis," in Eric Helleiner, Stefano Pagliari, and Hubert Zimmermann (eds) *Global Finance in Crisis: The Politics of International Regulatory Change*. London: Routledge.
Kondo, S. 1999. Kerun samitto no seika to nihon [ケルン・サミットの成果と日本] (The achievements of the Köln summit and Japan). Sekai keizai hyoron. September 8–28.
Kwack, S.-Y. 2004. "An Optimum Currency Area in East Asia: Feasibility, Coordination, and Leadership Role," *Journal of Asian Economics*, 15, 153–169.
Lee, Y. W. 2006. "Japan and the Asian Monetary Fund: An Identity–Intention Approach," *International Studies Quarterly*, 50(2), 339–366.
Lijiazui Forum. 2008. Lujiazui Forum 2008: Deepening Financial Reform – China and the World. 9–10 May. May 10, 2010).
Lingdao Canyue [Leadership Reference Reading]. 2008. Woguo ying jiji canyu bing zhudao yazhou zhaiquan shichang de fazhan [Our country should actively participate in and lead the Asian Bond Market]. September 15.
Miyazaki, N. 1998. G7 oyobi ichiren no kokusai kaigi ni tsuit [G7及び一連の国際会議について](About G7 and the series of international conferences). Fainansu. November 32–42.
Nordhaug, K. 2005. "The United States and East Asia in Age of Financialization," *Critical Asian Studies*, 37(1), 103–116.
Ogata, S. 1989. "Shifting Power Relations in Multilateral Development Bank," *The Journal of International Studies*, 22, January.
Pekkanen, S. M. (ed.) 2012. *Asian Designs: Interests, Identities, and States in External Institutions*. Book manuscript.
Peng, D. 2002. "Invisible Linkages: A Regional Perspective of East Asian Political Economy," *International Studies Quarterly*, 46(3), 423–447.
Putnam, R., and C. R. Henning. 1989. "The Bonn Summit of 1978: A Case Study in Coordination," in Richard N. Cooper, Barry Eichengreen, Gerald Holtham, Robert Putnam, and C. Randall Henning (eds) *Can Nations Agree? Issues in International Economic Cooperation*. Washington, DC: Brookings Institution.

Rabinovich, S. 2009. "China Officials Call for Displacing Dollar, in Time," *Reuters*, 6 July, 2009; http://www.reuters.com/article/idUSTRE5650WO20090706.

Rapkin, D. P., and J. R. Strand. 2003. "Is East Asia Under-Represented in the International Monetary Fund?" *International Relations of the Asia Pacific*, 3, 1–28.

Rozman, G. 2004. *Northeast Asia's Stunted Regionalism: Bilateral Distrust in the Shadow of Globalization*. London: Cambridge University Press.

Shambaugh, D. 2011. "Coping with a Conflicted China," *The Washington Quarterly*, 34(1), 7–27.

Sohn, I. 2005. "Asian Financial Cooperation: The Problem of Legitimacy in Global Financial Governance," *Global Governance*, 11(4) (October–December), 487–504.

Sohn, I. 2007. "East Asia's Counterweight Strategy: Asian Financial cooperation and Evolving International Monetary Order," *G-24 Discussion Paper Series*, No. 44. March.

Sohn, I. 2008. "Learning to Cooperate: China's Multilateral Approach toward Asian Financial Cooperation," *The China Quarterly*, 194 (June), 321–325.

Sohn, I. 2011. "Toward Normative Fragmentation: An East Asian Financial Architecture in the Post-Global Crisis World," *Review of International Political Economy*. DOI: 10.1080/09692290.2011.613350 (Online First).

Strange, S. 1994. *States and Markets*. London: Pinter Publishers.

Takei, T. 2009. IMF Kaikaku no Hitsuyousei to Kinyukiki no Eikyou; IMF Kameisochiho Kaiteian [IMF改革の必要性と金融危機の影響:IMF加盟措置法改正案], *Rippo to Chosa* No. 295. August 2009.

Terada, T. 2003. "Constructing an 'East Asian' Concept and Growing Regional Identity: From EAEC to ASEN+3," *The Pacific Review*, 16(2), 251–277.

Wade, R. 1996. "Japan, the World Bank, and the Art of Paradigm Maintenance: The East Asian Miracle in Political Perspective," *New Left Review*, May/June.

Wade, R. 1998. "The Asian Debt-and-development Crisis of 1997–?: Causes and Consequences," *World Development*, 26(8), 1535–1553.

Walter, A. 2010. Chinese Attitudes Towards Global Financial Regulatory Co-operation: Revisionist or Status Quo? In E. Helleiner, S. Pagliari, and H. Zimmermann, eds. *Global Finance in Crisis: The Politics of International Regulatory Change*. New York: Routledge.

Webber, D. 2001. "Two Funerals and a Wedding? The Ups and Downs of Regionalism in East Asia and Asia-Pacific after the Asian Crisis," *The Pacific Review*, 14(3), 339–372.

Wen, J. 2009, FOCAC: Transcript of Press Conference by Premier Wen Jiabao. *Pambazuka News*, November 12, Issue 457 http://pambazuka.org/en/category/africa_china/60182 (accessed January 19, 2010).

Wesley, M. 1999. "The Asian Crisis and the Adequacy of Regional Institutions," *Contemporary Southeast Asia*, 21(1), 54–73.

World Bank. 1993. *The East Asian Miracle: Economic Growth and Public Policy* (World Bank Policy Research Reports). New York: Oxford University Press.

World Bank. 2011. *East Asia and Pacific Economic Update*. Washington, DC: World Bank.

Xinhua News. 2012. Hu Urges Fair, Orderly World Financial System. June 20. http://www.china.org.cn/world/G20_2012/2012-06/20/content_25693822.htm (accessed on July 16, 2012).

Yang, J. 2010. A Changing China in a Changing World. February 5 (on July 16, 2012).

Yi, G. 2009. Statement of Dr. Yi Gang, Deputy Governor of the People's Bank of China at the Twentieth Meeting of the IMFC in Istanbul, October 4. http://www.imf.org/external/am/2009/imfc/statement/eng/chn.pdf (accessed July 16, 2012).

Yoshitomi, M., and K. Ohno. 1999. "Capital-Account Crisis and Credit Contraction: The New Nature of Crisis Requires New Policy Responses," *ADB Institute Working Paper Series*, No. 2, May.

Zhou X. 2009. Reform the International Monetary System. People's Bank of China. March 23. http://www.pbc.gov.cn/english//detail.asp?col?6500&ID?178 (accessed July 16, 2012).

7
The Financial Statecraft of Emerging Powers: How, Why, and So What?

Saori N. Katada and Leslie Elliott Armijo

From China to Brazil, and India to Venezuela, emerging powers of the world have made their presence felt in multiple ways in the first decades of the 21st century. Not only are their economic and financial capabilities growing, but they also have begun to utilize their newly found material capabilities as the basis for developing active foreign policy tools. What types of financial statecraft (FS) are they engaging in? What motivates the players? What are their constraints, and what are the implications of their FS strategies for global economic governance? These are the questions we asked at the start of this project.

In the last several years, particularly in the aftermath of the global financial crisis (GFC), the rise of emerging powers has captured headlines in many ways. The alarmists, on the one hand, have pointed to China and stressed its rapid rise and autocratic system to caution that the time is near when China will eclipse the United States, destroying the liberal economic world order as we know it by its sheer economic weight and distinctive economic approach. Despite the visible increase of China's presence on the global economic scene, however, we emphasize the need to understand the intensely nuanced ways in which the governments of emerging powers, including China, are using their countries' newly acquired financial power. The skeptics, on the other hand, would dismiss the rising importance of emerging economies as a cursory phenomenon soon to disappear as their economies hit the "middle income trap" and stagnate. While fluctuations in these economies' growth rates are real, we caution that it is important to decipher certain trends among emerging powers in utilizing their financial capabilities to protect their economies and promote their agenda.

In this book, we have analyzed the FS of these emerging powers, identifying both opportunities and challenges associated with the use of financial capabilities as instruments of broader national foreign policy strategies. In general, we found that, with their enhanced financial capabilities, emerging powers are expanding the repertoire of their FS strategies beyond their earlier tactics of merely defensive and reactive measures, such as protecting their economies from bilateral dependence and imported financial crises through defaults and nationalizations. Today, many emerging powers have seized the more sophisticated options of targeting defensive FS measures at the systemic level or have undertaken bilateral offensive FS tactics intended to influence smaller neighbors. Larger or more ambitious emerging powers even mount modest challenges to the inherited institutions and practices of systemic global financial governance managed by traditional great powers. Moreover, these FS measures extend from the monetary realm of reserve currencies, to capital controls (which influence both money and credit), to the overtly financial realm, as through international sovereign lending extended by emerging country governments. Thus far, one can still argue that the impact of these "new kids on the block" in changing the agenda of global governance has been limited – nor do most of these rising powers necessarily wish to restructure the global economic system in any fundamental way. Still, the voices of emerging powers advocating reform are starting to be heard. Hence, emerging powers have come a long way in devising their FS from the days when scholars assumed that such measures were only available to a select few large, advanced industrial economies.

This chapter concludes the volume by bringing together and analyzing the arguments and findings of the five empirical chapters. The next section summarizes and compares our collective findings about the types of FS employed in the early 21st century by important emerging powers in Latin America and Asia, in light of the overall analytical framework set out in the introduction (Armijo and Katada, Chapter 1). The section following that discusses the motivations for certain FS options, as well as their costs to their users. The chapter's final section reviews our expectations and predictions for the future, with particular focus on the implications for the advanced industrial countries that currently dominate global governance institutions.

The "old" FS of developing countries

The traditional FS strategy among emerging market economies (EMEs), large and small, centered around bilateral and emergency defensive measures as these countries struggled to cope with pressure from creditors abroad. Their ability to implement FS depended in the first instance on their capabilities for independent action in the interstate system. In Chapter 3, Armijo and Echeverri-Gent observed that, in the 1930s and 1940s, both Brazil and India had in common their major foreign creditor: Britain. Brazil, an independent country, was able to challenge Britain, and later the United States, by playing off different foreign creditors and potential allies against one another. During this period, India unfortunately lacked sovereignty and the capability to implement any FS measures on its own behalf. As a colony, its foreign economic policies were managed from the seat of British imperial power in London. Brazil's comparative freedom of action in the interwar years was unusual: historically the only option available to poorer or weaker countries had been default, which often left the debtor exposed to invasion as the creditor country send troops to seize customs houses until the debts were repaid (Marichal 1989).

Following World War II, the attractiveness to developing nations of bilateral and defensive FS measures has waxed and waned. Weaker countries have been most willing to run the risks of engaging in bilateral, defensive FS when their economies faced political or financial crises. Thus, India broke off its relations with Washington in the 1970s in favor of strengthening political, financial, and military ties with the Soviet Union, which seemed to Prime Minister Indira Gandhi to be a more generous and tolerant partner. The exacerbation of the 1980s' Latin American debt crisis eventually convinced Brazil's government to declare a moratorium on repayment of its foreign debt principal in 1987. Yet overall, the financial crises of the 1980s and 1990s tended to reinforce the trend toward economic liberalization and external economic integration among most of these middle-income economies. As the international norm shifted toward financial globalization and trade openness, coupled with domestic economic reform emphasizing macroeconomic prudence, blunt use of bilateral/defensive FS strategies became outdated for most emerging economies – with some exceptions, as in populist Argentina and Venezuela in the 2000s, as detailed by Labaqui in Chapter 2.

Across the Pacific, India, China, and Southeast Asian economies were relatively more protected from financial crises until recently, as their economies were less open to international commercial borrowing, and especially to short-term foreign capital flows, up until the 1990s. Nonetheless, governments in these countries were very keen on protecting their economies from instabilities while they strove for growth. Hamilton-Hart (Chapter 4) discusses the structure of domestic political incentives that supported the financial and monetary mercantilism pursued by Southeast Asian economies during the era of export-led growth prior to the Asian Financial Crisis (AFC) of 1997–1998. During this period, their respective governments' control over the financial sector allowed for rapid growth of manufacturing production. In most Southeast Asian countries, where reliance on foreign direct investment (FDI) long has been high, governments presided over an implicit bargain between foreign investors in export-oriented manufacturing industries and privileged domestic groups in the nontradable sector, resulting in a powerful domestic coalition favoring government support of exports. China, too, relied heavily on inward FDI to achieve its impressive GDP growth, and it has also applied stringent capital controls to block short-term inflows. Most of this panoply of capital controls remained intact as the People's Bank of China (PBOC) launched its cautious campaign to internationalize its currency, the RMB, in the late 2000s (Chapter 5, Volz).

International financial globalization and liberalization coincided with a slow shift in the interstate balance of overall material capabilities. The decades of the 1980s and 1990s mark the start of the time when the emerging economies, particularly the larger ones such as China, India, and Brazil, began to capture a significantly larger share of global material capabilities (Armijo and Katada, Chapter 1). Furthermore, the 2008–2009 GFC, during which the United States and Europe found themselves submerged under toxic assets and sovereign debts, did much to discredit the so-called "Washington Consensus" and the ideological attractiveness of neoliberalism. Quick recovery of the EMEs in the aftermath of the GFC (Wise, Armijo, and Katada, under review) ushered in new opportunities for these emerging powers to experiment with several alternative FS strategies in terms of their targets, goals, and tools.

The "new" FS of emerging powers, deconstructed

In order to understand and systematize the wide variety of FS strategies implemented in recent years by rising powers, this volume has demarcated three fault lines among these strategies (Armijo and Katada, Chapter 1). First, the target of a state's FS may be either a specific country or the global financial system in general. Second, the goal of the FS strategy may be defensive and oriented toward protection of its domestic economy or its financial system, or the policy may be directed toward a more offensive (or assertive) purpose, intended to alter either the behavior of others (bilateral) or the norms and structure of international markets or global financial governance (systematic). Third, the instruments of any of these broad types of FS strategies may be either financial or monetary. Financial instruments include borrowing and debt manipulation, credit and aid extension, and financial reforms and regulations, while the monetary dimensions of FS include macroeconomic policies such as balance-of-payments maneuvers, including exchange rate and currency strategies intended to promote emerging powers' foreign policy strategies.

Table 7.1 replicates the framework initially presented in the first chapter's Table 1.1, and then incorporates specific country examples of each type of FS identified. As we did in the introduction, we begin with the upper left-hand cell. Examples of *bilateral and defensive* FS begin with sovereign default on foreign debt, once common but now comparatively rare, especially among middle-income countries. However, in 2001, Argentina engineered the largest ever sovereign default in history (Labaqui, Chapter 2). Although there clearly have been costs, many in Argentina see the strategy as a success, which has satisfied the political goals of the country's leadership. Moreover, the action has implications beyond Argentina as serious foreign observers have urged other countries such as Greece, whose situation in the European Monetary Union (EMU) in 2010–2012 arguably paralleled that of Argentina with its creditors a decade earlier, to follow Argentina's lead and default (cf. Corcoran 2011).

However, global trends toward trade and financial liberalization beginning in the 1980s and intensifying in the 1990s have raised the costs to EMEs of default and nationalization, both reputational and directly economic. Nationalizations of FDI (or its functional equivalent of radically and unilaterally altering the terms of previously negotiated contracts, causing transnational firms to decide to exit) are relatively uncommon today. Nonetheless, this volume's empirical chapters refer to two such episodes in the 2000s, one of Venezuela vis-à-vis foreign petroleum firms and the other of Bolivia, which suddenly nationalized natural gas fields for which it had previously sold long-term exploitation rights to Brazil's state petroleum firm, Petrobras, plunging Brazil's leftist president into a difficult situation (see Chapters 2 and 3).

A more proactive, rather than simply reactive, form of bilateral and defensive FS is for EMEs to diversify their sources of foreign financial resources including loans, FDI, and aid.[1] Recent examples of this move may be seen in the choices of Latin American, East Asian, and African governments to become recipients of Chinese financial flows (Gallagher,

Irwin, and Koleski 2012; Brautigam 2010). Latin American and African countries also receive Brazilian financial flows, mostly of FDI, although these are much smaller than those from China (CEPAL 2013). Also in the 2000s, Venezuela extended special petroleum financing to a number of small and left-leaning Caribbean and Central American nations. Argentina's strategy of defying global capital markets was also assisted by joint issue of sovereign bonds with Venezuela (see Chapter 2).

Such diversification has opened up increased political room for borrowing-country leaders to manuever their domestic affairs as they manage to obtain financial support from variety of sources. If a government is averse to intervention in its human rights practices, for example, it can obtain support from Chinese sources. However, it seems doubtful that sovereign debtors to China, Venezuela, or Brazil (or private firms backed by an implicit sovereign guarantee from their governments) are better protected per se in times of international financial crisis than those with financial obligations to institutions based in advanced industrial countries: having a multiplicity of different creditors may be helpful, but borrowers should not expect "Southern" creditors to be more lenient. With respect to bilateral and defensive monetary statecraft, we note that a number of East Asian countries have diversified the currencies they employ for international transactions to include a greater share of RMB. However, this seems to be less of a conscious strategy of reducing dependence on the U.S. dollar than a simple reflection of their close and growing trade ties with China.

The second set of strategies belongs to the upper right-hand cell of Table 7.1, which shows evidence from our cases of *bilateral and offensive* FS. Several emerging powers have now become bilateral international creditors, particularly to other emerging or developing countries. This tactic is the counterpart to the bilateral, defensive tactic employed by relatively weaker countries of diversifying their sources of foreign capital by turning to other Southern countries, in the hope of reducing dependence on the advanced industrial countries or the traditional international financial institutions. For the Southern creditors, both commercial and political motivations may be at play. Among our cases, Brazil's loans and investments abroad have been largely motivated commercially (Armijo and Echeverri-Gent, Chapter 3), while China's strategy comprises a mix of ensuring export markets and a guaranteed supply of essential raw materials, including fuel, for the future. Meanwhile, international political motivations behind the use of financial resources are clearly demonstrated by Venezuela's schemes of extending advantageous financing for petroleum to smaller neighbors with leftist governments. Venezuela

Table 7.1 Emerging powers in Asia and Latin America: modalities of FS, 2000–2013

	Defensive	Offensive/Assertive
Bilateral	*Financial* * Default (Argentina) * Nationalize FDI (Venezuela, Bolivia) * Diversify sources or modalities of foreign sovereign borrowing (EME debtors to China, Venezuela, Brazil) *Monetary* * Diversify reserve currency holdings (East Asian holders of RMB)	*Financial* * Use credit or aid to exert control over smaller neighbor (China, Venezuela, Brazil?) or challenge a major power (Venezuela) *Monetary* * Promote RMB as reserve currency (China) * Encourage local currency trade invoicing with smaller neighbor (China) * Employ regional financial cooperation to discipline smaller neighbors (China, Japan)
Systemic	*Financial* * Capital controls (all EMEs profiled) * State banks (India, Brazil, China, Argentina, Venezuela) *Monetary* * Accumulate reserves (all EMEs profiled, especially East Asia) * Regional swap arrangements (ASEAN+3, FLAR) * Other regional financial initiatives (Banco del Sur)	*Financial* * Become regional financial hub (China, Brazil, South Korea) * Fill a niche in global financial markets (India) * Promote changes in international regulation and governance – e.g., global bankruptcy legislation; development as goal of financial governance; expansion of SDRs as reserve currency (South Korea, BRICS, both collectively and individually) *Monetary* * Seek active participation in global monetary governance (BRICS) * Use of CMI/CMIM as counterweight strategy toward IMF (China, Japan)

also cemented its relationship with similarly left-leaning Argentina by floating three issues of a joint sovereign bond between 2005 and 2008, as Argentina's acrimonious and ongoing negotiations with its private international creditors stemming from the 2001 default had shut the country off of international commercial borrowing (Labaqui, Chapter 2). China, with by far the world's largest foreign exchange reserves of over $3 trillion, has been the most active among all emerging economies in employing bilateral monetary statecraft to win friends and influence. Chinese leaders have actively encouraged trade invoicing in RMB (Volz, Chapter 5), and, as of mid-2012, China had currency swap arrangements with Argentina, Australia, Belarus, Brazil, Iceland, Indonesia, Kazakhstan, Korea, Malaysia, New Zealand, Singapore, the United Arab Emirates, and Uzbekistan.

The third category of FS includes policies that are *defensive but systemic*, shown in lower left-hand cell of Table 7.1. Leaders of the active states employ their national financial capabilities in an attempt to shield their country not against a particular foreign state but rather against systemic influences, whether coming from global markets or from the rules and institutions of global financial governance. By far the most important type of defensive and systemic international financial policy is the implementation of controls on the free cross-border movement of capital. All of the states profiled in this volume employ extensive capital controls.

Historically, governments have worried about capital flight, and have thus imposed limits on the ability of their own citizens and investors to exchange local currency for foreign hard currencies. In that sense, virtually all developing and middle-income states anywhere in the world have used some controls to capital *outflows*, as have some advanced industrial countries. In contrast, during the 2000s, most EME governments focused their energies on *inward* capital controls. They do so in order to prevent financial instability arising from capital inflows in large and unpredictable quantities, when the local interest rates are higher than those in advanced economies, only to flood out rapidly during a subsequent crisis. Most often, the semi-permanent capital controls in both Latin America and East Asia (see all of the country case chapters) today aim at limiting potentially volatile financial inflows of short-term capital such as investments in interest-bearing deposits. For example, Argentina's central bank imposed a 30 percent reserve requirement on short-term inflows of capital to discourage speculative investment and prevent the Argentine peso from appreciating (Labaqui, Chapter 2), while Brazil for a period simply taxed all cross-border financial transactions (Armijo and Echeverri-Gent, Chapter 3).

We have also considered interventionist counter-cyclical credit expansion through public sector banks as a part of defensive and systemic "international" FS. During the height of the GFC in 2008–2009, finance ministers in emerging powers – including but not limited to China, India, Brazil, and Indonesia – funneled emergency liquidity through state-owned banks (Chapters 3, 4, and 5). Policymakers in these countries subsequently and proudly noted that they were in a position to insist that the banks, in turn, loaned these funds to business borrowers. Such measures set the EMEs apart from crisis-ravaged European countries such as Spain and France, in which large private banks were accused of accepting public sector bailout funds – but then of preferring to invest these funds back in government securities rather than in loans to hard-hit, and therefore risky, private businesses. Meanwhile, Argentina's government used its control of state banks and regulatory authority over other sources of savings, including employee pension funds, to make its strategy of unilateral foreign debt restructuring viable (Labaqui, Chapter 2). When the Argentine government was shut out of global capital markets, it leaned on administrators of domestic financial institutions to "invest" in its public debt. This type of financial repression historically has been routine in many now emerging economies, and even today remains the norm in China and frequent in India.

Larger EMEs also have employed FS in the realm of monetary policy. By far the most important strategy in this area has been to build up official foreign exchange reserves, a choice made by every country profiled in this volume.[2] Following the recurrent international financial crises of the 1980s and 1990s, most Latin American countries (except Venezuela) by the early 2000s had adopted flexible exchange rates with capital controls. Helped by booming commodity exports (including oil), especially to China, over the last decade, these countries also managed to accumulate relatively large foreign exchange reserves as a buffer against speculative attacks on their currencies. The FS strategy of foreign exchange accumulation also has been sustained by the desire on the part of governments in countries where domestic political elites have counted on export-led economic growth, such as those in Southeast Asia, to maintain export competitiveness via managed exchange rate policies through a strategy of "monetary mercantilism," although the region's countries, especially those that have democratized more thoroughly, gradually are moving away from this earlier pattern as its costs become more apparent (Chapter 4, Hamilton-Hart). In Southeast Asia, as in China (Volz, Chapter 5 and Katada and Sohn, Chapter 6), the export surpluses resulting from sales of manufactures abroad enabled accumulation of foreign exchange war chests.

Overall, capital controls and the closely related buildup of large foreign exchange reserves have been the most widely used types of defensive and systemic FS employed by contemporary emerging powers, as well as those with the most significant practical effects thus far. Recently, emerging economies' large foreign exchange buffers played a very significant role in enabling them to weather the 2008–2009 "global" financial crisis.[3] Foreign exchange reserves also constitute real resources controlled by national governments, permitting some of the bilateral and assertive FS already discussed. Venezuela, for example, transferred some of its official reserve holdings to the national development fund, Fonden, to spend, and Argentina's president ordered that foreign exchange reserves be used to pay down the country's foreign debt, a policy the head of the central bank unsuccessfully opposed (Labaqui, Chapter 2).[4]

In the volume, we highlight the fact that the most dramatically new defensive and systemic type of FS has been cooperative South–South or intra-regional financial efforts. In the past, collective action among developing countries was viewed with suspicion and met with resistance. For example, a 1984 effort by Colombia's president to gather his Latin American counterparts simply to discuss the possibility of a common front vis-à-vis their international creditors (dubbed by the North American press a debtors' "cartel") was met by a combination of international scorn, excessive fear, and furious diplomatic activity by the United States. At that time, the *New York Times* reported that "adroit maneuvering" had been necessary to prevent Latin American countries from "ganging up" on the United States (Silk 1984).[5] As emphasized by Katada and Sohn (Chapter 6), even in the late 1990s, at the height of the AFC, the U.S. Treasury Secretary and other officials went to great lengths to discourage a regional stabilization initiative, the Asian Monetary Fund (AMF), proposed by Japan, a fellow democracy, close political ally, and at the time the world's second largest economy.

In this context, the construction of the Chiang Mai Initiative (CMI), originally a series of bilateral swap agreements linking poorer Southeast Asian countries to China, South Korea, and Japan, and its expansion into a multilateral institution, the CMIM, with $240 billion pledged, is a new and structurally significant departure in the FS of Asia's "new kids." As Katada and Sohn emphasize in Chapter 6, the CMI process has in the last ten years developed beyond a simple regional swap agreement to include an early warning system against financial crises with establishment of a cooperative research arm, and an increasingly institutionalized consultation process. This initiative is significant because it is an exclusively East Asian undertaking.[6] Moreover, China, Japan, and South Korea, three countries which are politically at odds among themselves on a host of delicate issues, have managed to cooperate and to reassure the members of ASEAN that this financial guarantee through CMIM is viable and useful, although prudent Southeast Asian countries will continue to rely on their own official reserves as the first line of defense (Hamilton-Hart, Chapter 4).

The FLAR, a regional swap arrangement in the North Andean region and Central America, unlike the CMI/CMIM, has actually been accessed on a few occasions by member states. It is at present relatively small, both in number of members and in terms of the size of the total assets pledged to be available for emergency swaps, although this could change if Brazil decided to join (see Armijo and Echeverri-Gent, Chapter 3). Similarly, the Banco del Sur has been formally agreed but not yet implemented in the region. Although not yet significant, this arrangement that is originally a Venezuelan project has been publicly supported not only by members of the Venezuela-led ALBA grouping but also by the MERCOSUR trade and economic community organized by Brazil and Argentina.[7]

The fourth major category, *offensive and systemic* FS, shown in Table 7.1's lower right-hand cell, represents the most dramatic departure for emerging powers from their past experiences. Arguably the most significant change in international financial relations discussed in the volume would be if China's RMB became widely used as an international reserve currency. However, this development could not occur without active promotion by China's leaders, who at present remain quite ambivalent (Volz, Chapter 6). We also would place in this cell all FS moves intended by national government actors to alter the rules, operations, or institutions of international financial markets or global financial and monetary governance. Offensive and systemic FS represents demands by rising states to compete actively in world markets and to have their voices heard in global governance. In the realm of finance, our case study chapters have mentioned efforts by emerging powers to break into global private markets. Both China and Brazil have attempted to expand their roles as regional financial hubs among neighboring "Southern" economies (see Chapters 5 and 2). India, which has much less congenial relations with most of its immediate neighbors, has a different strategy for cracking global financial markets; one focused on selling financial and information technology services to advanced industrial country markets.

Most importantly, emerging powers also have wielded their national financial capabilities as a sword to assert their views, especially within the G20 and the BRICS clubs, and to cleave a path to enhanced global systemic influence. For instance, the BRICS members have effectively created a caucus within the G20 to amplify their displeasure with the proposals coming from Washington, DC or London such as the implementation of a global "Tobin Tax" for financing European financial rescue efforts. Although IMF reform has stalled in recent months, BRICS members pitched in with contributions to its enhanced subscription in explicit exchange for more voice in the institution (Chapter 3, Armijo and Echeverri-Gent; Chapter 5, Volz; Armijo and Roberts 2014).[8] On some occasions, emerging powers have pushed for specific policy positions, including global bankruptcy legislation, an expansion of the use of IMF "Special Drawing Rights" (SDRs) as an alternative global reserve asset, an explicit inclusion of "development" as one of the goals of cooperative international financial regulation, and recognition of a norm that both deficit and surplus countries may need to adjust in cases of global imbalances.[9] Regional financial shields, although ostensibly defensive as discussed above, could also provide offensive capabilities. Thus, for China and Japan, regional monetary cooperation through the CMI/CMIM mechanism could be construed as a challenge to global financial governance in the form of an alternative mechanism to the IMF to tackle financial crises. As Katada and Sohn (Chapter 6) argue, however, both Japan and China are also interested in creating a regional structure to make other smaller (and more crisis-prone) economies behave.

In sum, with greater relative capabilities have come expanded foreign policy options. In contrast to the time when developing countries focused narrowly on protecting their economies through bilateral and defensive FS measures, the variety of FS strategies available for and employed by emerging powers both large and small has since expanded. Although some countries still employ traditional bilateral and defensive FS measures mostly motivated by domestic and political interests, many have moved on. Emerging powers have begun to utilize offensive measures to influence others and target the global system, rather than simply to defend themselves against their respective bilateral creditors.

Common themes: motives and costs of FS

The analysis provided by the five case chapters reveals several patterns in the motives and costs associated with FS strategies. First, emerging powers with active FS strategies governments profiled in this volume, including Argentina, Brazil, and Venezuela in Latin America, and China, India, Indonesia, Malaysia, and Singapore in Asia, have turned to capital controls (often although not always focused on inward flows) and the accumulation of official foreign exchange reserves as buffers against international financial and monetary volatility. These policies were implemented after the several waves of emerging market financial crises of the 1990s, and represented learning on the part of incumbent leaders of these countries. We observe, nevertheless, another group of EMEs, including Mexico, Colombia, and Chile in Latin America and South Korea in Asia, that have turned instead toward greater international financial integration, trusting their defense in future international financial crises to flexible exchange rates, relatively sophisticated domestic financial systems dominated by private (and often foreign) banks, and conservative macroeconomic policies of the sort long promoted by the international financial institutions. The former group of emerging powers, those profiled here, have more interventionist tendencies. Their political leaders explicitly perceive their countries' national *financial* resources as components of the nations' broader *political* capabilities as well.

Second, although most of our discussion in this volume has been couched in terms of FS as a strategy of international relations, incumbents' international policy choices very often have their roots in domestic politics.[10] We observe that asserting strong, principled opposition against external threats, both real (as with debt, currency, and imported banking crises) and imagined (as with a supposed U.S. plot to infect Latin American leaders with cancer, suggested by President Hugo Chávez to fellow cancer victims, Presidents Lula da Silva and Cristina Fernández de Kirchner, in 2011), has been a staple of every populist politician worldwide, and clearly played a role in Venezuela and Argentina in the 2000s (see Chapter 2). Loud demands made by these leaders that global capitalism end its exploitation of the world's poor and reform itself, despite being issued from high-visibility international pulpits at the United Nations or the G20 heads of state summits (to which Argentine though not Venezuelan leaders are invited), clearly are primarily aimed at domestic constituents.

Domestic politics and entrenched inter-sectoral national political economic bargains also play a particularly large role in Hamilton-Hart's analysis of FS in Southeast Asia (Chapter 4) and Volz's observations about China (Chapter 5). "Monetary mercantilism" in Southeast Asia rested on an alliance of foreign direct investors and associated domestic interests that would profit from exports, but meanwhile held down the real incomes of domestic consumers and workers. As countries such as Indonesia have democratized, this has tended to weaken the hold of the entrenched special interests who benefitted from artificially-induced undervaluation. In China, the de facto coalition supporting export-led growth has included the public sector banks and large state-owned manufacturing enterprises, while the relative losers have been consumers, workers, and small to mid-sized private businesses. Volz in fact concludes that much of the enthusiasm within Chinese officialdom for RMB internationalization and its promotion as a reserve currency probably originates with economists and policymakers pursuing a domestic economic reform agenda. China's finance ministry and central bank, the PBOC, support domestic financial liberalization for its own sake, viewing it as essential for securing more stable, long-term economic growth. By encouraging domestic support for the RMB's use as an international reserve currency, which appeals to the nationalist pride of ordinary citizens, the pro-financial liberalization alliance furthers its own cause, since domestic bank and interest rate reforms are logically prerequisite to greater RMB internationalization, and to increasing its attractiveness as a global reserve currency.

In the same vein, Armijo and Echeverri-Gent (Chapter 3) attribute Brazil's greater willingness, as compared to India, to challenge the United States on global financial issues in direct and vocal fashion in part to the two countries' different domestic politics of financial reform. In Brazil, there is broad de facto agreement among most economists involved in public policy debates on a relatively market-oriented financial system, responsive to price signals, yet one in which large public sector banks also participate.[11] In contemporary India, as in the Chinese case, the topic of domestic financial liberalization continues to be much more polemical. Thus far, senior Indian policymakers have often refrained from grandiose statements in multilateral financial governance fora at least partly because they did not want to complicate delicate negotiations and gradual shifts toward financial liberalization that were quietly in process back at home.

A third recurrent theme in the country studies concerns the costs, economic and otherwise, to the user of the various FS tactics surveyed. This is an understated theme, which needs to be highlighted. As was implicit in our first comparative observation in this section, the emerging powers most inclined to employ FS, whether for desperate bilateral defense (such as international loan default) or assertive systemic rebalancing (as through demands for IMF quota readjustment), tend to be those EMEs with somewhat statist or interventionist overall economic policy regimes, whose incumbent leaders insist on retaining some financial policy levers to employ on a discretionary basis. Any such strategy implies real costs on several grounds. On a purely economic level, markets are almost always more efficient at allocating resources and promoting overall growth in the long run than is centrally organized allocation. Consequently, reserving large quantities of resources (such as foreign exchange war chests) to be deployed by government technocrats is seldom the most pro-growth policy choice. On a mostly political level, once a given national economic regulatory strategy is adopted, particularly one involving barriers to free market allocation and resulting in a particular set of distributional outcomes within the country, then entrenched special interests tend to grow up around it. As such, it becomes difficult to shift away from that strategy, even when the initial rationale for its adoption disappears.

In this book, Hamilton-Hart (Chapter 4) makes these points most explicitly. The economic opportunity costs of large foreign exchange reserves – particularly those invested in low-yielding U.S. Treasury securities – are considerable. Although some Southeast Asian countries have managed to set up fairly large Sovereign Wealth Funds (SWF) to diversify their overseas investments, Hamilton-Hart argues that such accumulation of foreign exchange reserves, mostly for defensive purposes, has not fostered any useful offensive FS capabilities for the governments. On the contrary, it has introduced dependence and vulnerability on the part of these small economies. Despite such costs, in country after country, the entrenched political economies that have grown up around these interests are difficult to alter. Similar comments could easily be extended to other country cases (and see also Volz, Chapter 5).

Fourth and finally, none of the rising powers examined have pursued goals that could be construed as system-challenging or revolutionary. Even today's most direct challenge to the existing financial governance structure, the push for RMB internationalization, largely reflects China's campaign to promote domestic financial reform. Support for greater global use of the RMB from China's fellow BRICS is equally complicated in terms of motives, and likely quite unreliable in practice (see Chapters 3 and 5). These powers have also engaged in the efforts to foster South–South cooperation and building of regional structures to reduce dependence on the global financial system (Chapters 2 and 6). However, to date, these efforts are either explicitly supplemental to the global system (particularly the CMI) or too small to have much leverage to counterweigh the existing institutional and power structure.

Conclusions and implications for the future

What have we learned? This project has considered and catalogued the various types of FS engaged in by contemporary emerging powers. Through careful study of several cases, we have uncovered policymakers' apparent motivations and the nature of contemporary domestic economic policy debates in several important Asian and Latin American countries. In this section, we would like to go a step further to ask the question of what, if anything, these trends mean for international political economy and international relations more generally. We close with the following observations.

First, while the distribution of overall material capabilities has shifted notably toward the emerging economies, particularly China and the other original BRICS countries, the distribution of global *financial* (including international monetary) capabilities still overwhelmingly favors the advanced industrial countries. The direction of change in favor of emerging powers is clear, but the financial resources available to these powers are at most growing rapidly from a very low base, and hence these powers remain vulnerable to changes in the global macroeconomic and financial environments.

At the onset of this collaborative project, the editors and the contributors speculated that possession of ample official reserves might be the sine qua non of an EME whose leaders wish to engage in FS. Control over large foreign exchange reserves has indeed expanded both the national financial security and the international influence of rising powers. China's enormous foreign exchange reserves are, for example, correctly seen as a source of international power and influence. Some of this volume's empirical case studies, however, guide us to nuance this hypothesis with a better understanding of the motives and costs of reserve accumulation (Chapters 4 and 5, in particular). When the vested interests and domestic politics guide a country's foreign economic strategy to favor export promotion and dollar dependence, the resulting large reserve accumulation also may introduce challenges and vulnerabilities to these emerging powers. Furthermore, the G7 countries continue to dominate in all of the most sophisticated international financial markets.[12]

One can interpret these same facts in several contrasting ways. One interpretation would be that the different types of financial capabilities of emerging powers give to their possessors surprising and potent forms of international influence. This perception leads to an alarmist view of the world in which these emerging powers are seen as unknown and worrisome threats. A second, more skeptical interpretation would note that, excepting in the single category of official foreign exchange reserves accumulation, the EMEs remain relatively inconsequential in global finance. Consequently, the advanced industrial countries have nothing to worry about. Neither of these interpretations is necessarily wrong. However, this study would instead emphasize a different trend: a number of important emerging powers, including many of those profiled here, have cleverly parleyed these still small financial capabilities into large reputational and influence gains.

Nonetheless, these emerging powers remain susceptible to shocks in the global economy. Recent volatility in EMEs associated with the U.S. Fed's 2013 monetary taper has reminded the leaders of emerging powers of how vulnerable they remain.[13] By the time Fed Governor Bernanke announced the actual details of the planned taper in mid-December 2013, governments in all of the EMEs dubbed the "fragile five" (Brazil, India, Indonesia, Turkey, and South Africa) had responded to downward pressure (especially in U.S. dollar terms) on their currencies and securities markets with a combination of temporary new outward capital controls and domestic interest rate hikes (*Financial Times* 2013). For example, India's central bank, the RBI, placed new and stringent limits on gold imports in 2013, which many Indians have continued to see as a better and safer investment than any financial asset, but which causes Indian financial ministers to despair, as it constitutes unproductive investment from the perspective of the economy as a whole. This more difficult international environment casts doubt on some of the inflated rhetoric of 2008–2010, such as Brazilian President Lula da Silva's bold suggestion that investors worried about the safety of U.S. Treasury securities should instead invest in Brazilian government bonds (Chapter 3)! Once again, as so often in the recent past, emerging power governments are struggling to bolster their international financial credibility.

Second, today's emerging powers are rising in a global context within which there is a clear international consensus on at least one important goal of global economic governance: no country wants spreading financial crises or meltdowns. The fact that even countries such as the United States, Britain, and France have recently been rocked by financial crisis – and that Japan has still not fully emerged from its enormous domestic financial implosion of two decades ago – has made, or logically should have made, the substantial similarity of interests among major governments (such as G20 members) quite obvious. This environment marks quite a departure from the 1990s, an era when major financial and banking meltdowns were assumed to be limited to EMEs. At that time, there was a stark contrast in views regarding the causes and solutions of these crises between the major creditor countries and their financial institutions, on the one hand, and the debtor countries, on the other hand (Devlin 1989; Wade 1998; Armijo 2001; Katada 2005). Furthermore, the previously immense political power and social prestige of those nimble private financial firms ("speculators") active in some segments of global financial markets has (at least apparently or temporarily) waned in the face of scathing public criticism of the harm they caused in the late 2000s.

Possibly, then, the optimistic international scenario presented by G. John Ikenberry's (2009) vision of "liberal internationalism 3.0" is viable in the issue arena of global finance.[14] In essence, Ikenberry suggests that hegemonic and hierarchical international economic cooperation organized by the United States in the postwar period ("liberal internationalism 2.0") can be replaced if the status quo powers, the major advanced industrial countries, make concerted efforts to enmesh rising powers in existing global economic governance regimes, so that they will judge it too costly to pull out.[15] In other words, something like the postwar ("Bretton Woods") open international economic order could continue, but with an expanded set of participants. Of course, banks and financial firms everywhere bitterly resist regulation, and most especially hate collaborative multilateral regulation (Brown 2013). But there is no *government*, including those such as the United States and United Kingdom that have historically allowed outsize political influence to the private financial sector, that desires international financial volatility. This fact suggests that international financial regulatory cooperation, both formal and ad hoc, could continue, even in an increasingly multipolar world.

Nonetheless, and thirdly, many emerging powers remain quite suspicious of the intentions of advanced industrial countries when it comes to the "contributions" that these rising powers have been requested to make for the upkeep of global financial governance. Where opinion leaders in core capitalist economies have seen mostly public goods provided by post-World War II global financial governance (e.g., highlighting the crucially important and positive role played by the U.S. dollar in acting as the world's major transaction and reserve currency), policymakers and scholars in emerging markets often have highlighted the unequal advantage accruing to the core economies (including the privilege of unlimited seigniorage for the United States and the inability of developing countries to contract international finance in their home currencies) (see Armijo and Echeverri-Gent 2014, forthcoming). Chinese leaders are also concerned about their government being drawn in (as was the case for Japan in the 1990s) and asked to contribute limitlessly to support arrangements that "bail out" private investors headquartered in advanced economies and sustain the power and influence of these governments (Katada and Sohn, Chapter 6). Observers in the global "South" were never as likely as scholars in the "North" to believe that international financial relations were characterized by free-wheeling markets that had outrun the control of national governments (cf. Cohen, this volume's Preface). The perception gap over the role and intentions of the United States as leader of global markets and the free world not only remains largest in China (Nathan and Scobell 2012) but also is present in most of the globally consequential rising powers, including all five of the BRICS countries.

For the foreseeable future, therefore, we anticipate an uneasy truce in most EME statehouses between an impulse to employ the shield and sword of international FS to promote *national* foreign policy purposes, as in many of the case studies presented in this volume, and competing incentives and pressures to participate actively and "cooperatively" (a la "liberal internationalism 3.0") in global financial governance. The medium-term trend toward greater global multipolarity, and consequent greater ambitions of emerging powers, is clear. Fortunately, Ikenberry (2009) seems correct in observing that the international political and economic governance institutions that exist today are – at least in comparative historical perspective – remarkably open, even-handed, and easy to join. We are therefore cautiously optimistic about the future of both FS by emerging powers – and cooperative global financial governance with the active participation of these same countries.

Notes

1. In previous decades, there was also much discussion in the finance ministries of developing countries of the pros and cons of encouraging different types of capital inflows, such as foreign bank loans, direct investment, or portfolio investment in emerging stock markets (e.g., Armijo 1999). As other FS options have become available, these earlier debates have receded in importance.
2. In 1995, China's official reserves were 5.5 percent of global reserves; by mid-2010, they were over 31 percent. Over this same period, the share held by the remaining BRICS almost doubled, from 6.2 to 11.4 percent. Meanwhile, the shares controlled by the major advanced industrial countries of the G7 halved, falling from 33.6 to 16.1 percent (Lane and Milesi-Ferreti 2007, as updated to 2010).
3. Some analysts have renamed the GFC the "North Atlantic financial crisis" in recognition of the quick rebound of most EMEs (see, e.g., Mohan, Patra, and Kapur 2013).

The Financial Statecraft of Emerging Powers   181

4. Analytically, the buildup of foreign exchange reserves *for the purpose* of sustaining an export surplus would constitute offensive and systemic FS, as Hamilton-Hart's discussion in Chapter 4 recognizes. Unfortunately, empirically distinguishing between offensive and defensive systemic reasons for reserve accumulation is quite difficult.
5. Meanwhile, sovereign creditors and private creditor banks during the debt crisis coordinated their efforts through meetings organized by the International Monetary Fund (IMF), and through establishment of the Paris Club and Bank Advisory Committees (Aggarwal 1996; Katada 2001).
6. It is noteworthy that in the early 1990s when the then Prime Minister of Malaysia Mahathir Mohamad proposed an exclusively East Asian caucus within the Asia-Pacific Economic Cooperation (APEC) process, the U.S. government vehemently opposed the idea. The same membership of the unrealized caucus, ASEAN+3 now constitutes the CMI members.
7. With the passing of President Chávez in 2013, and the establishment of the alternative Pacific Alliance aimed to deepen the economic links of the more neoliberal Latin American countries Mexico, Colombia, and Chile and the United States in the region, the Banco del Sur project, which had represented ambitious systemic FS within South America that was at once both defensive and potentially offensive, has lost its earlier momentum.
8. There are subtle differences among this volume's contributors in how they assess the increments to their global financial voice achieved by EMEs, with Hamilton-Hart (Chapter 4) the most skeptical and Armijo and Echeverri-Gent (Chapter 3) more willing to see increased influence for emerging powers. Katada and Sohn (Chapter 6) emphasize that China hasn't yet decided in what direction it would like to push international financial reforms.
9. However, the last point is not a position endorsed by the largest emerging power, China.
10. The prominent role of domestic political and policy debates in each of our country cases remind us (as this volume's contributor, Ulrich Volz, already has) of the trenchant observation "all politics is local" made famous by former U.S. Speaker of the House Thomas "Tip" O'Neill.
11. The fact that Brazil's major public sector banks also must raise capital in private markets helps to keep them honest.
12. These major advanced industrial countries, for example, own 60 percent of the assets of all international banks (against only 4 percent for the BRICS) and are the issuer of record for 46 percent of outstanding international bond issues (compared to less than 4 percent for the BRICS, plus Hong Kong, Mexico, Singapore, and South Korea) (BIS 2013).
13. In the aftermath of the GFC of 2008–2009, the U.S. Federal Reserve Bank instituted several rounds of "quantitative easing" to stimulate the U.S. economy. As of early 2013, these constituted $85 billion in monthly financial asset purchases. Many international actors – notably including the IMF under Managing Director Christine Lagarde – were eager to see the continuation of the global stimulus created by leakage from U.S. monetary policies. Others, including the finance ministers of all of the BRICS countries, complained that U.S. policies were exposing them to excessive monetary volatility.
14. The arguably somewhat favorable conditions for multilateral financial regulatory cooperation would seem to contrast with, for example, the structurally

more difficult challenge of multilateral cooperation in preventing or reversing global climate change, where the politics of blame and the allocation of cutbacks have many more zero-sum aspects (Porter 2013).
15. The World Trade Organization, which both China and Russia campaigned long and hard to join, may be the best example of how this beneficial binding might operate.

References

Aggarwal, Vinod K. 1996. *Debt Games: Strategic Interaction in International Debt Rescheduling*. Cambridge: Cambridge University Press.

Armijo, Leslie Elliott. (ed.) 1999. *Financial Globalization and Democracy in Emerging Markets*. New York: Palgrave/St. Martin's.

Armijo, Leslie Elliott. (ed.) 2001. *Debating the Global Financial Architecture*. Albany, NY: SUNY Press.

Armijo, Leslie Elliott, and John Echeverri-Gent. forthcoming 2014. "Absolute or Relative Gains? How Status Quo and Emerging Powers Conceptualize Global Finance," in Thomas Oatley and William Winecoft (eds) *Handbook of International Monetary Relations*. Cheltenham: Edward Elgar (in press).

Armijo, Leslie Elliott, and Cynthia Roberts. 2014. "The Emerging Powers and Global Governance: Why the BRICS Matter," in Robert Looney (ed.) *Handbook of Emerging Economies*. New York: Routledge.

Bank for International Settlements (BIS). 2013. *BIS Quarterly Review, December 2013*. Basle: BIS.

Brautigam, Deborah. 2010. *The Dragon's Gift: The Real Story of China in Africa*. Oxford: Oxford University Press.

Brown, Gordon. 2013. "Stumbling Toward the Next Crash," *Financial Times*, December 18. www.ft.com (accessed December 20, 2013).

Comisión Económica para América Latina y el Caribe (CEPAL). 2013. *La Inversión Extranjera Direta en América Latina e El Caribe*. Santiago, Chile: CEPAL.

Corcoran, Patrick. 2011. "Argentina 2001 vs. Greece 2011: The Parallels and Pitfalls of Comparison," *Washington Diplomat*, November 1. http://washdiplomat.com (accessed December 28, 2013).

Devlin, Robert. 1989. *Debt and Crisis in Latin America: The Supply Side of the Story*. Princeton: Princeton University Press.

Financial Times. 2013. "'Fragile five' Countries Face Taper Crunch," *Financial Times*, December 17. www.ft.com (accessed December 28, 2013).

Gallagher, Kevin P., Amos Irwin, and Katherine Koleski. 2012. "The New Banks in Town: Chinese Finance in Latin America." *Inter-American Dialogue Report*, February.

Ikenberry, G. John. 2009. "Liberal Internationalism 3.0: America and the Dilemmas of Liberal World Order," *Perspectives on Politics*, 7(1), March, 71–87.

Katada, Saori N. 2001. *Banking on Stability: Japan and the Cross-Pacific Dynamics of International Financial Crisis Management*. Ann Arbor: University of Michigan Press.

Katada, Saori N. 2005. "Balancing Act: Japan's Strategy in Global and Regional Financial Governance," in John English, Ramesh Thakur, and Andrew F. Cooper (eds) *A Leaders 20 Summit: Why, How, Who and When?* Tokyo: United Nations University Press, pp. 97–120.

Lane, Philip R., and Gian Maria Milesi-Ferretti. 2007. "The External Wealth of Nations: Mark II," *Journal of International Economics*, 73, November, 223–250. Data updated to 2010.

Marichal, Carlos. 1989. *A Century of Debt Crises in Latin America: From Independence to the Great Depression, 1820–1930*. Princeton, N.J.: Princeton University Press.

Mohan, Rakesh, Michael Debabrata Patra, and Muneesh Kapur. 2013. "The International Monetary System: Where are We and Where do We Need to Go?," IMF Working Paper 13/224, Washington, DC: IMF, November.

Nathan, Andrew J., and Andrew Scobell. 2012. "How China Sees America," *Foreign Affairs*, 91(5), September/October, 32–47.

Porter, Eduardo. 2013. "Rethinking How to Split the Costs of Carbon," *New York Times*, December 24. www.nytimes.com (accessed December 29, 2013).

Silk, Leonard. 1984. "Economic Scene: Acting to Avert Debtor Cartel," *New York Times*, June 20. www.nytimes.com (accessed November 10, 2013).

Wade, Robert. 1998. "The Asian Debt-and-development Crisis of 1997–?: Causes and Consequences," *World Development*, 26(8), 1535–1553.

Wise, Carol, Leslie Elliott Armijo, and Saori N. Katada. (eds). Under review. *Unexpected Outcomes: How Emerging Markets Survived the Global Financial Crisis*. Book manuscript.

Index

Abertura Petroleros, petroleum deregulation law (Venezuela), 34–35
Acción Democrática (AD) (Venezuela), 23, 25
AMRO (ASEAN Macroeconomic Research Office) and regional financial surveillance, 140–42, 146, 154
Argentina, politics and financial statecraft of, 22–33, 164, 166, 186, 169, 170, 171, 174
   financial crisis & default (2001–02), 25, 166–67
   nationalization of pensions, 28–29
ASEAN (Association of Southeast Asian Nations), 96, 126, 77–98, 138–156
ASEAN+3, 96, 126
ASEAN+6, 154
Asian Bond Market Initiative (ABMI), 148, 154–55
Asian Development Bank, 141, 145
Asian financial crisis (AFC)
   and China, 146–47
   consequences in Southeast Asia, 80
   and Japan, 142–45
Asian Monetary Fund, 142–45
Aso, Taro (Prime Minister of Japan, 2008–09), 145

Banco del Sur (Bank of the South), 37–38, 60
Basel Committee on Banking Supervision (BCBS)
   and China, 149
Beijing Consensus, 153
Bharatiya Janata Party (BJP) (India), 68, 70
BNDES (National Economic and Social Development Bank, Brazil), 57–59, 68

Brazil, politics and financial statecraft, 3–5, 47–73, 164, 165, 166, 167, 168, 169, 170, 172, 174–75, 178
   differences with India, explained, 63–71
   geopolitical constraints, 66
   relations with U.S., 67
Brazilian Central Bank (BCB), 48, 53–54
Brazilian Social Democratic Party (PSDB), 69
BRICS (Brazil, Russia, India, China, and South Africa) countries, 13, 63, 89, 95, 127–28, 130, 173, 176
   BRICS bank, 62
   and China, 127–28
   and G20, 63
   and global governance, 72–73
Brown, Gordon (Prime Minister of Britain, 2007–10), 5
Bush, George W. (U.S. President, 2001–09), 70

Caldera, Rafael (President of Venezuela, 1994–99), 24
capital account liberalization, *see* capital controls
capital controls
   in Argentina, 31
   in Brazil, 55–57
   in China, 108–22
   in India, 55–57
   in Venezuela, 35–36
Cardoso, Fernando Henrique (President of Brazil, 1995–2002), 60, 69
Central Leading Group on Finance and Economic Affairs (CLGFEA), China, 119
Chávez Frías, Hugo (President of Venezuela, 1999–2013), 25, 33–39
   coup attempt against, 33
   coup attempts by, 24

186 *Index*

Chiang Mai Initiative (CMI/CMIM), 126, 138, 139–42
China, politics and financial statecraft, 1, 3–5, 6, 11, 14, 108–56, *see also* Chinese foreign policy
Chinese Communist Party, Third Plenary Session of the 18th CCP Central Committee
Chinese foreign policy, 125–29, 138–56, *see also* China, politics and financial statecraft
  in Asian financial crisis, 146–47
  and exchange rate policy, 14
  and financial regionalism, 147–49
  "realpolitik multilateralism" versus realism, 151
Clinton, Bill (U.S. President, 1993–2001), 57, 70
CMI/CMIM, *see* Chiang Mai Initiative
commodity prices, international, 40
Communist Party of India-Marxist, CPI(M), 69
Congress Party (India), 68–70
Contemporary Capabilities Index (CCI), 4
Convertibility Act (Argentina), 23
COPEI (Social Christian Party) (Venezuela), 23, 25
counterweight strategy
  defined, 138–39
  in East Asia, 147–48, 155
currency board (Argentina), 23
currency competition, currency hierarchy, 103, 105–08, *see also* currency internationalization
currency internationalization, China, *see also* renminbi internationalization
"currency war", 61
  politics of, 116–22

debt crisis, Latin America (1980s), 5, 22, 24, 33, 51, 164
De la Rúa, Fernando (President of Argentina, 1999–2001), 25
Deng Xiaoping, 151
Duhalde, Eduardo (President of Argentina, 2002–03), 24

emerging powers (aka rising, middle, or intermediate powers), 7, *see also* multipolarity
exchange rate policy, exchange rate management
  in China, 14, *see also* renminbi internationalization
  and financial statecraft, 174
  in Malaysia, 84
  in Singapore, 84–86
  in Southeast Asia, 82–87, *see* mercantilism, monetary
  in Venezuela, 35–36
export promotion, export-driven growth, 80–81

Fernández de Kirchner, Cristina (President of Argentina, 2007–), 25, 27–29
financial reform, China, 122–25
financial regionalism, in East Asia, 138–56
financial statecraft (FS)
  and capital account liberalization, 174
  defined, 2, 8–14
  and domestic politics, 174–75
  hypotheses about, 15, 71–72
financial statecraft (FS), defensive and bilateral, 10–11, 163–64, 166–67
  in Argentina, 27–32
  in Brazil, 51–52
  in India, 51–52
financial statecraft (FS), defensive and systemic, 12, 165, 169–72
  in Argentina, 27–32
  in Brazil, 52–58
  in India, 52–58
financial statecraft (FS), offensive and bilateral, 11–12, 167–69
  in Brazil, 51–52
financial statecraft (FS), offensive and systemic, 12–13, 149–55, 172–73
  in Argentina, 32–33
  in Brazil, 58–63
  in India, 58–63
FLAR, South American regional swap arrangement, 172
Fonden (Venezuela), 35

Index 187

foreign exchange reserves, *see* also exchange rate management; mercantilism, monetary
 in Brazil, 57
 in China, 82, 88, 91
  dual character of, 78, 87–93
 in India, 58
 in Japan, 145
 vulnerability of high reserve-holding countries, 92–93

Global Development Horizons (World Bank), 1
global financial crisis (GFC), 2, 4, 12, 41, 48, 53–58, 145, 147, 148, 149, 150, 162, 170
 and Japan, 145
 transmission to Southeast Asia, 98
Green Party (Brazil), 69
Group of 7 (G7), xi, 3, 4, 16, 62, 144, 149–50, 152, 177
Group of 20 (G20), 61–62
 and China, 94–95
 first summit, Washington, D.C., 2008, 4–5
 London summit, 2009, 5
 Seoul summit, 2010, 13
 and Southeast Asia, 94–97

hegemony, international (or hegemonic power), 150
 and U.S. dollar dominance, 105–08
Herrera Campíns, Luis (President of Venezuela, 1979–84), 24
heterodox economic policies, evaluated, 39–41
Hu Jintao (President of China, 2003–13), 148

India, politics and financial statecraft, 3–5, 6, 47–73, 174, 175, 178
 differences with Brazil, explained, 63–71
 geopolitical constraints, 66
 relations with U.S., 67, 69–70
Indonesia, politics and financial statecraft, 86–87, 95, 169, 170, 174, 175, 178
 and Asian financial crisis, 146–47

 and G20, 94–95
International Monetary Fund (IMF)
 and Argentina, 25–26
 and BRICS, 63
 and China, 94
 and East Asia, 126
 and Japan, 145
 Manila Framework, 144
 and Southeast Asia, 94
Iran, non-proliferation, and Turkey-Brazil diplomatic initiative, 5

Japan, politics and financial statecraft, 142–46, 150, 152
 during Asian financial crisis, 142–45
 Manila Framework, 144

Kirchner, Cristina Fernández de, *see* Fernández de Kirchner, Cristina
Kirchner, Nestor (President of Argentina, 2003–07), 25–28

Landless Movement (MST) (Brazil), 69
Lehman Brothers, 2
"lost decade", *see* debt crisis, Latin America
Lusinchi, Jaime (President of Venezuela, 1984–89), 24

Malaysia, politics and financial statecraft, 80, 83–84
Malvinas Islands, Argentina (aka Falklands Islands, UK), 22
Manila Framework (of IMF in East Asia), 144
Mantega, Guido (Finance Minister of Brazil, 2006–), 60–61
Market-oriented reforms (aka pro-market reforms, neoliberalism), *see* neoliberalism
Menem, Carlos (President of Argentina, 1989–99), 22
mercantilism
 classical, 78–79
 embedded, 79
 monetary, 77–98
MERCOSUR (Common Market of the South), 60

Mexican peso crisis, 57
monetary policy and financial statecraft
  in Brazil, 53–55
  in China, 119–20
  and currency internationalization, tradeoffs, 115–16
  in India, 53–55
monetary statecraft, 1–17, 162–180, *see also* capital controls; currency competition; currency internationalization; exchange rate policy
multipolarity (in the international system), x–xi, 1, 3–6, 165

National Democratic Alliance (NDA) (India), 68, 70
National Development and Reform Commission (NDRC) (China), 116, 117, 119, 120
neoliberalism (aka neoliberal economic paradigm, pro-market reforms, market-oriented reforms, and the "Washington Consensus"), 4–6
  in Argentina, 22–23
  costs of reversing reforms, 39
  in Venezuela, 24
New Miyazawa Initiative, 144–45
"North Atlantic financial crisis", 180n. 3
NRI (Non-Resident Indian) investors, 56

Obama, Barak (U.S. President, 2009–), 5, 70

Pacto de Punto Fijo (Venezuela), 23
PDVSA (state petroleum firm, Venezuela), 34–35
People's Bank of China (PBOC), 108–14, 116, 119–21, 123, 147
Pérez, Carlos Andres (President of Venezuela, 1974–79, 1989–93), 24
power (international)
  defined & discussed, 4
PSDB (Brazilian Social Democratic Party), 69

PT, *see* Workers' Party, Brazil

Qualified Foreign Institutional Investors (QFIIs), in China, 113

Rajan, Ragunathan (Governor of Reserve Bank of India, 2013–), 59
realism (in international relations theory), 3, 151
renminbi internationalization, 103–31
  domestic politics of, 116–22
  economic costs and benefits, 115–16
reserve accumulation, *see* foreign exchange reserves
Reserve Bank of India (RBI), 49, 54–55, 178
Rousseff, Dilma (President of Brazil, 2011–), 53, 69

sanctions, economic and financial, 7–9, 11, 15
security dilemma (in international relations theory), 14
self-insurance
  and foreign reserves, 88
Silva, Luiz Inácio ("Lula") da (President of Brazil, 2003–10), 47, 52–53, 56, 60, 68–69
Singapore, politics and financial statecraft, 84–86, 89–90
Singh, Manmohan (Prime Minister of India, 2004–14), 47, 62–63, 67, 69–70
sovereign wealth funds (SWFs), 84–86, 89
state banks
  in Brazil, 57–59
  in China, 116–17, 128
subprime mortgage crisis, 2
swap arrangements, bilateral currency
  with China, 32–33, 113
  with U.S., 57

Tobin tax
  and India, 61–62

UNASUR (Union of South American Nations), 32, 37, 60, 66

United Progressive Alliance (UPA) (India), 68–69
U.S. dollar dominance, 105–08, see also currency competition; currency internationalization
U.S. Federal Reserve Bank, international crisis management, 12, 57, 141

Vajpayee, Atal Behari (Prime Minister of India, 1998–2004), 70
Venezuela, politics and financial statecraft of, 23–25, 33–39, 164, 166–68, 170, 171, 172, 174
challenge to U.S., 37–38
coup attempt (April 2002), 33
Pacto de Punto Fijo, 23
and United States, 37–38

"Washington Consensus", 165, see also neoliberalism
and Argentina, 26, 39
and Japan, 143, 150, 152–53
Workers' Party (PT) (Brazil), 68–69
World Bank
globalization, views of, 1
WTO (World Trade Organization), 52, 56, 72, 97, 121, 142

Xi Jinping (President of China, 2013–), 124

Printed and bound in the United States of America